Hegel's Rabble

Bloomsbury Studies in Philosophy
Series Editor:
James Fieser, *University of Tennessee at Martin, USA*

Bloomsbury Studies in Philosophy is a major monograph series from Bloomsbury. The series features first-class scholarly research monographs across the whole field of philosophy. Each work makes a major contribution to the field of philosophical research.

Hegel's Rabble

An Investigation into Hegel's Philosophy of Right

Frank Ruda

Bloomsbury Studies in Philosophy

B L O O M S B U R Y
LONDON · NEW DELHI · NEW YORK · SYDNEY

Bloomsbury Academic
An imprint of Bloomsbury Publishing Plc

50 Bedford Square	175 Fifth Avenue
London	New York
WC1B 3DP	NY 10010
UK	USA

www.bloomsbury.com

First published by Continuum International Publishing Group 2011
Paperback edition first published 2013

British Library Cataloguing-in-Publication Data
A catalogue record for this book is available from the British Library.

ISBN: HB: 978-1-4411-5693-8
PB: 978-1-4725-1016-7

Library of Congress Cataloging-in-Publication Data
Ruda, Frank.
Hegel's rabble : an investigation into Hegel's Philosophy of right /
Frank Ruda; with a preface by Slavoj Žižek.
p. cm. – (Continuum studies in philosophy)
Includes bibliographical references.
ISBN 978-1-4411-5693-8
1. Hegel, Georg Wilhelm Friedrich, 1770-1831–Political and social views.
2. Hegel, Georg Wilhelm Friedrich, 1770-1831. Grundlinien der Philosophie
des Rechts. 3. Poor–Political aspects. I. Title. II. Series.
JC233.H46R83 2011
320.092–dc23
2011016510

Typeset by Newgen Imaging Systems Pvt Ltd, Chennai, India
Printed and bound in Great Britain

Contents

Abbreviations

Hegel:

HA1   Hegel, *Aesthetics. Lectures on Fine Art*, vol. I, New York: Oxford/New York/Toronto: Oxford University Press 1975.

HA2   Hegel, *Aesthetics. Lectures on Fine Arts*, vol. II, Oxford/New York/Toronto: Oxford University Press 1975.

HENZ3   Hegel, *Enzyklopädie der philosophischen Wissenschaften im Grundrisse (1830), Dritter Teil: Die Philosophie des Geistes. Mit den mündlichen Zusätzen*, in: ders., *Werke*, Bd. 10.

HGPR   Hegel, Grundlinien der Philosophie des Rechts oder Naturrecht und Staatswissenschaft im Grundrisse. Mit Hegels eigenhändigen Notizen und den mündlichen Zusätzen, in: ders., Werke, Bd. 7.

HLH   Hegel, *The Logic of Hegel. Translated from the Encyclopedia of Philosophical Sciences*, Oxford: Clarendon Press 1892.

HLHP 1   Hegel, *History of Philosophy 1825–6. Volume I: Introduction and Oriental Philosophy*, Oxford/New York: Oxford University Press 2009.

HLHP 3   Hegel, *Lectures on the History of Philosophy 1825–6. Volume III: Medieval and Modern Philosophy*, Oxford/New York: Oxford University Press 2009.

HOPR   Hegel, *Outlines of the Philosophy of Right*, Oxford/New York: Oxford University Press 2008.

HPH   Hegel, *The Philosophy of History*, New York: Cosimo Inc. 2007.

HPM   Hegel, *Philosophy of Mind*, Oxford/New York: Oxford University Press 2008.

HPN   Hegel, *Philosophy of Nature. Part Two of the Encyclopedia of Philosophical Sciences (1830)*, Oxford/New York: Oxford University Press 2004.

HPR 1   Hegel, *Lectures on the Philosophy of Religion. Vol. 1. Introduction and the Concept of Religion*, Oxford/New York: Oxford University Press 1984.

HPR 2   Hegel, *Lectures on the Philosophy of Religion. Vol II. Determinate Religion*, Berkeley/Los Angeles/London: University of California Press 1987.

HPS   Hegel, *Phenomenology of Spirit*, Oxford/New York: Oxford University Press 1977.

HSL   Hegel, *The Science of Logic,* Cambridge: Cambridge University Press 2010.

HVAE2   Hegel, *Aesthetics: Lectures on Fine Art,* Vol. II, Oxford: Oxford University Press 1998.

HVORL 1   Hegel, *Vorlesungen über Rechtsphilosophie, 1818–1831.* Edition und Kommentar in sechs Bänden von Karl-Heinz Ilting, Erster Band, "Der objektive Geist" aus der Heidelberger Enzyklopädie 1817, mit Hegels Vorlesungsnotizen 1818–1819. "Naturrecht und Staatswissenschaft" nach der Vorlesungsnachschrift von C. G. Homeyer 1818/19. – Zeitgenössische Rezensionen der "Rechtsphilosophie", Stuttgart-Bad Cannstatt 1973.

HVORL 2   Hegel, *Vorlesungen über Rechtsphilosophie, 1818–1831.* Edition und Kommentar in sechs Bänden von Karl-Heinz Ilting, Zweiter Band, Die "Rechtsphilosophie" von 1820. Mit Hegels Vorlesungsnotizen 1821–1825, Stuttgart-Bad Cannstatt 1974.

HVORL 3   Hegel, *Vorlesungen über Rechtsphilosophie, 1818–1831.* Edition und Kommentar in sechs Bänden von Karl-Heinz Ilting, Dritter Band, Philosophie des Rechts. Nach der Vorlesungsnachschrift von H.G. Hotho 1822/1823, Stuttgart-Bad Cannstatt 1974.

HVORL 4   Hegel, *Vorlesungen über Rechtsphilosophie, 1818–1831.* Edition und Kommentar in sechs Bänden von Karl-Heinz Ilting, Vierter Band, Philosophie des Rechts. Nach der Vorlesungsnachschrift von K.G. v. Griesheims 1824/25, Der objektive Geist. Aus der Berliner Enzyklopädie zweite und dritte Auflage (1827 und 1830), Philosophie des Rechts. Nach der Vorlesungsnachschrift von D.F. Strauß 1831 mit Hegels Vorlesungsnotizen, Stuttgart-Bad Cannstatt 1974.

HPRV   Hegel, *Die Philosophie des Rechts. Vorlesung von 1821/22,* Frankfurt a. M.: Suhrkamp 2005.

Others:

ATS   Theodor W. Adorno, *Three Studies,* Cambridge/London/ Massachusetts: MIT Press 1993.

AHT   Shlomo Avineri, *Hegel's Theory of the Modern State,* Cambridge: Cambridge University Press 1974.

BBE   Alain Badiou, *Being and Event,* New York/London: Continuum 2005.

HPIF   Axel Honneth, *The Pathologies of Individual Freedom: Hegel's Social Theory,* Princeton: Princeton University Press 2010.

MCHR   Karl Marx, *A Contribution to the Critique of Hegel's Philosophy of Right.*
          Introduction (1843–4), in *Early Writings*, London: Penguin 1972,
          pp. 243–58.
MCH   Karl Marx, *Critique of Hegel's 'Philosophy of Right'*, Cambridge:
          Cambridge University Press 1977.
MEPM   Karl Marx, *Economic and Philosophical Manuscripts (1844)*, in *Early*
          Writings, London: Penguin 1972, pp. 279–400.
RHS   Franz Rosenzweig, *Hegel und der Staat. Zweiter Band. Weltepochen*
          (1800–1831), München/Berlin: Scientia 1920.

Acknowledgments

Thinking would be impossible if one were to be alone. The same goes for the present book. It is the product of a *general intellect* composed of the friends, comrades, colleagues and teachers who have made it possible. Although I present the following investigations exclusively in my own name, I owe a lot to: Alain Badiou, Bruno Besana, Lars Bullmann, Sarah Campbell, Lorenzo Chiesa, Tom Crick, Sophie Ehrmanntraut, Felix Ensslin, Oliver Feltham, Mike Lewis, Peter Hallward, Anselm Haverkamp, Christoph Menke, Mark Potocnik, Gerd Ruda, Anneliese Ruda, Cornelia Schmidt, Ralf Schmidt, Manfred Schneider, Aaron Schuster, Ozren Pupovac, Jan Völker and Slavoj Žižek. I also have to thank the doctoral program "Forms of Life and the Know How of Living" for their support.

The Politics of Negativity

Slavoj Žižek

Frank Ruda's *Hegel's Rabble* is one of those remarkable books which, although focused on a specific topic, implicitly deals with the most fundamental philosophical questions: his close reading of a couple of paragraphs on the *Poebel* in Hegel's *Philosophy of Right* effectively crystallizes not only the vast domain of what is called "Hegel's politics," but also the crucial topic of the post-Hegelian break in the history of philosophy.

This break has two aspects which are not to be confused: the assertion of the positivity of actual being as opposed to notional mediation, and the assertion of pure repetition which cannot be contained in the idealist movement of *Aufhebung*. Although the first aspect was much more in the foreground, it is the second aspect which bears witness to a true philosophical revolution. There is no complementarity between these two aspects, they are mutually exclusive: *repetition relies on the blockage of direct positive affirmation*, we repeat because it is impossible to directly affirm. Another axis of the opposition between these two aspects is the one between finitude and infinity: the great motif of the post-Hegelian assertion of positive being is the accent on material, actual, finitude, while the compulsion-to-repeat introduces an obscene infinity/"immortality," not the spiritual immortality, but the immortality of "spirits," of living dead.

If, however, death-drive/compulsion-to-repeat is the heart of negativity, how are we to read Freud's famous claim that the unconscious (as exemplified by the universe of dreams) knows no negation? It is all too easy to empirically refute this claim by way of noticing that, not so many pages after making this claim, Freud provides a series of ways of how dreams can render negation of a certain state of things. Freud's example of *Verneinung* (when a patient says, "I don't know who is the woman who appears in my dream, but one thing is sure—she is not my mother!," one should interpret this assertion as an unambiguous confirmation that the woman in the dream is the patient's mother) remains pertinent here: negation belongs here to the level of conscious/ preconscious, it is a way for the conscious subject to admit the unconscious incestuous fixation. The Hegelian negation as universalizing abolishment of particular content (say, negation of the empirical wealth of an object in its name), this violence inherent to idealization, is what is missing in the Freudian unconscious. However, there is a weird negativity which also pervades the entire sphere of the unconscious, from brutal aggressivity and self-sabotaging to hysteria with its basic experience, apropos every object, of *ce n'est pas ca*, so that it is as if (in accordance with Freud's insight that the multiplicity of phalluses is a sign of castration) the suspension of negation is paid by its multiplication. What is the foundation and status of this all-pervasive "negativity" which eludes the logical form of negation? Perhaps, one of the ways to resolve this problem is to read negation itself as positive fact (in the same way in which, in a differential system, the absence itself can be a positive feature, or, to refer to the best-known line from Sherlock Holmes stories, the fact that the dog didn't bark is in itself a curious accident). The difference between the system of conscious/preconscious and the unconscious is thus not simply that, in conscious/preconscious, there is negation, while the unconscious is too primitive to know the function of negation; it is rather that the system of conscious/preconscious perceives only the negative aspect of the negation, i.e., that it sees negation only in its negative dimension (something is missing, etc.), ignoring the positive space opened up by this negation.

Freud deploys a whole series, system even, of negations in the unconscious: throwing-out of the Ego (*Ausstossung*), rejection (*Verwerfung*), repression (*Verdraengung*, itself divided into primordial repression—*Ur-Verdraengung*—and "normal" repression), disavowal (*Verleugnung*), denial (*Verneinung*), up to the complex mode of how acceptance itself can function as a mode of denial, as is the case in so-called isolation (*Isolierung*), where a traumatic fact is rationally accepted, but isolated from its libidinal-symbolic context. What further complicates the scheme are objects and signifiers which somehow overlaps with their own lack: for Lacan, phallus is itself the signifier of castration (this introduces all the paradoxes of the signifier of the lack of signifier, i.e., of how the lack of a signifier is itself "remarked" in a signifier of this lack), not to mention *l'objet petit a*, the object-cause of desire which is nothing but the embodiment of lack, its place-holder. The relationship between object and lack is here turned around: far from lack being reducible to the lack of an object, the object itself is a spectral positivization of a lack. And one has to extrapolate this mechanism into the very (pre)ontological foundation of all being: the primordial gesture of creation is not that of an excessive giving, of assertion, but a negative gesture of withdrawal, of subtracting, which only opens up the space for creation of positive entities. This is how "there is something rather than nothing": in order to arrive at something, one has to *subtract from nothing its nothing(ness) itself*, i.e., one has to posit the primordial pre-ontological Abyss "as such," AS NOTHING, so that, in contrast to (or against the background of) nothing, something can appear.

The underlying problem is here which of these negations is the primordial one, i.e., which one opens up the space for all others. From the Lacanian perspective, the most obvious candidate may appear to be the notorious "symbolic castration," the loss which opens up and sustains the space of symbolization—recall, insofar as the Name-of-the-Father is the bearer of symbolic castration, how Lacan plays on the French homophony between *le Nom-du-Pere* (the name of the father) and *le Non-du-Pere* (the no of the father). But it seems more productive to follow a more radical path of thinking beyond father (*pere*) to what is even worse (*pire*). Again, the most obvious candidate for this "worse" is (death-)drive, a kind of Freudian correlate to what Schelling called the primordial "contraction," the obstinate repetitive fixation on a contingent object which subtracts the subject from direct immersion into reality.

Drive as such is death-drive—not in the sense of longing for universal negation/dissolution of all particularity, but, on the contrary, in the sense of the "spontaneous" life-flow of generation and corruption getting "stuck" onto some accidental particularity and circulating endlessly around it. If Life is a song played on an old LP (which it definitely is not), drive arises when, due to a scratch on the LP surface, the needle gets stuck and the same fragment is repeated. The deepest speculative insight is that a universality can only emerge when a flow of particularity get stuck onto a singular moment. And this Freudian notion of drive brings us to the radical ambiguity of Hegel's dialectics: does it follow the logic of drive or not? Hegel's logic is a logic of purification, of "unstucking": even when a subject puts all of his libidinal investment into a contingent fragment of being ("I am ready to risk everything for that!"), this contingent fragment—the Lacanian *objet petit a*—is, in its indifferent accidentality, an operator of purification, of "unstucking" from all (other) particular content—in Lacanese, this object is a metonymy of lack. The subject's desire is here the transcendental void, and the object is a contingent ontic filler of this void. In drive, in contrast, *objet a* is not only the metonymy of lack, but a kind of transcendental stain, irreducible and irreplaceable in its very contingent singularity, not just a contingent ontic filler of a lack. While drive is a mode of being stuck onto a contingent stain-object, dialectical negativity is a continuing process of un-stucking from all particular content: *jouissance* "leans on" something, hanging onto its particularity—this is what is missing in Hegel, but operative in Freud.

There are good reasons to link the Freudian unconscious to the self-consciousness as self-reflexivity: "self-consciousness is an object," i.e., in an object-symptom, I reflexively register a truth about myself inaccessible to my consciousness. This, however, is not quite the same as the Hegelian unconscious: it is a particular (singular) unconscious, a kind of contingent transcendental, a contingent knot-*sinthom* holding together the subject's universe. In clear contrast to this Freudian unconscious, the Hegelian unconscious is formal: it is the form of enunciation invisible in the enunciated content; it is systemic, not a contingent *bricolage of lateral links (what Lacan calls lalangue)*, i.e., it resides in the universal symbolic form on which the subject unknowingly relies, not in the contingent "pathological" desire which transpires in the slips of tongue. Hegel's unconscious is the unconscious of self-consciousness itself, its own necessary nontransparency, the necessary overlooking of its own FORM ("*das Formelle*") in the content it confronts. Unconscious is the universal form of particular content: when Hegel says that the truth is in what I say, not in what I mean (to say), he means the universality of the meaning of words as opposed to the particular intention.

The relationship between Hegel's negativity and Freud's death-drive (or compulsion to repeat) is thus a very specific one, well beyond their (hidden) outright identity: what Freud aimed at with his notion of death-drive—more precisely, the key dimension of this notion for which Freud himself was blind, unaware of what he discovered, is the "non-dialectical" core of the Hegelian negativity, the pure drive to repeat without any movement of sublation/idealization. The paradox here is that pure repetition (in contrast to repetition as idealizing sublation) is sustained precisely by its *impurity*, by the persistence of a contingent "pathological" element to which the movement of repetition remains stuck.

In the Kierkegaard-Freudian pure repetition, the dialectical movement of sublimation thus encounters itself, its own core, outside itself, in the guise of a "blind" compulsion-to-repeat. And it is here that one should apply the great Hegelian motto about the internalizing of the external obstacle: in fighting its external opposite, the blind nonsublatable repetition, the dialectical movement is fighting its own abyssal ground, its own core; in other words, the ultimate gesture of reconciliation is to recognize in this threatening excess of negativity the core of the subject itself. This excess has different names in Hegel: the "night of the world," the necessity of war, of madness, etc. And, perhaps, the same holds for the basic opposition between the Hegelian and the Freudian negativity: precisely insofar as there is a unbridgeable gap between them (the Hegelian negativity is idealizing, mediatizing/"sublating" all particular content in the abyss of its universality, while the negativity of the Freudian drive is expressed as being-stuck onto a contingent particular content), the Freudian negativity provides (quite literally) the "material base" for the idealizing negativity—to put it in somewhat simplified terms, every idealizing/universalizing negativity has to be attached to a singular contingent "pathological" content which serves as its "sinthom" in the Lacanian sense (if this sinthom is unravelled/disintegrated, universality disappears). The exemplary model of this link is, of course, Hegel's deduction of the necessity of hereditary monarchy: the rational state as universal totality mediatizing all particular content has to be embodied in the contingent "irrational" figure of the monarch.

It is at this point that Ruda's book enters the stage: he discerns the same matrix on Hegel's treatment of rabble—Hegel fails to take note how the rabble, in its very status of the destructive excess of social totality is the "reflexive determination" of the totality as such, the immediate embodiment of its universality, the particular element in the guise of which the social totality encounters itself among its elements, and, as such, the key constituent of its identity. (Note the dialectical finesse of this last feature: what "sutures" the identity of a social totality as such is the very "free-floating" element which dissolves all fixed identity of any intrasocial element.) One can even establish a link between Hegel's residual anti-Semitism and his inability to think pure repetition: when he gives way to his displeasure with the Jews who stubbornly stick to their identity, instead of "moving forward" and, like other nations, allowing their identity to be sublated /*aufgehoben*/ in historical progress, is his displeasure not caused by the perception that Jews remain caught in the repetition of the same?

This is why Ruda is fully justified in reading Hegel's short passages on the rabble as a symptomatic point of his entire philosophy of right, if not of his entire system. What makes the notion of rabble symptomatic is that it describes a necessarily produced "irrational" excess of modern rational state, a group of people for which there is no place within the organized totality of the modern state, although they formally belong to it—as such, they perfectly exemplify the category of singular universality (a singular which directly gives body to a universality, bypassing the mediation through the particular), of what Rancière called the "part of no-part" of the social body. We can easily perceive here the link between the eminently political topic of the status of the rabble and Hegel's basic ontological topic of the relationship between universality and particularity, i.e., the problem of how to understand the Hegelian "concrete universality." If we understand "concrete universality" in the usual sense of the organic subdivision of the universal into its particular moments, so that universality is not an abstract feature in which individuals directly participate, and the participation of the individual in the universal is always mediated through the particular network of determinations, then the corresponding notion of society is a corporate one: society as an organic Whole in which each individual has to find its particular place, i.e., in which I participate in the State by fulfilling my particular duty or obligation. There are no citizens as such, one has to be a member of a particular estate (a farmer, a state official, mother in a family, teacher, artisan . . .) in order to contribute to the harmony of the Whole. This is the Bradleyian proto-Fascist Hegel who opposes atomistic liberalism (in which society is a mechanic unity of abstract individuals) on behalf of the State as a living organism in which each part has its function, and within this space, the rabble has to appear as the irrational excess, as the threat to social order and stability, as outcasts excluded and excluding themselves from the "rational" social totality.

But is this truly what Hegel aims at with his "concrete universality"? Is the core of the dialectical negativity not the short circuit between the genus and (one of) its species, so that genus appears as one of its own species opposed to others, entering a negative relationship with them? In this sense, concrete universality is precisely a universality which includes itself among its species, in the guise of a singular moment lacking particular content—in short, it is precisely those who are without their proper place within the social Whole (like the rabble) that stand for the universal dimension of the society which generates them. This is why the rabble cannot be abolished without radically transforming the entire social edifice—and Hegel is fully aware of this. While he enumerates a series of measures to resolve the problem (police control and repression, charity, export of rabble to colonies . . .), he himself admits that these are only secondary palliatives which cannot really resolve the problem— not because the problem is too hard (i.e., because there is not enough wealth in society to take care of the poor), but because there is too much excessive wealth—the more society is wealthy, more poverty it produces.

Hegel is of course aware that objective poverty is not enough to generate the rabble: this objective poverty must be subjectivized, changed into a "disposition of mind," experienced as radical injustice on account of which the subject feels no duty and obligation toward society. Hegel leaves no doubt that this injustice is a real one: society has a duty to guarantee the conditions for a dignified free autonomous life to all its members—this is their right, and if it is denied, they also have no duties toward society. There are, however, profound ambiguity and oscillation in Hegel's line of argumentation here. He first seems to blame the poor themselves for subjectivizing their position as that of the rabble, i.e., for abandoning the principle of autonomy which obliges subjects to secure their subsistence by their own labor, and for claiming as their right to receive means for survival from society. Then he subtly changes the tone, emphasizing that, in contrast to nature, man can claim rights against society, which is why poverty is not just a fact but a wrong done to one class by another. Furthermore, there is a subtle *non sequitur* in his argumentation: he passes directly from indignation against the rich/society/government to the lack of self-respect (implied by the demand to receive from society subsistence without working for it)—the rabble is irrational because they demand decent life without working for it, thus denying the basic modern axiom that freedom and autonomy are based on the work of self-mediation. Consequently, to quote Ruda, the right to subsist without labor

> can only appear as irrational because Hegel links the notion of right to the notion of the free will that can only be free if it becomes an object for itself through objective activity. To claim a right to subsist without activity and to claim this right at the same time only for oneself, according to Hegel, therefore means to claim a right that has neither the universality nor the objectivity of a right. The right that the rabble claims for Hegel is therefore a *right without right* and . . . he consequently defines the rabble as the particularity that unbinds itself also from the essential interrelation of right and duty.

But indignation is not the same as the lack of self-respect: it does not automatically generate the demand to be provided for without working. Indignation can also be a direct expression of self-respect: since the rabble is produced necessarily, as part of the social process of the (re)production of wealth, it is society itself which denies them the right to participate in the social universe of freedoms and rights—they are denied the right to have rights, i.e., their "right without right" is effectively a meta-right or reflexive right, a universal right to have rights, to be in a position to act as a free autonomous subject. The demand to be provided for life without working is thus a (possible superficial) form of appearance of the more basic and in no way "irrational" demand to be given a chance to act as an autonomous free subject, to be included in the universe of freedoms and obligations. In other words, since members of the rabble were excluded from the universal sphere of free autonomous life, their demand is itself universal—their

> claimed *right without right* contains a latent universal dimension and is itself not at all a mere particular right. As a particularly articulated right it is a right that latently affects anyone and offers the insight into a demand for equality beyond the existing objective statist circumstances.

There is a further key distinction to be introduced here, a distinction only latent in Hegel (in the guise of the opposition between the two excesses of poverty and wealth) elaborated by Ruda: members of the rabble (i.e., those excluded from the sphere of rights and freedoms) "can be structurally differentiated into two types: there are the poor and there are the gamblers. Anyone can nonarbitrarily become poor, but only the one that arbitrarily decides not to satisfy his egoist needs and desires by working can become a gambler. He relies fully on the contingent movement of bourgeois economy and hopes to secure his own subsistence in an equally contingent manner—for example by contingently gaining money on the stock-market." The excessively wealthy are thus also a species of the rabble in the sense that they violate the rules of (or exclude themselves from) the sphere of duties and freedoms: they not only demand from society to provide for their subsistence without work, they are *de facto* provided for such a life. Consequently, while Hegel criticizes the position of the rabble as being the position of an irrational particularity that egoistically opposes its mere particular interests against the existing and rationally organized universality, this differentiation between the two distinct rabbles demonstrates that only the rich rabble falls under Hegel's verdict: "While the rich rabble is, as Hegel judges correctly, a mere particular rabble, the poor rabble contains, against Hegel's judgment, a latent universal dimension that is not even inferior to the universality of the Hegelian conception of ethicality."

One can thus demonstrate that, in the case of the rabble, Hegel was inconsistent with regard to his own matrix of the dialectical process, *de facto* regressing from the properly dialectical notion of totality to a corporate model of the social Whole. But does this mean that all we have to do here is to enact the passage from Hegel to Marx? Is the inconsistency resolved when we replace the rabble with the proletariat as the "universal class"? One can argue that, on the contrary, the position of the "universal rabble" perfectly renders the plight of today's new proletarians. In the classical Marxist *dispositif* of class exploitation, capitalist and worker meet as formally free individuals on the market, equal subjects of the same legal order, citizens of the same state, with the same civil and political rights. Today, this legal frame of equality, this shared participation in the same civil and political spaces, is gradually dissolving with the rise of the new forms of social and political exclusion: illegal immigrants, slum-dwellers, refugees, etc. It is as if, in parallel to the regression from profit to rent, in order to continue to function, the existing system has to resuscitate premodern forms of direct exclusion—it can no longer afford exploitation and domination in the form of legal and civil authority. In other words, while the classic working class is exploited through their very participation in the sphere of rights and freedoms, i.e., while their *de facto* enslavement is realized through the very form of their autonomy and freedom, through working in order to provide for their subsistence, today's rabble is denied even the right to be exploited through work, its status oscillating between that of a victim provided for by charitable humanitarian help and that of a terrorist to be contained or crushed; and, exactly as described by Hegel, they sometimes formulate their demand as the demand for subsistence without work (like the Somalia pirates).

One should bring together here Hegel's two failures (by his own standards), rabble and sex, as the aspects of the same limitation. Far from providing the natural foundation of human lives, sexuality is the very terrain where humans detach themselves from nature: the idea of sexual perversion or of a deadly sexual passion is totally foreign to the animal universe. Here, Hegel himself commits a failure with regard to his own standards: he only deploys how, in the process of culture, the natural substance of sexuality is cultivated, sublated, mediated—we, humans, no longer just make love for procreation, we get involved in a complex process of seduction and marriage by means of which sexuality becomes an expression of the spiritual bond between a man and a woman, etc. However, what Hegel misses is how, once we are within the human condition, sexuality is not only transformed/civilized, but, much more radically, *changed in its very substance*: it is no longer the instinctual drive to reproduce, but a drive that gets thwarted as to its natural goal (reproduction) and thereby explodes into an infinite, properly metaphysical, passion. The becoming-cultural of sexuality is thus not the becoming-cultural of nature, but the attempt to domesticate a properly un-natural excess of the metaphysical sexual passion. THIS is the properly dialectical reversal of substance: the moment when the immediate substantial ("natural") starting point is not only acted-upon, trans-formed, mediated/cultivated, but changed in its very substance. We not only work upon and thus transform nature—in a gesture of retroactive reversal, nature itself radically changes its "nature." (In a homologous way, once we enter the domain of legal civil society, the previous tribal order of honor and revenge is deprived of its nobility and all of a sudden appears as common criminality.) This is why the Catholics who insist that only sex for procreation is human, while coupling for lust is animal, totally miss the point, and end up celebrating the animality of men.

Our advice to a reader of Ruda's book is thus: you are holding in your hands a classic, so allow yourself to be swallowed by the vortex behind the "marginal" topic of the *Poebel*—in this way, you enter the risky domain of authentic thinking.

Introduction: From the Rabble to the Proletariat

I think what we fundamentally owe to Hegel is a powerful reflection on the negative.
(Alain Badiou)[1]

It is not the worst reader who provides the book with disrespectful notes in the margin.
(Theodor W. Adorno)[2]

The present book starts with a fiction. Such a beginning might seem unusual or even illegitimate. But the fiction with which the present book begins is neither merely unreal nor simply feigned. Rather it is an attempt to deal with a problem that Adorno had already diagnosed, albeit in a different context. His seminar on Kant's *Critique of Pure Reason* on the twelfth of May 1959 begins with the following remark: "Let me begin with the fiction that you do not yet know anything about the *Critique of Pure Reason*." He continues his investigations by claiming that such a fiction is "simultaneously legitimate and illegitimate." It is illegitimate because everyone present has

> undoubtedly . . . heard that Kant's so-called Copernican Revolution consisted in the idea that the elements of cognition that had previously been sought in the objects, in things-in-themselves, were now to be transferred to the subjects . . .

Such a fiction is at the same time, Adorno continues, legitimate because the "formulae to which philosophies are commonly reduced tend to reify the actual writings . . . and to make a genuine interaction with them all the harder."[3] The fiction of the present book shares Adorno's diagnosis that the ordinary formulae tend to make it more difficult to access some philosophical works and make it impossible to grasp what is at stake. A specific perspective is introduced when this diagnosis is related back to what is usually called "political philosophy." How are we to draw nearer to the works of those thinkers—such as Hegel or Marx—who first developed the theory of reification if our interaction with their works is itself ossified by reification? The initial fiction of the present book serves to open up the reification and functions as an implement with which to fight against it. The concrete point of entry of the present book is the relation between Hegel and Marx. It begins with the fiction that 'we' do not know anything about the transition from the one to the other.

This fictitious assumption is also both legitimate and illegitimate. That it is illegitimate seems obvious insofar as this transition is one of the most frequently discussed moments in the entire history of modern philosophy.[4] There are countless works which have thought through this transition, and to anyone working in 'political philosophy,' the various versions of the infamous formulae of transition are well known: with Hegel dialectics is still standing on its head, with Marx it is set on its revolutionary feet; it is a transition from idealism to materialism, from an idealist theory of the state to the critique of political economy. My preliminary hypothesis is that all of these formulae tend to fall into the very gesture that Adorno criticizes. They all tend to make it more difficult to interact with the works in question by obstructing their proper philosophical stakes.[5] In the same way, "the Marxist tradition did not know how to say much more concerning the relation of Hegel and Marx than Marx did . . . turn the Hegelian dialectic upside down."[6] Therefore, the present book assumes that these formulae of transition have become part of a philosophical *doxa* that obstructs and reifies that which is at stake in the transition from Hegel to Marx. One effect of this reification is manifest in the fact that this transition is often treated as a purely *philosophical* problem. The transition in this version becomes a question which is the exclusive preserve of 'political philosophy' as the administrator of its own history. Therewith one begins from a presupposition that considers "politics—or rather, the political—as an objective datum, or even an invariant, of universal experience"[7] and that the task of the philosopher resides in articulating its essence in the register of philosophy. Thereby the relation of Hegel and Marx becomes a relation between two philosophical positions that remain commensurable because they encounter and confront one another within the same register, the register of philosophy. Hegel and Marx become philosophers of the political and their relation becomes a question of philosophy and its categories.

In this way it is also presupposed that politics presents itself as an objective invariant given so that the—idealist or materialist—philosopher can turn toward it with a gesture of sovereignty and uncover its always stable essence. The difference between Hegel and Marx is seen from the perspective of 'political philosophy' as a difference between two philosophical perspectives, between two different theories. Politics or *the* political is a category of philosophy and the transition from Hegel to Marx is nothing but a transition from one philosophical position to another: a transition from (political) philosophy to (political) philosophy *within* philosophy. How to grasp the transition from Hegel to Marx thus becomes a question that philosophy solely addresses to itself and philosophy alone answers.

It is from this diagnosis that the initial fiction of the present book gains its legitimacy. Because to again raise the old question of thinking the transition from Hegel to Marx it is necessary to displace it and extract it from all prefigured philosophical knowledge. This displacement I understand in a way that follows "the *incessant displacement* of an object of thought from which very soon emerges the insight that it cannot be reduced to the theses in which it formerly appeared."[8] This means that the fiction of not knowing anything about the transition from Hegel to Marx distinguishes itself from the already mentioned and purely philosophical formulae of transition. This is due to the fact that this fiction is a supposition that is precisely putting into question the *relation* of philosophy to politics in a new way. But if politics is not to be made into a philosophical category whose stability, objectivity and invariance one presupposes, then here one encounters a possible perspective on what a nonphilosophical politics could be. Politics as a nonphilosophical domain would then be the site of a subject and the place of a transformation which could not easily be fitted into philosophical categories of stability, possibility, change, and so on. Politics would rather be something that was able to trouble philosophy and to confront it with exigencies which would demand a transformation of philosophy itself. Politics would then be a condition of philosophy. The present book wishes to follow such an irritation of philosophy by politics as it takes place in the transition from Hegel to Marx. My thesis will be that this transition relates to the singularity and peculiarity of one form of politics. In the following I do not begin with reflections on an already established philosophical knowledge—which will also borne in mind—but with a suspension of that which one is tempted to believe that one knows about this transition. The hypothesis of the book is thus that it is precisely the relation between philosophy and politics—politics being an irritation of philosophy—which helps us to grasp the transition from Hegel to Marx.

Maybe it is not surprising that this irritation of philosophy is indicated in the form of a problem. Shlomo Avineri has remarked that Hegel leaves one problem peculiarly unsolved in his *Philosophy of Right*—in this work which one assigns to his 'political philosophy':

> Though his theory of the state is aimed at integrating the contending interests of civil society under a common bond, on the problem of poverty he ultimately has nothing more to say than that it is one of "the most disturbing problems which agitate modern societies". On no other occasion Hegel leaves a problem at that. (AHT, 154)

In Hegel's theory of the state, which proposes to expound the necessary deployment and the rational structure of an ethical polity, Hegel is, according to Avineri, confronted with a problem that fundamentally runs contrary to his own claim. In what follows I want to take up Avineri's remark but also to alter it. In the first place, while I also start from the idea that Hegel in his *Philosophy of Right* is confronted with a problem that he is unable to resolve and that is closely related to the problem of poverty, I differ from Avineri in that I intend to show how poverty is only the necessary condition of a more fundamental problem that Hegel addresses under the name, 'rabble.' The subject of this book therefore finds its place within philosophy, the 'political philosophy' of Hegel, but it is not thereby a subject of philosophy *stricto sensu*. It will have to be shown that the 'appearance' of the rabble in Hegel's philosophy is a problem *of* philosophy and *within* philosophy but a problem with something other than philosophy: a problem with politics. The peculiar logic of politics, as I will show, breaks into the Hegelian *Philosophy of Right* in a way that the latter is indeed able to perceive as a problem but which it is unable to come to terms with. The present book aims to show that one can observe in Hegel's *Philosophy of Right* that the philosophical description of the constitution of politics— under the aegis of the state—fails, and in such a way that its failure offers a perspective on the *peculiarly singular logic of politics*. The name of this problem is 'rabble.' Finally I will show that, with the failure linked to the rabble, a different transition from Hegel to Marx becomes thinkable.

But how should a book on a specific problem of Hegelian philosophy also be a contribution to the debate surrounding Hegel and Marx? When Marx remarks that "Hegel is not to be blamed for depicting the nature of the modern state as it is, but rather for presenting what *is* as the *essence* of the state" (MCH, 64), his claim already entails the dialectical emphasis with which the present book begins.

If Hegel even in his failure accurately depicts what is, and if the place of his failure is a theory of the modern state, then one can claim that his description is even able to present the place of his own failure. In his short remarks on the rabble, Hegel offers all the resources that we need in order to trace the failure of his own 'political philosophy' and its conception of the state. In a certain sense Hegel's adequate description of the *logic of politics* turns against the *logic of philosophy*. But Marx's remark about Hegel can also be instructive for the following investigation: If Hegel adequately depicts what is, then one can claim that Marx—the thinker of "real conditions"[9]—starts from precisely the point where Hegel fails. Given that Marx was driven by Hegel's failure to pronounce the necessity of transforming philosophy and its categories, this means that the rabble—the problem in respect of which Hegel's 'political philosophy' fails—can be conceived of as the starting point of Marx's enterprise. If on the one hand the transition from Hegel to Marx is due to a problem that can be understood as a fundamental irritation of philosophy by politics, and if on the other hand this irritation makes it necessary to transform philosophy, then it becomes clear that this transformation has to start from the point at which Hegel's 'political philosophy' fails.

The assumption of the present book is thus that the transformation of philosophy introduced by Marx starts from the rabble. The way of the fundamental restructuring of philosophy begins with the rabble, but it does not end with it. Rather, the transition from Hegel to Marx is, I want to claim, is the transition from the rabble to the proletariat.[10] If Hegel's theory is, as Marx had it, a theory of the *modern* state, it is because within it Hegel attempts to link two things: 1. the free self-realization of rational subjects whose historical advent he relates to the Reformation and 2. the condition of a legally regulated equality and justice that emerges with the French Revolution. If Hegel fails because of the rabble, this failure takes place under specifically modern conditions. The Marxian transformation of philosophy therefore has to be grasped as a transformation that attempts to be appropriate to the historical conditions of modernity. If Hegel's *Philosophy of Right* is marked by its claim to think a relation between a conception of subjectivity in which the active realization of freedom is inscribed and a notion of justice—under the condition of a state-secured system of rights—one already attains the essential coordinates according to which the Marxian transformation of philosophy orients itself: subject, justice, equality.

The formula of the transition from Hegel to Marx—from the rabble to the proletariat—is therefore a formula that no longer hinges upon an invariant givenness of the political which philosophy only has to interpret in different ways, but a formula that understands politics, that breaks into philosophy under the name of 'rabble' as an irritation and a disturbance that introduces the necessity of a transformation of philosophy, as an essentially subjective event in which issues of justice, equality and freedom are addressed. But to do justice to this transformation of philosophy one needs a systematic understanding of Hegel's failure that Hegel himself marks under the name of the 'rabble.'

Chapter 1

Luther and the Transfiguration of Poverty

As at the time it was a monk, so now it is the philosopher in whose brain the revolution begins.

(Karl Marx)[1]

Luther profanes poverty. Thus might one encapsulate the result of "the all-enlightened *Sun*" (HPH, 412) of the reformation. The reformation ousts poverty from its holy throne and destroys in this way the privilege of a class that imagines itself to be the sole possessor of truth. Luther thereby shatters the medieval economy of salvation that had become dilapidated and that had previously been able to assign a seemingly fixed place to poverty. Before Luther, voluntary rejection of property and refusal of worldly possessions is integrated into an economy of salvation by the fact that the beggar is "promised spiritual support"[2] in return. The alms therefore amounts to a micro-(salvational-)economic letter of indulgence whose effectiveness is assured by the authority of the church that in turn initially allows for the contractual form on a macro-(salvational-)economic level. But already in medieval times—the "dawn" (HPH, 412) before Luther—the frontier between the *pauperes cum Petro* (the voluntary clerical poor) and the *pauperes cum Lazaro* (the involuntary poor) becomes questionable. Because what comes with the profession of the beggar is an inescapable suspicion of fraud.[3] The alms get caught in a functional-economic ambiguity: either it is the vanishing mediator that is able to ensure the salvation of the soul or it is a form of ultimate fraud. The result of a wrongly given alms is not only material damage, but rather it produces—and this is the mark of its danger—the uncertainty and deception concerning the purportedly secured life. In this sense it is in the last instance always uncertain if the *pauper* is a *pauper sacer*, a *pauper cum Petro* or not. It is uncertain whether the transaction which is supposed to redeem the sins reaches the divine addressee or silts up in worldly channels, bread or other things. This dangerous ambiguity of the alms[4] ultimately stems from the contradictory constitution of the clerical authority itself. The possibility of buying eternal salvation through the donation of alms is confronted with the fundamental indistinguishability between voluntary and nonvoluntary poor.

"The followers of voluntary poverty and the involuntary poor had regarding their values nothing in common. But sometimes by virtue of external similarities of dress, appearances and way of life the aura of sanctity was extended to the latter group."[5] Because of this, the legitimacy that the churchly authority allotted to the clerical poor rebounds onto the worldly poor and perverts its own principle in two ways. First, every pauper is now suspected of being a fraud, and secondly, this means that the authority that aligns poverty with sanctity itself becomes dubious because it cannot offer reliable means with which to differentiate between the competing forms of poverty. The authority of the church in relation to poverty is revealed in all its contradictory nature: 1. the microeconomic problem makes the letter of indulgence also macroeconomically dubious; 2. the assigned sanctity of poverty suspends the possibility of distinction and therefore of rational insight by leading into a problem of indistinguishability.

The whole economy of salvation, secured by the church, thus becomes unhinged. In and against the church there is for the first time a logic of suspicion which for Hegel plays a role in any revolution (of spirit).[6] The exterior indistinguishability of the poor with Peter and the poor with Lazarus that inaugurates the logic of suspicion will now be overcome in Luther by rendering all the poor—whether voluntary or not—poor in the way of Lazarus, Lazzaroni. Luther frees the believers from their exterior ambiguity and thereby purifies the believer of the former barriers of churchly authority. Luther's mediation between the believer and god—a mediation without barriers and through faith alone—signifies for Hegel that the subject is fundamentally purified of its exterior bond to authority and the insertion of a place in the "inner sanctum of humanity" (HLHP, 55) that makes it such "that all externality disappears at the point of the absolute relationship to God" (HLHP3, 77). "The principle became a moment of religion itself . . ." (Ibid., 77). Luther produces a new, historically powerful criterion of truth that amounts to a decisive determination of Hegelian modernity: Because from now on, the true is what "authenticates and evidences itself in my heart" (Ibid., 79). With it the distinction of laity and cleric also disappears, with regard to the Mass. The Reformation that takes place by way of a book of the people—the Bible—enables any subject whatsoever to examine his conscience by means of his own interpretation, guided by reason, and thereby to posit himself as a legitimate and general authority due to his rational capacities and solely by his own efforts. The Protestant principle is marked by a refusal "to recognize in one's disposition of mind anything not justified by thought" (HOPR, 15). In this structure one can also recognize an essential turn in the interpretation of poverty. If Luther smears the dishonest humbleness of the Catholics and the exterior poverty affiliated with it, for Hegel, he at the same time introduces a new principle which transfigures world history: the principle of activity or action [*Tätigkeit*]. In this way the Lutheran Hegel[7] can interpret the Reformative profanation of poverty as a principal turn in the progression of history. Now man is not what he is by nature, but only comes to himself and to truth after an active process of (re-) formation or education [*Bildung*]. Through the Reformation the rational and active subject becomes for Hegel the essential determination of modernity. What is valid for the subject is valid for its foundation, the free will: what it is it can only become through labor.[8]

> The repudiation of work no longer earned the reputation of sanctity; it was acknowledged to be more commendable for men to rise from a state of dependency by *activity*, intelligence and industry, and make themselves independent. It is more consonant with justice that he who has money should spend it even in luxuries, than that he should give it away to idlers and beggars . . . (HPH, 423)

To make oneself independent by one's own activity names the central formula of the subjectivity that is free in itself and that arrives in the world with the Reformation and which becomes the subjectivity of "*all mankind*" (Ibid., 416). The subject becomes the truth of itself by abandoning its particularity and by taking possession of the substantial and rational truth. It is only in this way that "all men can in their subjectivity become as free men subjects of a political, legal and social order."[9] But this process of taking into possession is fundamentally bound to the moment of activity that first had itself to take possession of the truth of history in a (re-)formation of history. "Time, since that epoch, has had no other work to do than the formal imbuing of the world with this principle . . . Law, Property, Social Morality, Government, Constitutions, etc., must be conformed to a general principle, in order that they may accord with the idea of Free Will and be Rational." (HPH, 417)

It is already possible to predict at this stage why with the Reformation "the entire revolution in our mental attitude has come about" (HLHP3, 139). Because now all notions have to be conceived of under the aegis of free, rational activity which has become the *conditio sine qua non* for any subjectivity. Also, "industry, art, and the like uphold the principle of my own activity too, insofar as my activity accords with what is right" (Ibid., 76). From this background the notion of poverty is given a momentous destiny in the 'political philosophy' of Hegel. Because before Luther "poverty was considered to stand higher than living from one's own hands labour; but now it is known that poverty is an aim not more ethical. Rather it is more ethical to live from labour and to be happy about what one brings before onself" (HVORL 3, 49). The profanation of poverty transforms all paupers into Lazzaroni who no longer have any place in the referential system of the salvational economy that is detached from the church's authority, since a "human being has to acquire for himself the position which he ought to attain; he is not already in possession of it through instinct" (HOPR, 173). The barring of the salvation of salvational economy leaves the poor in the precarious state of being a mass whose only place from now on will be the worldly economy, civil society and philosophy, if it wants to depict the state in its rationality, it has to confront these poor.

Chapter 2

Pauper-Rabble: The Question of Poverty

What disorganizes the unity of logical reason equally disorganizes actuality.
(G. W. F. Hegel)[1]

If Hegel's *Elements of the Philosophy of Right* attempts "to render to the state its lost consecration, sanctity" on the ground of the "autonomous thought"[2] prepared by Luther, then what is at stake in this project can hardly be underestimated. Hegel attempts to accomplish in the rational exposition of the notion what Luther began in the sentiment of faith: the divine will as spirit expressing itself in reality should be thought and developed in its unfolded reality, this is in its present statist organization. Already just a year and a half after Hegel's death, Eduard Gans had remarked—on the occasion of a famous edition of Hegel's works—in a "prophetic"[3] preface that the *Philosophy of Right*—a work "wrought from the metal of freedom"—will, as a part of Hegel's philosophical system, stand or fall with it.[4] What is at stake with the following analysis is a reversal of Gans' prophecy: not only does the *Philosophy of Right* stand or fall with the Hegelian system; the Hegelian system stands or falls with the *Philosophy of Right*. At this juncture it will not be my primary aim to reconstruct the *Philosophy of Right* in its entire structure. Rather, the examination will follow the emergence of the post-Lutheran, which is to say profane, poverty and its place to first trace the historically powerful effect that for Hegel begins with the Reformation and whose historical mark is still present in his 'political philosophy' and, secondly, to bear in mind that the Hegelian 'political philosophy' is a philosophy of the state that has to cope with poverty from the state's perspective.

"The important question of how poverty can be remedied is one which agitates and torments modern societies especially," as Hegel writes in his addition to paragraph 244 of the *Philosophy of Right*. But what is the agitating and what is the tormenting aspect that civil society is confronted with in poverty? Hegel defines poverty as the state in which all the advantages of civil society,[5] including the guarantee of one's subsistence, are lost, though all needs are preserved. The poor is the one who either due to an arbitrary-irrational commerce with the means that are necessary for the assurance of one's own existence or due to "contingencies, physical conditions and factors grounded in external circumstances" (HOPR, 219) has lost all possessions. Or he is the one who constitutively lacks "his own immediate assets (his capital)" (Ibid., 192), since it is always purely contingent "what and how much I possess . . ." (Ibid., 63). Who is or becomes poor depends on their particular, individual fates, but that there is poverty is a necessary result of the stabilizing and driving dynamics of civil society. First of all, it is imperative to unfold some of the central elements of the setting that civil society and its movement provide for the question of poverty: one central effect is that besides their property the poor also lose the possibility of acquiring their own subsistence which "leaves them more or less deprived of all the advantages of society . . ." (Ibid., 220). Therefore the effects of integration are not working for the poor anymore. Initially the civil society presents a logically higher[6] level within the ethical system. Family is the ethical substance in its immediate and natural form that after the loss of its unity[7] releases the educated person into their autonomy into civil society. It releases its members from the precautions and the bond of felt unity with the other, into the formal generality of equal needs and the administration of rights. Both lead to the fact that persons encounter one another in an exterior way on the "stage of *difference*" (Ibid., 180)[8]—civil society—under the loose "bond of connection" (Ibid., 52) and of right.

Hereby the two fundamental principles of civil society are indicated: 1. the concrete person as totality of its needs and 2. the person in its relation to the other person: interpersonality or intersubjectivity. Civil society is thus the unity constituted by similarities of different persons. If each person is only interested in the satisfaction of its own needs the unavoidable relation to others—that seem to be mere means of satisfaction—generates a form of generality, universality. "I further my ends, I further the ends of the universal, and this in turn furthers my end" (Ibid., 182). This is a "system of needs"(Ibid., 215) wherein the well-being and the right of each particular individual are formally in relation to all of the others. This is why Hegel can call civil society in its totality the "territory of mediation" on which "there is free play for all idiosyncrasy, every talent, every accident of birth and fortune and where waves of every passion gush forth . . ." (Ibid., 181). That this only delineates a formal universality—a universality without universal content—is clearly articulated in Hegel. This is why he can claim: "In these conflicts and complexities the civic society affords a spectacle of excess, misery, and physical and social corruption" (Ibid., 224). This spectacle, that resembles a "medley of arbitrariness" (Ibid., 187) is itself maintained by a internal, unconscious necessity whose central elements are the particularized needs and the labor needed to satisfy them.

The capacity that emerges here, and one that is specifically human, is the possibility of reflecting the circle of concrete needs that is predetermined by instinct and to achieve a multiplication of needs by way of analysis and differentiation. Civil society is therefore also an all-embracing differentiation of needs that results from those human capacities that are marked by an affiliated differentiation of conditions of labor and production. With the differentiation of needs, the means of satisfying those needs are themselves differentiated, and the seemingly contingent dependence on the products of those others who satisfy my needs becomes necessary and universal. "[E]verything particular becomes something social" (Ibid., 189) insofar as the satisfaction of my particular needs necessitates that I work and in this way contribute to the satisfaction of the needs of everyone. Everyone enjoys, produces and acquires for himself and produces therewith at the same time the satisfaction of the needs of the others. Furthermore, this differentiation logically implies a dissection of the processes of labor that causes labor to become simpler and ultimately more mechanical, "until finally the human being is able to step aside and let a machine take his place" (Ibid., 191).

The decisive thesis is as follows: from a certain historical-logical moment in the necessary economical development onwards, civil society cannot grant everyone the access to labor and therewith the autonomous assurance of subsistence. This historical moment is the becoming-industrial of labor in the factory in which the machine takes the place of the human being. If the dynamics of civil society is untrammeled in its effects it produces a constantly enlarged population and at the same time a constantly diminished possibility of maintaining subsistences. A consequence of this is "disproportionate wealth" (Ibid., 221) in the hands of a few, and reciprocally an augmentation of "dependence and distress" in "the class tied to work of that sort" (Ibid.). What becomes clear here is that out of the internal dynamic of civil society there is an unavoidable production of poor or impoverished masses. Without limiting its own effectiveness, civil society is always confronted with the problem of its own development, with poverty. As Joachim Ritter rightly remarks, for Hegel it is at the same time valid that "any advice to return to a former world" is a "way to take refuge in impotence. . . ."[9] Inescapably, civil society has therefore to confront the product of its own dynamic. But it is precisely unable to grant this to everyone to whom it must if it is to remain faithful to its own principle: that for everyone, one can secure one's own subsistence by one's own labor.

Also the state seems to be impotent here: the poor appears after the dissolution of the family as an autonomous person facing other persons but, and this is essential, does not find a representation in an estate that structures civil society. What is an estate? An estate constitutes itself through the mediation of collective labor and need and therefore emerges as a logical product of the economical movement and its differentiation. The estate appears besides the family as the second basis of the state.[10] Hegel distinguishes between three types of estates: 1. the immediate or substantial estate that is dedicated to the formation of its own land—its real estate—and which is dependent upon products of nature; 2. the reflective or the formal estate that mediates the formed natural material into mediation through the needs and works of others and therefore becomes differentiated/gets split up into the estate of artisans, manufacturers and commerce; 3. the general estate that is relieved of direct labor by private property or by state supply and that fulfills political-representative functions. The estate to which an individual belongs is contingent but *that* he belongs to one is necessary. "When we say that a human being must be 'somebody' [*etwas*], we mean that he should belong to a specific estate, since to be somebody means to have a substantial being" (HOPR, 197). Simply by belonging to an estate man makes himself into an element of civil society through his own determination; this is carried out by his own labor, which forms him, and he strives to conserve society and, through the mediation of the universal, he strives to conserve himself. Now, what does it mean *not* to belong to an estate? Hegel answers: "A person with no estate is a mere private person and does not enjoy actual universality" (Ibid.). Or to use a formulation of Neocleous: "[. . .] not being a member of an estate means that a person is nothing, nobody."[11] The poor who cannot develop the natural product of their own property and who is not an artisan, manufacturer or trader and cannot participate in the political-representative estate counts as nothing and is a nobody for the rational political order of the state. He is merely socioeconomically present, that is to say he appears in the social space and in the space of economy. But as a detached human being without an estate he does not stand within the rational political order of the state. If he "loses standing" (HOPR, 271, transl. mod.) with regards to its subsistence, Hegel can deny existence to the poor and to the whole *un-estate* of poverty. "[S]ince in civil society that which is common to particular persons only *exists* if it is legally constituted and recognized" (Ibid., 226). Poverty has in and for Hegel become an *un-estate*, it has become that which does not really exists because it does not exist adequately. Therefore he can note with absolute certainty: "The concrete state is the whole, articulated into its particular groups. A member of a state is a member of such a group, i.e. of an estate, and only as determined in this objective way does he come into consideration in relation to the state" (Ibid., 294). Being without an estate means to fall out of the representative frame of the state. Against this background, the poor or impoverished masses in Hegel's *Philosophy of Right* can easily be identified with what Jacques Rancière calls the *part sans-part*, the part without a part.

Nonetheless I shall demonstrate that Hegel does explicitly and implicitly offer proposals as to how we might solve the question of poverty, and by reconstructing these proposals I will demonstrate that he does not leave the problem of poverty untreated—as, for example, Avineri believes. The peculiar problem that Hegel recognizes is rather that he sees that something else emerges with poverty, that is connected to it. Although, as I will show, all of Hegel's solutions fail for internal logical reasons and it becomes clear that the problem of poverty points to a much greater problem, one that initially seems to be mediated by the problem of poverty: that of the emergence of the rabble.

Chapter 3

The Emergence of the Rabble from the Un-Estate of Poverty

With regards to poverty one can state that it will always exist within society and ever more so wealth increases.

(G. W. F. Hegel)[1]

Civil society produces poor and impoverished masses. This judgment is explicit in Hegel's deduction of its laws of movement. But because civil society in the organic framing of the state has to preserve the existence of its citizen, it has to confront the inescapable product of its own movement. Its movement generates the poor; the struggle now is to find solutions for this problem without arresting its own dynamic. The treatment of this specifically modern problem is thus dependent on the means that modern society provides which do not halt its own movement. One can find seven propositions in Hegel which attempt to broach a solution to the problem of poverty. All of them, I wish to claim, in a first approach, are, for different internal logical reasons, insufficient,[2] and in their failure make it possible to precisely mark the place which the rabble names. The seven solutions are[3]: 1. the treatment of the poor by civil society itself; 2. public begging; 3. the right of distress; 4. colonization; 5. redistribution of labor; 6. the corporation and its ethics (of responsible consumption); 7. the police, and in combination with it, religion (in the form of charitable institutions).

1. The "civil society must" following its own entitlement "protect its members" (HOPR, 218) and is responsible for "feeding" them (Ibid., 219) because it "takes the place of the family where the poor are concerned . . ." (Ibid., 220). Thus the support of the poor is demanded of civil society and its own resources, capital. But this seems impossible, as Hegel claims in an infamous sentence, because civil society is *"not rich enough"* (Ibid., 222) to assure the subsistence of those without labor, the poor. But behind this formula is most notably the insight buried that a redistribution of accumulated capital—through direct taxation, for example—would contradict the principle of civil society. This principle is the accumulation of the necessary means of subsistence for one's

own life by one's own labor. Civil society would commit a wrongdoing against its own principle and would therefore be led into a suspension of its constitutive continuity of mediation if it was to take from those who assure their own subsistence by laboring and give it to those who are not laboring, the poor. In Hegel's own words: "In either case, however, the needy would receive subsistence directly, not by means of their work, and this would violate the principle of civil society and the feeling of individual independence and honour in its individual members" (Ibid., 221).

In this sense, within poverty the contradiction of civil society with itself is crystallized: it should assure the livelihood of its members, but it can only grant it by committing a misdeed against its own principle and would consequently harm the fundamental conditions of its own existence. Therefore it has to give up either its claim to support its members or its principle. But the problem entails a further component: not only would such a contradiction with its own principle produce outrage in those who are able to support themselves by laboring; the contradiction would moreover generate in the poor the false insight that they are on the level of isolation, that is, of civil society, still linked to quasi-undivided, familial caring relations. Therefore, it would nourish not only the poor but also the belief that they could participate in a common property without the necessity to enter into the relations of mediation that are generated by labor. The poor would as a consequence lose the insight into and the desire for the necessity of a true existence, of a legal life and the threat of the emergence of a work-shy, lazy, careless mass would arise. In short, the threat of the emergence of that which Hegel calls the rabble. Therewith one of its central determinations is already named: the secondary loss of the insight into the necessary and active assurance of subsistence that supplements poverty. In this way the excessive surplus of the movement of civil society that is embodied in the poor leads, in the attempt to overcome it, to an even bigger excess, to the rabble. "One increases the evil that one wanted to cure" (HPRV, 224).

2. "[T]he most direct measure against poverty," Hegel claims, "has turned out to be to leave the poor to their fate and instruct them to beg from the public" (HOPR, 222). This formulation indicates that begging is able to maintain a minimal standard of attitude [*Gesinnung*], i.e. at least the formal stabilization of a will to work and to be active. Hegel seemingly wants to determine begging in this way as a residual and minor form of labor and to conceive of it in such a way that it can hinder the emergence of the rabble. With begging there seems to be the assurance of a minimal measure of activity or attitude. But Hegel also clearly sees the concomitant and dangerous effect of a tendency to restore pre-Reformation circumstances. The alms would reward the post-Lutheran idler who does not take his place in the mediating field of activity and would in this way also produce the condition for the emergence of the rabble. The consequence of his fidelity to Luther is articulated by Hegel when he speaks of

a difficulty related to begging: "Someone who has begged once soon loses the habit of working and he thinks he is entitled to live without working" (HPRV, 220). But as Hegel continues, "in civil society everyone is entitled to exist through his work" (Ibid., 222), which is to say that, in it one can only live an honorable life by laboring. Therefore, begging, contrary to first impressions, leads again to the emergence of what Hegel calls "the most horrible rabble that even fantasy cannot imagine" (Ibid., 223). The lazy, work-shy, dishonorable mass, the rabble, emerges inescapably also with begging.

3. The right of distress opens up a complex problem. Because on the one side there is, as Hegel claims, if it is necessary for the preservation of one's own life, the "right to life," that can legitimate an unlawful action: for example, "the stealing of a loaf of bread" (Ibid., 240). This means that there is a right also in contradiction with and opposed to the property of others. Without it someone whose life is endangered would be without rights and the greatest wrong would appear, namely the negation of a particular existence of freedom. With this Hegel wants to avoid the possibility that there can be particular victims of the general preservation of (abstract) right as a result *of* that very preservation.[4] The right of distress is a *right to avoid the victims of right*. It can only be justified through the "necessity [*Not*] of the immediate present" (HOPR, 125), but Hegel reminds us in the same context that human beings are rational beings and are therefore not simply given over to the instant, to the immediate present. In the necessity of the instant the poor can call upon the right of distress as a last resort to rescue their minimal life-preserving well-being. But within the state a deed committed out of distress initially still appears in the form of a crime.[5] The rational human being has to accept the necessity of the existing laws and to transcend his immediate indigence because "my conviction does not change the right of objectivity" (HPRV, 246); and one can add that it does not change the objectivity of right. The right of necessity seems to entail the possibility of a demand for the minimal security of subsistence. But it leads into the necessity of the distinction between a deed committed out of necessity and a simple crime. Implicitly, Hegel indicates a measure of necessity in his *Philosophy of Right*. It is determined by the magnitude of the lack of differentiation of needs.[6] If the need is solely directed toward one object then it reaches its most extreme form: desire. The right of distress is in fact a right to be exempted from worldly laws. But the legitimacy of the exception is still decided by (worldly) right itself. This ensures the primacy of right. Only a third instance can judge the crime that is committed out of necessity and, if justified, grant "pardon [*Gnade*]"[7] (HOPR, 129). But therefore the measure of necessity has to be inspected in order to make it possible to distinguish it from mere criminality.

So the deed performed out of distress always appears as a crime that retroactively can be judged as justified or not justified by a court of law. The court will inspect it in order to determine whether the deed was a mere "momentary blindness" or not (HOPR, 129). If the right of necessity does not apply then the reason for the judgment cannot refer to momentary blindnesses or to the "strength of sensual impulse" to not judge the criminal "as abstractly momentary" but according to his "honour due to him as a human being" (Ibid.). He has thus to be judged in the way that he is "as subject to *this* single moment alone" but as "essentially something universal" (Ibid.). It is clear that the right of distress only applies to actions of desire that imply the most intensive lack of a differentiation of needs. This is the subjective condition which objectively appears as a necessity [*Not*]. Hegel defines desire explicitly as "immediate singular [will] (desire)" (HGPR, 200), i.e. as a will that is without any distance and immediately directed to something that is exterior to itself and wants it for its own. But the immediate will is a merely natural will that, in order to be transformed into a truly free will, must be negated. In support of my reading, one can find in Hegel the following passage: "*immediate* will; natural will, freedom—to be with oneself—through negation of the *natural* will" (Ibid., 307). Any will has to immediately relate to something that is exterior to it (at least initially) in order to give itself existence, or, to put it differently: even to preserve itself as an individual will. What the will under conditions of necessity wills as universal is on the one hand a self-preservation as (at least) residual, that is, the minimal realization of (the particular) freedom; and, on the other hand, it wills this universal in a way that addresses its self-preservation.

In indigence, the need that founds all interactions of civil society regresses to mere and immediate desire, drive. In other words, in desire, freedom regresses to the state of the drive of a natural will. In desire, the universality and the demand for self-preservation (of the will) occurs in a particular and at the same time fundamental form. If the peculiar rationality of the illegal action performed out of desire and necessity can only be judged and found retroactively, one can here draw a further consequence from Hegel's conception of the right of distress: to him who looks rationally upon the crime (done out of desire), the crime in turn presents a rational aspect. This relation is mutual. The difficulty which I want to remark here is the following: that desire as undifferentiation of all needs and in consequence as the direction of all actions to one object introduces into desire a peculiar primacy of the natural. Desire means the concentration of a free will on the mere preservation of life. This concentration reduces the options of actions and needs and therefore indicates at the same time, as the foundation of the right of distress, the rationality of illegal actions and a moment of irrationality within them. If man is nothing but an absolute *conservare sui* when desire determines his actions, then the rationality of his actions, to which the right of distress has merely to refer becomes indistinguishable from the irrationality of an unfree animal.[8] Because as Hegel claims somewhere about the immediate will: "the immediate will is precisely one that acts on immediate fantasies and caprices, rather than on reasons and ideas [*Vorstellungen*]" (HOPR, 173).

Only when the rationality proper to man makes it necessary (for him) to concentrate all his actions and his free will on mere self-preservation, only when man follows one of his mere drives to assure his survival, does the right of distress apply. It therefore finds its place at the point where man and animal nearly have become indistinguishable. It applies to illegal actions that structurally come very close to what Hegel wants and has to keep out of the judging of criminals: the intensity of sensual impulses.[9] Any judgment that purely relates to desire as the intensity of sensual impulses and in this sense declares a necessary momentary blindness judges man, contrary to Hegel's intention, not as man but as close to what he calls a "beast" (HOPR, 145). One can find in Hegel a passage which points in the same direction when he argues that momentary blindness should not be used as explanation of a punishment. He enumerates there all that has to be excluded in order to finally add an important hint with regard to the solution of the problem I have been discussing. What cannot be taken into consideration for a judgment is "momentary blindness, the goad of passion . . . or, in a word, what is called the strength of sensual impulse (excluding impulses which are on the basis of the right of distress) . . ." (Ibid., 129). The argument is clear. The intensity of sensory impulses cannot be referred to as long as the judge does not deal with a crime committed out of distress. Therefore, the right of distress does not judge man according to his honor as a human being but as infamous. A handwritten note of Hegel is quite telling in this context: "Indigence [*Not*] is a sacred word, if truly. . . ." (HGPR, 240)

Indigence is a sacred word because it names the resort that protects life from right itself. Therefore the holiness of the word indigence is always already related to the life appearing in relation to it. Indigence is a holy word and life, being in indigence, is a holy life. And thus is supposed to be protected by the right of distress. But in the same breath it is sentenced to be in the status of a malicious form of life that fully expresses the whole ambiguity of the word *sacer*.[10] Because the judgment of the right of distress that follows the Hegelian axiom, "right—must have life" (Ibid., 241), paradoxically, by not judging it according to its honor, denies it the right to life. Because "life—life which only a person has, is a right . . ." (Ibid., 242). This means also that the judgment of the right of distress at the same time protects the life it judges and denies it the right to life. The right of distress always implicitly judges human beings as vicious, as malicious, and as animals. It is only valid for the being of actions that stem from desire and therefore it is only valid for man as malicious, irrational animal, as beast.

Also it needs to be stated that the exception from objective right that is the right of distress cannot be a permanent one because right itself decides over its exception. This is a further problematic consequence of Hegel's conception. If the right would install the permanence of actions out of distress it would become less entitled to be objective right and the right of objectivity.

Related to this is a problem of the reversal of quantity into quality on two levels. If, for the particular individual, the right of distress is valid in one case the momentous indigence is only overcome *for the moment*. Because, if there will be a reemergence of indigence, right can only be cleared by another trial. The right can decide only for *this* case. Otherwise, constant indigence would imply the constant possibility of an unrestrained legitimate claim for the right of distress. Every exception from right has to remain a specific and singular exception and does not at all imply a permanent repetition: "But the only thing that is necessary is to live now; the future is not absolute but ever exposed to contingency" (Ibid., 125). In addition, the same problem repeats itself on a secondary level because within civil society an always particular misery is multiplied in the sense of the production of the impoverished masses. On both levels the decision for a permanent justified applicability of the right of distress would come with a qualitative transformation of right itself. Right would lose (at least by trend) both the "force of reality" and the status of "being in some way known" as objectively actual. The question of poverty remains unresolved by the right of distress.

4. With the idea of colonization Hegel offers a historical and logical option that necessarily accompanies civil society. After having stated that civil society is necessarily driven beyond its own limits,[11] he goes on to explain the meaning of this claim. Civil society has to find "means of subsistence, in other lands" (Ibid., 222). But at the same time, the colonization of other peoples, due to its internal logic, offers no more than a temporal retardation of the problem of poverty. Hence it leads into a logic of bad infinity because it does not represent a solution to poverty as such but rather a temporary postponement. It generates an eternal return of the same problem in the framework of bad infinity that can be deduced from the extension of civil society itself. It is nothing but a postponement of the same problem.

5. Hegel discusses the possibility of giving those who are without work an employment at various times as a further option of fighting against poverty.[12] But he is also quite explicit that this idea would lead to destructive consequences for the whole of the economy of society. On the one hand, it would result in a disproportional increase of production that would lead at best to a mere redistribution of those who are poor. If one gives employment to the poor they produce products that are generally produced by others who would then would descend into poverty. Hegel gives the following example:

> In an area of the mountains live 1200 families of weavers, the consumption is such that in total 200 are without work; if one now gives employment to them they all produce as much as 1200 can produce, but they consume what a mere 1000 can accomplish and as a consequence of this 200 other families lose their work; the only difference is that 200 are helped and in contrast 200 others become beggars. (HVORL 4, 612)

The redistribution thus structurally leads to a repeated institution of the status quo and does not offer a qualified solution to the problem of poverty. Rather it can even have effects that lead to a debasement of the whole situation. By giving an employment to the poor, "the ensemble of production is increased. The evil [of this solution] consisted in the fact that too many products exist; the worker does not find a way to sell his commodities. One thus multiplies the evil one wanted to cure. Because in this way even those who formerly found buyers will be ruined" (HPRV, 224). Through this disproportionate overproduction there will consequently be a crisis that relates to the value of all goods and to the production of all commodities. Therefore it has a dangerous effect for the totality of the economic movement of civil society. Hegel refuses this option not just because it does not abolish poverty but because it has an intensifying effect of crisis.

6. Due to its logical constitution, the corporation seems to indicate a possibility of subduing the problem of poverty. The reflecting estate that is the most essential estate of civil society gathers in his branches (the artisan, manufacturer and merchants' estates) the majority of social activity.[13] Artisans, manufacturers and merchants now build on the shared fundaments of their modes of activity and work associations. Within the corporation that appears to its members as a "second family" (HOPR, 225), the particular individual gains its honor through a mutual recognition of the respective ability and furthermore through the commonality of work there emerges the "livelihood . . . stable resources." (Ibid.). In this way the construction of secure resources to which any active member contributes assures the support of all those members who sink into poverty. For Hegel, in the corporation, poverty loses "the unjust humiliation associated with it. The wealthy perform their duties to their fellow associates and thus riches cease to inspire either pride or envy . . ." (HOPR, 226). The corporation appears as an *institution of provisions* mediated by common labor. But: these provisions are exclusive. Because only the members of the corporation constitute the bonds of support that only they can demand in case of emergency. Here a subduing effect of economy and of the problem of poverty is reached. But because it is constituted exclusively by the common quality of work—that Hegel for this reason calls capability[14] [*Befähigung*]—it excludes all those who are not members of the corporation, i.e. who are incapacitated. The funding in common activity does make the capacity into an *exclusive* condition for the possibility of participation in the corporation.

An extension of this structure may be found in the attempt to read the Hegelian conception of the corporation as at the same time a genesis of an "ethic of responsible consumption."[15] One proponent of this idea is Joel Anderson, and it is necessary to discuss it here briefly since it presents a radicalized version of the function of subduing. Anderson starts from the assumption that the corporation produces an educational effect that accompanies the creation of an economic consciousness on the part of its members. In short this

means: The producer comes to realize that he is also a consumer. In this way
an economical and ethical investment in the particular property that would be
unthinkable for uncivilized peoples, becomes thinkable, as Anderson claims.
If they still show "a lack of consciousness of the way the use of my property is
disadvantageous for others"[16] in an "ethic of responsible consumption" civil
society would itself become an overly enlarged corporation. Only, this corpo-
rative society would not be marked by the essential feature of constituting a
common property. Rather it would appear in the form of an educational effect
and the emerging ethics of economically responsible consumers would be its
substantial result. In Anderson, this consequence is described as follows: "The
general principle, however, is that a society with stable employment patterns
will be a society in which consumers put their money where the jobs are."[17] The
attempt of civil society to become state,[18] as Marx defined the corporation,
would then have been realized. The rational state would be transformed into
a general society-corporation and its corresponding economical reason. But
the soothing assurance of certain of the social domains that the corporation is
able to introduce even in this tightened dialectic of producers and consumers
has a specific, qualified form of production—which is to say, a capacity—as its
precondition. The corporation is able to grant the security of its members. But
it knows the poor only as former, capable producers. Or to put it differently:
it only feeds and supports the poor that it knows. Hegel's conception of the
corporation excludes those that are not capable members of it; Anderson's
reading of it excludes those who have and have had no employment and who
therefore lack "immediate assets (capital)" (HOPR, 192) and a developed
capacity. The corporation always knows a remainder and this remainder is the
poverty of those that it does not know.

Here a further differentiation of the corporation becomes necessary. This
comes out of the determination of the specific right of the corporation. Because
it has the "right . . . to look after its own interests within its own sphere, . . . to
admit members qualified objectively by the requisite skill and rectitude, in the
numbers determined by the general context . . ." (Ibid., 224–25). Domenico
Losurdo has reconstructed in great detail the genesis of the liberal theories of
the Vormaerz-politics, and it is thanks to his work that we can now understand
more clearly how the conception of the corporation in the Hegelian *Philosophy
of Right* can be understood as an organizational model and political instrument of a working class at the time of its formation.[19] For the working class, the
corporation adopts a function that should not be underestimated. Losurdo
reads the Hegelian explanations of the corporation as a paradigmatic sketch
of a proto-trade union that would put the worker estate in a position to generate a form of organization that, on the one hand, could distance itself from
the fossilized structures of the medieval system of guilds and crafts and would
therefore be able, on the other, to influence economical factors as laboring
time regulations, wages and further general determinations that are linked to

the workers' estate. As Losurdo has shown, the vehement defensive reactions that are not only directed against workers associations in the period of their formation but also against the Hegelian *Philosophy of Right* can be convincingly read as symptoms of such a possibility. Losurdo rightly states that "with the diagnosis of the mercilessness of the dialectics [that leads to the inescapability of poverty in civil society] . . . nothing remains but the solidarity of the members of a certain category of worker which does not abolish poverty but to alleviate it."[20] But he neglects to take into consideration one essential category in the constitution of solidarity. Because solidarity can only be conceived of in Hegelian terms as a specific form of shared professional ethics [*Standesehre*] within the corporation that can only result on condition that another quality be present. Here the category of rectitude plays a central role. This can be clearly shown by referring to the fact that before a new member is affiliated with the corporation his rectitude has to be detected by an inspection. If rectitude is the virtue that "displays itself solely as the individual's conformity with the duties associated with the circumstances to which he belongs . . ."[21] (HOPR, 192, trans. mod.), then by investigating rectitude, the economical effects of the dynamics of civil society return through the backdoor.

Rectitude is, as a result of its structure, one of the forms of the appearance of the good whose basic determination Hegel stated in a handwritten note to paragraph 18: "α.) good, what is in adequacy with my end, for example my sentiment—paradigm; β.) the good—adequacy of the will to itself . . ." (HGPR, 69). Adequacy therefore can be understood as the conformity of the particular will with objectivity. Rectitude as the form of the appearance of the good means in this context also the adequacy to the duties associated with the circumstances, which also means conformity to them. This conformity is the object of the test that comes before any affiliation with any corporation. The testing of individual rectitude operates for Hegel with the distinction of day laborer [*Tagelöhner*] and merchant or craftsman [*Gewerbsmann*], which is to say with those who "are or want to become masters" and those who are not one and do not want to become one. "The elements need to have a certain skillfulness [*Geschicklichkeit*] . . . one therefore examines who wants to be in that particular trade" (HVORL 4, 629) and tests their capacities. If the corporation examines its members it tests their fundamental adequacy to the duties of the circumstances. In short: it examines that which Hegel calls attitude or conviction [*Gesinnung*]. If rectitude is that "which may be demanded of him by law or custom" (HOPR, 157), this means that the examination of whether or not someone lives in a way that is adequate to the circumstances is at the same time one that investigates whether this someone also fulfills the necessary conditions to develop a feeling of self [*Selbstgefühl*]. The feeling of self within the corporation means to be identical with the other members of the same corporation and to recognize the general resources.[22] However, the examination of the adequacy of the attitude of the individual necessarily excludes those who are not masters and do not want to become masters—the poor and uneducated. In short: the day laborer or the poor do not act according to the duties of the circumstances and therefore lose the possibility of becoming a member of the corporation. The adequacy of the individual to the circumstances in this way implies a participation in an estate and the assurance of one's own subsistence through labor. But if, as is the case for the poor, the adequacy is lacking, the whole problem crystallizes on one categorical side of the distinction with which the examination operates—on the side of the day laborer. He figures as an in-corporation[23] of the unskilled, of unwillingness, of inadequacy. The problem of exclusion from the corporation occurs in the same sense as the problem of attitude appears as a problem for civil society.

Also the alleged objection that a day laborer is only a day laborer because of the already functioning repressive capitalist politics that attempts to make any form of workers organization impossible[24] does not lead to a further solution. Either the power of contingent economical circumstances are again introduced and with it the dominance of one class, the capitalists, as Hegel often states from 1823 on, and this leads to a weakening of the function of the corporation. Or the discussion shifts onto another level, where it concerns the particular individuals and takes them as responsible for their exclusion from the responsible attitude—but then one falls behind Hegel's own diagnosis and understands poverty as individually generated. Either one explains the arbitrariness of economical movement with the arbitrariness of the obtaining of individual interests which have effects on the corporation—one explains the arbitrariness (within the corporation) by the arbitrariness (of bourgeois circumstances)—or one explains it by starting from individual errors (arbitrariness) that are abstractly separated from the movement of civil society. Neither position leads to a solution of the poverty question. Although Hegel refuses both explanations, the internal (conceptual) constitution of the corporation does not offer a sufficient solution either. The corporation, due to its structure, retains the function of an administration of the given conditions, although it is entitled to raise that which the particular interests have in common to the universal level. Because those who cannot articulate a legitimate particular interest within civil society, due to the fact that they do not participate in an estate, necessarily and a priori fall out of the corporation.[25] The corporation is in Hegel's conception a regulating institution of provisions whose regulating function always remains dependent upon the given dynamics of civil society; its fundamental illness, poverty, can be alleviated but never cured by it.

6. Apart from the corporation, the police are *the* decisive institution of exterior provisions.[26] They intervene to oppose the remaining contingencies in the system of needs and in the administration of justice, that is the legal safeguarding of civil society in its purely formal universality. The system of needs presents the well-being and the subsistence of the singular individual solely

as "a *possibility* whose actual attainment is . . . conditioned . . . by the objective system of needs" (HOPR, 215). The administration of justice takes care of the juridically anchored security of property and therefore of the assurance of the exterior appearance of personality and sublates its infringements as privately legal and penological jurisdiction. But all this it does only in a limited manner, because it can only act in "individual cases" (HOPR, 215). In this way, there is an opening of the floodgates to the obstruction of the universal possibility. The limitation of the administrations of judgment already marks the police's field of operation. The police act precisely in the domain in which the possibility of gaining one's own subsistence is guaranteed in its realization. It therefore assures the possibility *as* possibility. This is why it can be understood as an aid to realization because it assures the possibility that precedes the realization of a singular will on the level of formal generality. In it the assurance of the singular subsistence becomes a legal claim and therefore the police accomplish the mediation between the individual and the universal possibility. As the "universal authority by which security is ensured" (Ibid.), the police, while having many other tasks, for example do prevent and prosecute crimes and "penal justice" (Ibid., 216). But by still operating on the level of the infinity of understanding, i.e. civil society, it does not have an objective measure, no inherent limit,[27] that would mark what is damaging, what is to be forbidden or what is suspicious or dangerous. Because of this lack of objectivity an essential characteristic of the operational domain of the police is reflected back into it and introduces into its operation a certain arbitrariness, "a measure of odium" (Ibid., 216).

Also, there is no objective limit for its course of action and it may therefore sometimes "set to work very pedantically and inconvenience the day-to-day life of people" (Ibid.). In the last instance, its proceedings are justified by the understanding and the character of the policemen.[28] As "authority of order [*Ordnungsmacht*]" (HVORL3, 692) that work in, on and with contingencies it is directed against the arbitrarinesses of evil, against any merely particular will that opposes in the form of a wrong the general will and abstract right. But because the relations of civil society are exterior ones, i.e. subject to contingency, there can even be, involuntarily, in the course of a just action, for instance using my body or my property, a harm done to others. This harm, as Hegel claims, will consequently be more or less imputed to me "because the things that cause it are, indeed, mine, although it is true that they are subject to my control . . ." (HOPR, 116). Unlawful actions are thus not only constituted by the arbitrariness of a particular will but also by the contingencies of social life. There is a perpetual "possibility of harm" (Ibid., 260) with regard to the right of other singular wills that cannot be reduced to a mere particular possibility which depends solely on an isolated will. The possibility of hindering the realization of freedom is given in the exact same measure as the possibility of its realization.[29] The police find their place in the struggle between the two possibilities.

Important here is a hint that can be found in Griesheim's transcription of
the lectures on the philosophy of right from 1824/25. In it Hegel refers to the
fact that the possible harm that is produced by the usage of one's property is
the same as "the pauperies . . ." (HVORL 4, 591). The term "pauperies" refers
etymologically to poverty, but also to the actual form of cases in Roman Law
which name a harm generally induced by animals and that by association was
by a legal judgment imputed to the owners of the animals. The duty to compensate for the damages for which it was possible to file a suit (*actio de pauperies*) only originated in cases in which the animal acted in a way that was called
contra naturam sui generis. This means that one only had to cover the damages
in cases when the type and genus of the animal and its ordinary behavior did
not allow for an anticipation of the harm done. This duty expires if the owner
hands over the animal to the injured. This remark is important if one is to
conceive more precisely of the police operation,[30] because from it one can
conclude that the police proceed against any action *contra naturam sui generis*. I
will, after a few more general remarks, follow up on this lead.

The general determinations of the police can be grouped as follows: They
assist in the realization as a) an organ of inspection, surveillance and control
(in relation to the particular members of civil society) and as b) an instrument
of regulation and monitoring (in relation to the totality bourgeois economy).
One can claim that police provisions on the particular level include inspection, surveillance and control and that these functions become regulation and
monitoring on the more general level. Here it becomes clearer to what extent
the police represents another possible solution for poverty. Because as a) an
organ of inspection, surveillance and control it does have a broader function of
provisions than simply that of preventing crimes. It also ensures that any individual member of a particular family enters into the general one and becomes
"a *son of civil society* . . ." (HOPR, 218). If consequently the family does not
assume the function of providing the assurance of the well-being of its members, the police have to intervene. Because the family also appears as a person[31]
within civil society, the police are able to act against the arbitrary actions of
this familial person. And these arbitrary actions are first and foremost actions
that go against its own purpose and nature, actions that are *contra naturam
sui generis*. The police intervene, for example, if the child does not receive an
appropriate education—if so the right of the children to be educated and the
duty of the parents to provide them with it is unnaturally or even counternaturally suspended—or if the family wastes its "external reality" (HOPR, 171), its
property and in this way "the existence of its substantial personality" (Ibid.,
trans. mod.), that is constituted by its "permanent and secure . . . resources"
(Ibid.); or if its own preservation and subsistence is unnaturally endangered.
The police as organ of surveillance protect the right of the children to become
members of civil society and fulfill in this regard an explicitly sociopolitical
function. Already the education of the children in the family is supervised

by the police who can "compel parents to send their children to school, to have them vaccinated and so forth" (HOPR, 219). As organ of control it draws the consequences of the familial negligence by depriving the parents of the custody of their children. The interrelation of surveillance and control here leads directly to the question of "extravagance [*Verschwendung*]" (Ibid.) and clarifies its relation to the problem of poverty (and its consequences). Because civil society has the duty to guarantee subsistence to its members, "it also has the right to press them to provide for their own livelihood" (Ibid.). If a person acts against his duty and starts wasting [*Verschwendung*] rather than gaining its own subsistence, civil society has the right to take over their guardianship. This goes for all persons. Everyone stands under the surveillance of police as it prevents him from destroying himself *contra naturam sui generis*. The police as organ of surveillance and control do not only intervene when there is a sinking into poverty motivated by arbitrariness. It is not only about "starvation," as Hegel writes, "the further end is to prevent the formation of a pauperized rabble [*Pöbel*]" (Ibid.).

The police supervise the rights of individuals in order to control their fulfillment of their duties and to intervene against actions *contra naturam et sui generis*. Therefore they operate to conserve the general possibility of realizing the always particular well-being of each against the possibility of harm. It intervenes against unnatural actions because it secures any particular possibility even against the particularity itself, that is, it secures the general possibility even against the bearers of this possibility. The police come to the defense of the wastrel against himself. In this way, the struggle of possibilities even traverses any (singular) particularity. But it is also clear that Hegel wants to avoid a further problem here. The police as organ of surveillance and control prevent the emergence of the rabble. Because if the child lacks education or "if one allows children to do as they please . . .," they develop "a deplorable absorption in particular likes and dislikes, in peculiar cleverness, in self-centred interest—the root of all evil" (HPM, 58). The police thus want to eradicate the root of all evil[32] [*ausreuten*], as Hegel writes elsewhere, because it is that which engenders the rabble. It attempts to prevent the rise of the rabble by preventing actions *contra naturam et sui generis* which produce the condition of possibility for its genesis. On the one side the functioning of the family is supervised and if necessary there is an intervention to secure the reproduction of civil society. In this educational-political relation, the police seem to be victorious when it comes to the prevention of the rabble. But on the other side, the emergence of the rabble occurs because of the production of poor masses in civil society and not because of individual or personal failures—i.e. also not due to a failure of the familial person. If the possibility of surveillance and control on the part of the police is defined in such a way as to potentially obviate the descent into poverty as the result of singular and irrational arbitrary actions, it is limited even in this function. It cannot eradicate the principle on which the police operates and which it attempts to protect. Because for civil society, poverty is not in all cases *sui generis* although it is in all cases *contra naturam*, or in short: it is a contradiction. The police therefore do not offer a fundamental abolition of the problem of poverty. It always remains partial and never becomes fundamental in its actions against the formation of the rabble.

But the spectrum of the police tasks in civil society is not limited to supervision and control. For the discussion of the question of poverty the second function of the police, b) as an instrument of regulation and monitoring is important. For Hegel the police also undertake the far-reaching task of generally regulating the interests of the consumers of "regulating the market" (HVORL 4, 595). For this it has to care for "street-lighting, bridge-building, the pricing of daily necessities, and the care of public health" (HOPR, 218). It conducts passport controls,[33] cares for "country roads, harbors, communication across the water" (HVORL4, 595), the opening hours of shops (Ibid., 599) and undertakes the "protection of consumer interests" (Ibid.) by examining the quality of groceries, medicine and of the "health of the cattle" (Ibid., 597); it also controls the production of groceries—by introducing for example commodity-norms. In this regulating and monitoring function, the police are a (bio-politically operating) institution of provisions that devotes itself to "universal activities and arrangement of common utility" (HOPR, 217), to the "essential need" (HVORL 4, 595) in which all particular everyday actions have something in common. This field of many tasks also includes the supplementing of alms. The contingent help against poverty is supplemented by "public poor-houses, hospitals, street-lighting, and so forth" (HOPR, 220) whose administration is under the control of the police. It carries out a regulation of (the harm of) poverty, that is, an administration and a minimal accommodation of the existing poor masses. It should be mentioned here that the poor houses have a dual purpose. On the one hand they operate under the governance of a subsistential measuring device; in them one can read off the subsistential minimum of a society: "One can get to know the minimum of subsistence in the poor houses, hospitals, in them only the necessary is endowed, therein it can be seen what is considered to be the most marginal measure of needs" (HVORL 4, 608). On the other hand, the transition from the purely charitable *welfare of the streets* to the "administrative" (Ibid., 607) *welfare of the hospitals* takes place in these institutions. As institutions they represent the interface of the police and the religious sentiment of charity. Because the purely charitable benevolence is contingent in its relation to indigence and poverty and depends on the arbitrary moral determinateness of every singular will, in its institutionalization there is an increase and intensification of its effects. For Hegel such an increase is established by Christian religion in a twofold manner: first it *internally* 'institutionalizes' in any believer the feeling of charity and therefore achieves an increase in the effectivity of mere morality[34]; it increases the *welfare of the streets*. Secondly, it institutionalizes charity *externally* in the poor houses and thereby the *welfare of the hospitals* gains a stable existence. This is why, as Hegel claims, poor houses and hospitals can often be found in "catholic countries" (HVORL 4, 607) because it is first and foremost the religious fraternity, i.e. the Christian one, which "maintains hospitals . . ." (HPRV, 221). That also the "essential religiosity" (HVORL 4, 607) of Christianity and its double intensification of charity can only limit harm, not end it altogether, results from the fact that it can only provide minimal care. If the poor even "loses the consolation of religion" because he cannot enter the church "in rugs" and if "also the clerics prefer to visit the houses of the rich more than the barracks of the poor" (Ibid., 604),[35] in the poor houses—as their function as measuring device of subsistence shows—he is reduced to "mere survival."[36] In the poor-houses the poor is preserved *as* poor. This then means that a twofold problem is repeated here: 1. The preservation of the poor who do not subsist by their own labor also nourishes the rabble-like attitude of demanding subsistence without work[37] 2. the assurance of mere survival presents a merely temporary cessation of the problem of poverty because it cannot abolish the problem but only perpetuate the status quo. The poor remain poor and the rabble can arise at any time.

One can also find two things that are in the realm of police tasks which are closely related to the problem of poverty and the prevention of the rabble. Again, these are tasks that prevent actions *contra naturam sui generis*. The police are in charge of the right to strike and also of what one can call, in a more modern idiom, the management of production. The question of the right to strike is part of the (market-) regulating function of the police because in it the question of stopping the unhindered effectivity of the dynamics of civil society arises. Initially, all producers in the civil society have the "interest of satisfying their needs" (HPRV, 217). But by the fact that their egoistic production is part of the general system of needs with any singular process of production there arises a general claim for the producers that is directed toward the product manufactured by another particular producer. In any producer, by also necessarily being a consumer depending on the products of others, a demand (for the continuation of production) formally develops and this can also mean: a claim even against himself. The right to produce in civil society following selfish interests in this way turns into the duty to produce. This obligation to produce usually only "surfaces in some cases" (Ibid., 218) and remains invisible because it is no "properly physical necessity . . ." (HVORL 4, 598). Rather, this obligation appears at moments in which the individual misunderstands himself and reduces himself to the sole role of the producer. In this way he misapplies the (formally) universal demand of anyone to possess the products of his own labor. He forgets his own claim as consumer on the products of others that determine him. The formal universality appears in any particular producer as a split that divides him into producer and consumer. The interlocking of right and duty on the level of civil society can be understood as a logical intertwinement which presents the universal inherent in any particular individual. Against the background of this universal claim Hegel can justify the necessity of police intervention in the case of strikes. He notes in this context: "The journeymen agree upon the fact to not work anymore for their previous salary, this cannot be allowed by the police" (HPRV, 218). Because "the branch that has been covered by them must be satisfied; it is their duty to produce, the public has a claim on their work and can assert it" (HVORL 4, 598).

If anyone in civil society is a producer *and* a consumer then the claim of the consumer is structurally a claim that he himself makes against himself as producer. One can remark here that the nature of any producer is split and thereby the intervention of the police against strikes is again justified as an action *contra naturam sui generis*. If the producer strikes he does not act in accordance with his own interests as consumer and thereby acts against his own nature, his own purpose and claims in civil society. Striking therefore becomes an action which runs counter to one's own nature. The police have to intervene against these "dangers of arising upheavals [*gefährliche Zuckungen*]" (HOPR, 217), of striking particularities that disregard the universal and by suspending the production act against their own nature. In short: the police have to intervene to lead these particularities back to the universal. But for Hegel this means that any legal justification for a strike is impossible. Striking is nothing but the selfish promotion of particular interests that the police have to hinder in the interests of the universal, and this means in the interest of the consuming producer against the producing producer. Hence, any form of inner-economical blockage of the reduction of earnings or the prevention of poverty on the side of the producers becomes impossible. The problem is not only included in the strike but rather in the impossibility of anchoring a suspension of the universal claim within the effective system of right.[38] If civil society is "the battlefield where everyone's individual private interest meets everyone else's" (HOPR, 278), then it is clear that another terrain of this field of conflict is the inner split of each individual producer (into producer and consumer). On the level of civil society, it is unthinkable for Hegel that a particularity, here being the producer, incorporates the claims of the universal because it has always behind his back caught up with him.

The last regulating function of the police that is again closely related to the question of poverty is the management of production. To coordinate the production falls to the police, because "public care and direction" (HOPR, 217) is necessitated by the fact that "large branches of industry depend on foreign circumstances and remote combinations" (HVORL 4, 600) that cannot be overseen by any single individual. The management of production that the police as "governing office" (Ibid.) undertakes initially means regulating the production. Its measures are derived from the trade-related conjuncture in relation with other states. This regulation consists in finding "standards" to "help supposed evils" and, if necessary, "open a new outlet" (Ibid.). The police in this function are a sort of *visible hand* that intervenes in the functioning of the market if the monitoring of the trade-related situation leads to the diagnosis of a threat to the inner-economical stability. One can remark here that this regulative task of the police makes it appear to be a modern institution of provisions. It observes the production in its own and in other states and attempts to avert a crisis of overproduction and to create economic ways of relieving the market of surplus products. With that Hegel has implicitly extended the economic model of civil society into all other states. It is no longer limited to just one state, and this means that the economic conjuncture derives not only from intrastatist but also from interstatist interdependences that the police have to monitor.

But at the same time, Hegel could not be more explicit as to the fact that the unimpeded effectivity of civil society "thus drives it . . . beyond its own limits" (HOPR, 222). That fact that its own dialectical dynamic leads to the permanent surfacing of instability and impoverished masses does not change when this dynamic is extended as a model to cover other states and is under the control of a monitoring institution. The regulating power of the police has the principle and the laws of the dynamic of civil society itself as its inner limit. That for Hegel, the police, due to their rich field of tasks is "the ancient politics which once expressed the political constitution of civil society and the art of its government"[39] is clear. However, the police constantly struggles with the tendencies and the effectivity of civil society, under conditions that a priori make it impossible for it to win. Because it permanently attempts to stem the dangers of the economic excesses and of economic disintegration it becomes clear that as a "medium of administration" it is directed against the "existence of the rabble." The rabble then no longer represents, as it did for the "philosophical tradition of politics," the "positive limit" with which state justified itself historically, but the element that it attempts to "integrate."[40] That this attempt permanently fails due to the structural irresolvability of the problem of poverty is because the possibilities of regulation are always preconditioned by the movement of civil society that constantly produces Lazzaroni.

Chapter 4

Transition: From the Poor to the Rabble

'The vulgar' [Pöbel] usque recurret.

(Friedrich Nietzsche)[1]

What do all these solutions show? None of them eliminates the problem of poverty because "the free play of forces in capitalist society, whose liberal economic theory Hegel had accepted, has no antidote for the fact that poverty" exists (ATS, 29). The support by civil society is unsuitable because it either contradicts its own principle (and would be a deed *contra naturam*) or produces a wrong attitude and conviction in those who would receive it; begging also fails due to this problem of attitude; colonization is nothing but a retardation of the problem and not a fundamental solution; redistributed labor produces a crisis of overproduction; the right of distress is only valid in singular cases and at the same time reduces man to the status of an animal fighting for its mere survival; the participation in the corporation generates only an exclusive form of supplying the poor that excludes those who do not have the necessary capacity; the police remain always bound to the principle of civil society that itself is the reason for the production of poor masses. Poverty "remains inherent and endemic to modern society" (Ibid., 153) and consequently the poor fall out of the binding mechanism of civil society and the state because they do not follow the central implicit imperative of the *Philosophy of Right,* namely to be somebody. "When we say that a human being must be 'somebody' [*etwas*], we mean that he should belong to a specific estate, since to be somebody means to have substantial being" (HOPR, 197).

The poor, by being deprived of participation in an estate, is no longer something, but is rather a nothing that surfaces within civil society. The *un-estate* of poverty falls out of all institutional and representative forms of integration and stands as an unnatural fact, like an irremovable obstacle in the social economy and in the economically mediated social sphere of the state. In this regard one is justified in claiming that the poor can be conceived of as a part without a part in Rancière's sense or a singularity in the terms of Alain Badiou[2] because it is present socially just as much as it is present economically, but at the same time it is excluded from the mechanisms of representation—that are derived from the participation in an estate. Rancière and Badiou are both in agreement that this structural place in which the poor appear can be described as a place of transformation; a place in which something can happen, precisely due to its peculiar lack. What becomes clear in the *Philosophy of Right* is that all of the solutions proposed by Hegel perpetuate a more fundamental problem: that the unrecoverability of the question of poverty leads to the permanent and irrefutable possibility of the emergence of the rabble. Or to put it differently: from the *un-estate* of poverty leads a constantly possible way to the formation of the rabble. That all of Hegel's solutions fail indicates that his famous claim that civil society is never rich enough and never has enough of its own peculiar property has to be read in two ways: On the one hand, as already discussed, one needs to read it in a way that civil society is not able to live up to its own entitlement and assure the subsistence of every individual. But on the other hand—and this can be shown here—the Hegelian judgment has to be read as claim that civil society is internally marked by a lack that it cannot overcome. "When the civil society is in a state of unimpeded activity" (HOPR, 220), the effectivity of its inscribed lack is perpetuated and that leads to the production of poor and impoverished masses in consequence of which the rabble can emerge.

In this way civil society is incessantly compelled to recognize the inevitable production of that which it cannot recognize. If only that which is "common to particular persons really *exists* [and] is legally constituted and recognized" (Ibid., 226), one can discern in this constellation, invoked by the poverty problem, the fact that within Hegelian philosophy something else becomes thinkable, a 'something' which does not exist (as a legally constituted and recognized entity) but that is still 'there.'[3] To use a word of Adorno's: the rabble is emerging and "spirit knows that without being permitted to know it . . ." (ATS, 26). In this context Hegelian remark that the "movement of recognition and of being recognized" is "as social form of mediation embedded in the movement of the economic processes"[4] also gains an enlarged meaning. The structural lack in civil society is acted out in the excessive production of its own opposite. The internal rationality of its own nature appears for itself in incorporations of its own irrationality. Civil society appears in this perspective as an oversized network of action *contra naturam sui generis*, or to put it differently: the nature and purpose of civil society is opposed to its own nature; its own nature is counternatural. Because if poverty is in civil society a sort of counternature that is deprived of the mediating relations of work and exchange, it is still necessarily produced by the nature of civil society. *Sui generis* it encounters its other in poverty. *Sui generis et contra naturam*: this is the formula of civil society itself. That the purpose of civil society is to produce what contradicts its own nature inscribes into Hegel's thought the necessity that "the state is appealed to in desperation as a seat of authority beyond this play of forces" (ATS, 29).

For, "a *deus ex machina* is needed, which binds together necessity and contingency in law. This law that reconciles the social antagonisms and mediates the movement of the whole again with the movement of the particular is, for Hegel, the state . . ."[5]

The central instruments of the state's influence are the institutions—with the exception of the judicature—that are given in civil society for fighting poverty: the corporation and the police. As shown, neither leads to an abolition of the lack in civil society or its production of poor masses. The principal lack which is inscribed into the determination of the civil-social dynamic is even perpetuated in a radicalized 'form' in its excessive effects and, this will be my thesis, it will be inscribed in the state. For the contradiction that determines civil society leads to the (logical) coemergence of the state *and* the rabble. The name of this peculiar excess of civil society is 'rabble' whose emergence is unavoidable; whose possibility of surfacing cannot be escaped. But who or what is the rabble?

Chapter 5

Pauper-Rabble

Poverty in itself does not turn people into a rabble [. . .].

(G. W. F. Hegel)[1]

The rabble "makes itself [*macht sich von selbst*]" (HOPR, 221, transl. mod.).
For, although it is defined as the "lowest level of subsistence" Hegel remarks
afterwards that "poverty in itself does not turn people into a rabble" (Ibid.).
Poverty appears as a precondition of the rabble but when and where the
rabble occurs is contingent. To say this is also to say that its occurrence is
solely and decisively determined by a subjective operation or act. The rabble "is created only when there is joined to poverty a disposition of mind
. . ." (HOPR, 267). Since the rabble not only names the poor, but the poor
who apart from their property have lost also their honor to earn their own
subsistence through laboring, their participation in an estate and, moreover,
their insight into the rational whole of the organically structured state. "The
rabble is different from poverty . . ." (HVORL 4, 608); it is the poor who has
become disgraceful. "Within the state the citizen receives its honor through
the office that he occupies, through the business that he runs or through his
other working activities" (HENZ 3, 222). Anyone without office, business or
activity becomes dishonorable. The extended and deepened loss leads to the
fact that he is full of "inner indignation [*Empörung*] against the rich, against
society, against the government, etc." (HOPR, 221) because he considers himself to be "in a state that lacks rights [*Rechtlosigkeit*]" (HPRV, 222). This is
what Hegel calls "paltry rabble loutishness [*Pöbelhaftigkeit*]" (Ibid., 223), and
implicitly this renders more determinate what the rabble's extended loss is.
The term 'loutish [*dürftig*]' is significant in this formulation. It refers to the
Old High German word 'durft'[2] which names as much a need as nature's call
[*Notdurft*]. What Hegel also calls the "loutishness [*Notdurft*]"[3] of poverty, this
is the rabble. The rabble is loutish in two respects: first because it emerges
in the loutish, and, second, as soon as it emerges it is nothing but the excre-
mental, the exudation, the unbound of civil society. It is what is expelled even
from the poor. The rabble is generated from the needy, but is itself needier

than those in need because it is the product of a further, deepening privation. This further privation distinguishes it from the poor and it determines its peculiar loutishness. This is why it considers himself to be without rights. Because "in civil society everyone is entitled to exist through his work" (HPRV, 222) and while the poor cannot secure his subsistence in it "and because he [the rabble] knows that it has the right to find his subsistence, its poverty becomes a wrong, an injury of its right; this generates a dissatisfaction that at the same time takes the form of a right" (HVORL 4, 609). It measures it against the general claim that arises from its own nature and which cannot be upheld due to its inscribed lack. If civil society unavoidably produces the poor, with their existence comes an indignation about this existence. The rabble feels indignant about the excessive and counternatural effects of the economic movement of society because in them it becomes clear that the legal entitlement of everyone's existence can only be upheld on condition of the constant deprivation of rights of a huge mass of impoverished individuals, which becomes visible retroactively. The possibility of maintaining the right to subsistence of all in society means at the same time the impossibility to ensure the right of subsistence *for* all. It is this contingent insight into the counternature which creates the rabble and its indignation. It is, to speak with Marx, "in its abasement the indignation at that abasement, an *indignation* to which it is necessarily driven by the contradiction between its human *nature* and its condition of life, which is outright, resolute and comprehensive of that nature."[4]

That this indignation appears as "conviction without rights" (HVORL 3, 703) is, following Hegel, due to the fact that the rabble lacks "honour to secure subsistence by its own labour and yet at the same time" claims "the right to receive subsistence" (HOPR, 221) because "once society is established, lack [*der Mangel*] takes the form of a wrong . . ." (Ibid., transl. mod.). It is here that for the first time the complex structure of the problem of the rabble becomes clear: only that which is mediated through work and activity exists truly in civil society; its own dynamic produces something that cannot be mediated by work or activity; the indignation that might surface concerning this structural lack, which is its indignation about its own counternature, can appear to civil society only as counternatural. In the indignant voice of the rabble, civil society does not hear anything but the counternatural voice that it itself generates. The rabble becomes the counternatural entity which unbinds civil society and from its perspective appears as counternatural indignation. In this way the "loutish rabble-likeness" is a "consciousness of lack of rights under the condition of right" (HPRV, 223). Therefore Hegel can judge him as "impudent" and the whole attitude as "impudence" (Ibid.). The rabble drops the "subjective bases of society" (HOPR, 222)—shame and honor—and becomes "frivolous and shy of work . . . like the Napolitan Lazzaroni for example" (Ibid., 221, transl. mod.). In this way it fundamentally loses the "habit of working" and the "need for industriousness disappears" (HVORL 4, 609) and it abandons itself to "laziness and extravagance [*Verschwendung*]" (HOPR, 222). It becomes clear here, and this expands the rabble problem with one decisive component, that the lazy, impudent, shameless, frivolous rabble without habit does not originate only in relation to poverty.

"There is also a rich rabble" (HPRV, 222),[5] Hegel remarks far-sightedly in his lectures of 1821/22. In the posthumously published lectures he at the same point speaks about the distinction between proletarians and capitalists.[6] With this an essential structural comparability of the rabble and the proletarian is noted which I will carry along in the background in what follows. But it is worth making the implications of Hegel's remark on the rich rabble from the notes of his lectures explicit, for in this way one can better grasp decisive characteristics of this concept.[7] There is also a rich rabble. And it is marked by similar mechanisms of privation to those of the poor rabble. That there is this equation is due to the fact that, as Hegel diagnoses, the fact that it uses the "power of wealth" to "pull itself out of many things that would do no good to others" (HPRV, 222ff). The rich rabble pulls itself out of many things and unbinds itself from them. It appears therefore also as a result of a privation, although it initially does not appear to be a deepening privation. Already the meager rabble was marked by a loss of shame, honor, etc. This movement of loss is repeated with the rich rabble. The poor rabble is furthermore marked by denying its legitimacy to anything that is recognized and legitimate in civil society and it shares this judgment with the rich rabble. But the poor rabble declares all existing things null and void because it is driven by the indignant insight that the poor is himself a product of the socially repressed impossibility to uphold the right to subsist for anyone. It is indignant at the substantial deprivation of rights that befalls the poor and denounces the totality of civil society by taking its peculiar counternature as a basis to distance himself from it. Because the meager rabble denounces an injustice (which is also his own) it follows from that, that this injustice places it outside of right in general. As Avineri remarked, the rabble is "a heap of human beings utterly atomized and alienated from society, feeling no allegiance to it and no longer even wishing even to be integrated into it" (AHT, 150).

Atomization, alienation, unbinding, disintegration. These are the characteristics of the rabble. But in contrast to the poor rabble, the rich refuses to legitimate everything that exists for different reasons. It presupposes a "state of lack of rights" (HPRV, 223)—a sort of economical state of nature[8]— in which its wealth is the only power determining everything. Because a great many subsistences depend upon its wealth, it misunderstands their dependency as his power (over them). It misperceives itself as a sovereign, who decides upon their misery and therefore also their rights. In this way it opposes his purely economic power over the abstract right, over the universal legal right of anyone and thereby to the ethical community as such. It opposes with the whole of its fortune "the customs [*Sitte*]" (HPRV, 223). The rich rabble is marked by the "corruptness" which manifests itself in the fact that the rabble "takes everything for granted for itself" (Ibid.) because he also denies the right to exist to any of the ethical, legal or statist institutions. Therefore it understands itself to be beyond the (existing) right, because it assumes that it stands above right as such; or: it stands outside (existing) right because it thinks that it itself is the only valid right. It can only claim this by assuming an economically determined state of nature, in which it can also assume the economic right of the fittest.[9] The rich rabble pits its sovereign command of purely economical power against the sovereignty of the state and its institutions. It thereby sets up its (purported) right against the right (of the given). Thus it thinks of itself as the sole true instance of right and order: beyond the existing right of the ethical community there is a right, which it as sole sovereign. To put it differently: it does not recognize "the ethical substance and its laws and powers" (HOPR, 155) because he conceives of himself as the sole absolute. But if one can claim here that the meager rabble is fundamentally generated by a "dissatisfaction" (HVORL 4, 609) of the poor with regard to their own situation, how does the corruptness of the rich rabble originate? Or to put it differently: from which point on do the assets transform into such a power of wealth that the conditions of possibility of becoming-rabble are given?

These questions are all related to what Hegel calls "luxury" (HPRV, 229). To start, *ex negativo*, one can claim that as soon as the rich rabble appears within civil society the institutions that for Hegel are supposed to perform the transition to ethicality do not properly function. The corporation, for example, did not only have the task of opposing poverty but also of hindering the concentration of wealth and with it the origin of luxury. This is why Hegel determines the corporation not only in such a way that in it the contingency of alms is abolished. It should also produce general resources that support its members and should take "the arrogance of wealth in its duties against the cooperative [*Genossenschaft*] and the envy it can cause" (HVORL 3, 689). The concentration of wealth in the hands of the few *always* engenders envy outside the corporation and is *always* marked by the greed of the individual: this is Hegel's radical antiliberal diagnosis throughout. Wealth outside the corporation and the alms given to the poor is determined by arbitrariness. To put it differently: *any wealth outside the corporation and the estates is the property of the rich rabble*. In short: the rich man who is outside of both is always rich rabble. But to tame this double arbitrariness (of wealth, of the alms) the corporation is introduced by Hegel. It would mediate both with the common property. But "when complaints are made about the luxury of the business classes [*Klassen*] and their passion for extravagance—which have as their concomitant the creation of a rabble of paupers—we must not forget . . . this phenomenon has an *ethical* ground" (HOPR, 225).

The failure, as Hegel points out here, does not result from the constitution of the corporation. The ground lies rather in those single wills which are not members of a legitimate corporation and therefore its "isolation reduces his business to mere self-seeking . . ." (Ibid., 226). It is this reduction that delineates the fundamental condition of possibility of the rich rabble. Like the poor, it lives as a "mere private person" (Ibid., 197) without any form of universality within civil society because it, too, does not participate in an estate and consequently in no corporation. This is why the poor and the rich rabble live as private persons in an atomized, alienated, unbound, disintegrated manner. When Hegel defines the corporation as "the second *ethical* root of the state, the one planted in civil society" (Ibid., 226), one can conclude that both, the luxury- and the poverty-rabble are ethically uprooted. To be ethically uprooted means to live as a merely private person. But here one can find an important difference in the form of appearance of the two types of the rabble which can be read at the same time as a distinction between two different dimension of contingency. The poor depends on the alms and the public institutions, i.e. he ultimately depends on nothing but contingencies to maintain his subsistence. The private person who is reduced to the egoistic side of business, i.e. to the pure self-seeking accumulation of capital, is on the one hand also structurally dependent on contingencies. But it is decisive that he himself has contingently, which is to say, arbitrarily decided in favor of these contingencies. He who thirsts for luxury is subordinated to contingency, just as the poor man is. But one cannot claim that it is the same contingency in both cases. If the poor is *involuntarily* in the situation of depending on contingencies, nevertheless, the *voluntary* decision of a single private person precedes this dependence. This is why Hegel can claim that the arbitrary decision against the universality of the estate and the corporation generates the existence of the gambler.[10] When the individual becomes a gambler by deciding to depend and ground his existence and subsistence purely on the contingencies of civil society, for him, then, the whole economic dynamics becomes a gigantic roulette wheel and gambling table.

Here the general structure of the *Philosophy of Right* should be recalled briefly. The partition into abstract right, morality and ethicality is repeated in each individual step,[11] including the last one, ethicality. There, this partition is rendered in the form of the distinction between family, civil society and finally, the state. If one links each of these steps together, then morality and civil society stand on the same logical level and therefore one can understand civil society as the dimension of morality within ethicality. The sphere of morality is fundamentally determined by the fact that in it the subject determines by himself and in himself what his own good is; an always subjective and always singular determination of the good. Morality can be conceived of as a determination of the good in itself on the level of the will as free for itself. As Josef Derbolav writes: "Within abstract right men are recognized as merely formally free persons, morality does justice to them as subjects, that is as individual, willing and acting human beings."[12] It is only here that there appears that "which we call *human being*" (HOPR, 188) because only here does it move from the concrete needs to a determination of its own good, of an always singular concrete good. However, this good in itself must be objectified, i.e. realized, through actions, and it delineates only in an abstract way what can be considered as the end of an action that can only become an end in and through acting. If one structurally draws a parallel between morality and civil society, one can understand how the existence of the gambler is generated. As Hegel put it in his handwritten notes on the determination of one's own good, talking about the form in which the good initially appears in the subject: "with the individual, a matter of contingency, arbitrariness of his own particular decision . . ." (HGPR, 238). Or even more succinctly: "The Good is initially determined by the particular, by opinion [*Meinen*]" (Ibid.): opinion, one should add, because it depends on the possibility that contingency can err.

The individual becomes a gambler by his own contingent decision. Anyone is reduced to being a mere private person who voluntarily—or involuntarily—withdraws from participation in an estate and the corporation; in short: to someone who, whether voluntarily or not, does not want to be *something* (recognized). That is why Hegel can describe the appearance of the gambler in civil society as a contingent and particular determination of one's own good and purpose. The gambler is thus twice governed by arbitrariness. He becomes a gambler through his own arbitrariness and remains in consequence always subordinated to the same contingency (of the game). He therefore depends on all of the dimensions of contingencies within civil society. This is why gamblers just live from moment to moment without it being possible for their subsistence to gain any security or solidity. For one might claim that the gambler puts, due to his particular opinion, *the* contingent as such in the place of the universal. For him security exists "only for today" (HPRV, 230) and thus he does not receive through the mediation of an estate and the corporation any recognition and honor (as would be accorded to a master), he is in a state of lack. The lack of recognition he attempts to compensate through luxury[13]—which can only succeed if today's game ended happily. Luxury expresses the limitless exterior elaboration, the *"external evidence"* (HOPR, 225) of the wealth accumulated in the game. Thus, in luxury one can see the indefinite multiplication "of needs, means and enjoyments" (Ibid., 190) that are no longer produced by an external dependence or necessity. In this way, luxury, that is the constantly and increasingly differentiated and multiplied exterior elaboration of one's own satisfaction of needs, becomes a supposed medium of compensation for the lacking recognition. Luxury is a compensation for a lack of recognition but at the same time it also clarifies what the gambler as such is marked by. For the logic of the existence of the gambler is a logic of a double *happy few*. On one side, the game presupposes that not everyone can win in it, but only the happy few; on the other side, the winnings in this game are never lasting and persistent, rather it is the *few happy moments* that allow the gambler to ensure his subsistence.

The gambler who wins the game for today and so can secure his subsistence loses, like the poor, his honor but he is capable of seemingly regaining the refused recognition in "the most outrageous way" (HPRV, 230) through luxury. The gambler who wins for today is the rich rabble. Luxury designates in relation to the gambler the "external demonstration of his success" (Ibid.), of a success in the always ongoing game of contingency. This also means: Luxury exists only on the side and only because of the gambler. Luxury is always luxury of the rabble; or more precisely: luxury is the peculiar (external) form of appearance of the rich rabble. The general and recognized resources of the corporation and the poor without any resource stand opposite to him. In short and in a formula one can claim for Hegel: where there is luxury, there is the rich rabble; where there is the rich rabble, there is luxury. He assumes that there can be a logic of recognition beyond the mutual mediation through labor: the logic of luxury itself. For the rich rabble pretends that a being-recognized exists beyond the estates, without the honor of the estate, a recognizing without shame and honor. However the structure of recognition is itself suspended because the supposed recognition is a purely external and this means a purely momentary one. Although the gambler assumes that as soon as he extorts the winnings of the contingent game, he can even out the deficit of recognition and honor by the exterior demonstration of his success. However, this incorrect assumption drives him even deeper into mere externality and the semblance of recognition. He perverts the specific reciprocal reference that marks the logic of recognition by dissolving it into a purely exterior and moreover a one-sided relation. He applies all social relations only to his wealth in the same way that he thinks of all relations only with reference to it. With this move he wrongly presupposes a recognition without the (institutional and legal, i.e. ethical) structures of recognition of the other as equal. A recognition neither of the others as the same nor of the same as others, but a recognition of the one, the particular individual as isolated and particularized. The gambler and his wealth create and are the only thinkable universal in this logic. The external demonstration of his success that can, because of this, never know an end is bound to a logic of bad infinity. Over and over, he has to confirm himself and has to externally secure his supposed recognition. For Hegel, the gambler knows the universal only as an exterior relationship and therefore always remains merely external to it. Through the exterior demonstration of his property, any other property is always cut off from it.

At each moment, this supposed recognition can be lost again and it is always uncertain whether the luxury and splendor will ever be enough to be truly recognized. Although he is free from honor and shame the gambler assumes that he can gain recognition externally. He is driven further into shamelessness and the lack of honor because he exteriorizes himself further in and through luxury. In short, the gambler fails because he carries out a perversion of the logic of recognition which leads at the same time and immediately to the impossibility of recognition. This is also why the successful gambler and the poor are the two figures in which the rabble can originate. But one has to remark that the poor can be the failed gambler, and yet it does not have to be him. The lost game is only one possibility among many for the genesis of poverty, a contingent, and not a necessary one. But poverty is produced necessarily by the unhindered effectivity of civil society. The gambler trusts precisely in this unhindered effectivity that produces the poor, but he stands on the side of its contingencies and not on the side of its necessary result. If the gambler becomes poor, this means that the economic contingencies, to whose dependence he exposed himself, have turned on him and his success and wealth have proven to be what they always will have been in advance: absolutely momentary and merely particular. The failed gambler who cannot be caught up by any general resources and the gambler who loses his wealth fall back into poverty. There is always a path from gambling and luxury to poverty but no path from poverty to luxury.

But Hegel's worry, as one has to remark, concerns the successful gambler, who is the rich rabble. Because he has made an "acquisition . . . without labor," a "contingent winning" so that he produces, as Hegel notes in another passage: "an external, mindless and immoral [*gesinnungslos*] relationship" (HGPR, 331–2). The explanation of his peculiar danger that he poses again leads back to the question of recognition: The successful gambler is dangerous because he on the one side—and in contrast to the poor rabble—secures his subsistence without entering[14] into the mediating relations of work and activity and therefore he unbinds himself by a supposed legal entitlement[15] from any form of universality. For the successful gambler only the first fundamental definition of the level of civil society is valid: "In civil society each individual is his own end, everything else is nothing to him" (HOPR, 181). But this would not really be a problem, because it defines the formal constitution of "the *world of appearance [Erscheinungswelt] of the ethical—civil society*" (Ibid., 180) and therefore becomes the definition of any member of society. Rather the danger is generated by the fact that the second definition is not valid for him, which is that: "But except in contact with others he cannot attain the whole compass of his ends . . ." (Ibid., 181). The contingent winnings enable him to understand himself in a way that he is own end and all others are nothing to him. Thus he is no longer "conditioned by universality" (Ibid.). In a handwritten note to paragraph 155 of his *Philosophy of Right*, Hegel describes the form of the existing reciprocal recognition within the ethical as follows: "Not only: others have rights, I am equal to them, am a person like them, I shall have duties by their rights—as being equal to them I also shall have rights through these duties . . ." (HGPR, 305).

Only by addressing and presupposing the other in all my actions as equal can I reciprocally be recognized as equal. I as a person respect the other as a person if and only if all my actions presuppose that they can only succeed if I have already recognized the other as a person. Recognition essentially relies upon the form of reciprocity. The rich rabble—i.e. the successful gambler— interrupts this reciprocity. It considers his economic power, its wealth, as the sole right standing absolutely above the right of all others. Therewith it dissolves, as a direct dialectical consequence, its duty by them. And as it "holds in his hands many subsistences" (HPRV, 223) and it also renounces its duties by them, "it considers itself as a master of their misery and therewith also of many of their rights" (Ibid.). The rich rabble posits itself as the source of these rights. Because of the purely external dependence of a certain number of subsistences on its wealth, it considers himself not to be recognized as equal but as unequal, as fitter, as their master. Because of this dependence it considers itself to be recognized as (their) master. But this it can do only by understanding its economic power[16] as the sole legitimate power that opposes all other power and authority. In this way it misinterprets their dependence on his wealth as its mastery. It posits himself as individual and the power of an individual fortune as the only authorized and authorizing universal. Therewith it fundamentally posits *the* particularity, the particular of his position as sole legitimate universal, i.e. as the universal that befits it and only it and therefore it hypostatizes structurally *the* particularity (as such) as the universal. The rich rabble, in his understanding, is the only one who stands above the ethical universal of the state; the only one who due to its wealth can understand itself *as* being the real universal. The rich rabble is: the ego and its own, more precisely: the own(ed) is the ego, the only thing. In this way it takes the standpoint of those "principles . . . from . . . [which] follows the ruin of inner ethical life and the upright conscience, of love and right between private persons, no less than the ruin of public order and the law of the state" (HOPR, 11).

The rich rabble (is) atomize-s(-d), alienate-s(-d), unbinds (unbound), disintegrate-s (d). It posits itself as atomized individual in the place of the universal; therewith it alienates it in the form of mere particularity, unbinds itself from it and thereby disintegrates the logic of ethical community as such. Luxury therefore presents rather the expression of a mere semblance of recognition that can subside again any day. Because there can only be recognition of a purely egoistic interest if it is at least formally mediated with the universal of all egoistic interests. As Hegel notes, it is necessary

by one's own act, through one's energy, industry, and skill, to maintain oneself in this position, and to provide for oneself only through this process of mediating oneself with the universal, while in this way gaining *recognition* both in one's own eyes and in the eyes of others. (HOPR, 197)

The gambler as a merely private person already and necessarily cuts off this mediation, and the successful gambler, the rich rabble is only the obvious deepening of this lack of universality. This is why one can also find here a deepening loss that already marked the poor rabble, but which is decisively different. Recognition relies on a minimum of universality that the recognized and the recognizing share[17]: the sole universal that here remains is the unmediated egoism, the absoluteness of a particular position claiming it is the only legitimate one. Hegel writes as if he were thinking of the rabble: "If all rights were put on one side and all duties on the other, the whole would be dissolved . . ." (Ibid., 161). By way of the isolated claim to unite the whole of right in itself and by preserving the other only in his duty toward this, its right, the entitlement of the rich rabble that it constantly expresses in its external declaration of his power is constituted. But its entitlement is "insecure [nichts *Stehendes*]" (HOPR, 226) as one might put it with Hegel. This is because for the claim of the rich rabble to hold the absolute right is valid what we say for the claim to right in general: "A claim as such, [is] only an incomplete right" (HGPR, 181).

Through its wealth, subsistences are dependent upon it and it misjudges this external dependence by conceiving of it as his recognized power and of itself as master of these subsistences. One can speak of a *double misunderstanding on the part of the rich rabble*. Because it misunderstands itself as the master of the subsistences subordinated to it and misunderstands in this way what appears to be an external dependence and envy as a supposedly universal relation (of recognition) whose creation is due only to the rabble and it property. Therewith the rabble takes Hegel's comment "to *particularity* it [civil society] gives the right to develop and launch forth in all directions" (HOPR, 181) in a certain sense too seriously, because it transforms the "system of complete interdependence" (Ibid.) into a system of one-sided dependence. The rich rabble so interprets the envy of others as a compensation for its lack of recognition. But envy is already an effect of the movement of isolation and particularization that produced the gambler and has therefore lost the character of anything essentially universal. Through envy this movement of particularization now externally reflects back onto the rabble: what it presumes to see as recognition in the others is nothing but that which it itself is marked by—namely egoistic interests, in the form of envy (of his wealth). The universal that it assumes to create with its wealth dissolves in its exterior relation to others immediately into that which this supposed universal always already was: a selfish affect of a particular will. The semblance of recognition here appears as that which it essentially is: a mere semblance.

The rich rabble is a selfish particularity hypostatized to become a universal and this is precisely what appears again and again in any relation into which it enters: as luxury and envy. Here the logic of bad infinity appears again in absolute clarity: to compensate for the lack of recognition, it demonstrates its wealth externally as luxury; this does not generate recognition but rather envy; envy does not mean recognition of the rich rabble but is selfishly directed at the inequality of his wealth; the external demonstration of luxury thereby generates a relationship to it that is also purely external; the rich rabble considers itself thereby to be recognized as absolutely unequal, as master; but because its supposed power and rule is based solely upon the exteriority of its wealth, it has to repeat this external demonstration permanently in order to let his power not be seen as a mere semblance of power; therewith the rich rabble stands in a constant and unsurpassable dependence on the externality of its fortune; it follows a logic of "again and again" that continually subordinates its claim to be regarded as a legitimate universal and absolute right to the external contingency of his acquired wealth; consequently it is constantly subordinated to the laws (of externality) that have generated it: the master before whom the rich rabble bends its knees is, however, contingency. Here one finds the whole "incoherence of the unethical" (HOPR, 179, transl. mod.) that the rich rabble is marked by. One can state that the conditions of possibility of the rich rabble are produced subjectively. It is due to an arbitrary decision to posit oneself outside the ethical bond of mediation that the gambler will always depend on objective, i.e. external contingencies. This is why the rich rabble even lacks what determines the familial person, namely the need for "possessions specifically determined as permanent and secure . . . resources . . . permanent property" (HOPR, 171). Both in the rich rabble and in its form of appearance (luxury) there always appears another regent who is the reason for its inner instability: contingency. What follows after the subjective contingency of deciding to remain a mere private person and become a gambler is the external contingency which characterizes the game that is the bourgeois economy. The rich rabble remains within the heteronomous determination by chance.

Let me summarize what has been said thus far: the gambler does not care for recognition. By siding with contingency as such he always already posits himself in "a situation of slavery and dishonour" (Ibid., 147) and gets back what he is fundamentally determined by in the inverted form of envy, "as an alien subjective conviction" (Ibid.) that always remains alien to him, i.e. merely external. This is an example of successful communication.[18] The gambler refuses already through its hypostatization of the mere contingent particularity as such "the normative presuppositions that we adopt as soon as we take part in corresponding activity" (HPIF, 73). The only norm that is known to the gambler is contingency and particularity as such. Therefore he de-socializes, or better: a-socializes himself. Consequently, the successful gambler is also disintegrated and asocial. If, for example, the family—the first social unit in the state—is for Hegel fundamentally determined by a "consciousness that is not selfish" (HGPR, 323), then this is because, in it, the individual already stands in a relationship which accompanies the understanding that he would be lacking something if there were no others. The rich rabble however and already the existence of the gambler is lacking this form of sociality and he is stuck in "the arbitrariness of a mere individual's particular needs . . ." (HOPR, 171). To him one may apply the inversion of what Hegel describes in his handwritten note to paragraph 170, which deals with the resource of family as a general resource: "The rooster eats nothing for itself—searches the hens and chicks—moving" (HGPR, 324). The rich rabble even lacks the moving behavior of an animal; he rather represents a rooster who eats everything for itself.

The rich rabble, the successful gambler, is atomized and isolated in a double sense: following the temporal logic of the *few happy moments* and essentially, because it is the only one to whom its wealth is of any use; it is the incarnation of the *happy few*. In this it contradicts the formal universal of the mediation of needs and activity within civil society. If for Hegel civil society is integrated into the (rational) dialectical movement which leads to the state, then this is because it describes as formal universality a mediation of the contingency of each individual's egoistic will and the necessity of a universal, complete dependence. The presence of the rich rabble in luxury again refers to a contradiction of civil society with itself: If on the *side of universality*, i.e. of its necessary movement, there is a contradiction due to the production of poor masses, there is on the side of formality, i.e. of the particular selfish interests in their contingencies the contradiction that the contingent games of civil society can contingently produce a particular position which dissolves the mediation with the universal. This position is its own end as with everyone in civil society but it does not need others in order to attain it. Thus its particular end does not take "the form of *universality* . . ." (HOPR, 181). The successful gambler is rather the contingent particularity which posits itself *as such* as universal and absolute. In this context, one of Hegel's claims about the rabble gains another meaning: "It is precisely the excess of wealth by which civil society becomes too poor to control the excess of the rabble" (HVORL 4, 611). Civil society becomes too poor (concerning the degree of its universality) due to the excess of wealth which is the excess of the rich rabble. One can note here: There is a rabble on the side of necessity within civil society, which emerges from the poor, and a rabble on the side of contingencies within civil society, which emerges from the gamblers. Or, one can say: there is a *rabble of necessity* and a *rabble of contingency*. To reformulate this once again: there is a *universal and a particular rabble*.

The universality of the poverty-rabble comes from its contingent emergence from the necessarily produced poor, and this emergence provides a peculiar but irreversible insight. Its emergence reveals a logic that I will call the *logic of double latency*: Anyone within civil society and the state can, as a result of their singular fate, deteriorate into the *unestate* of poverty. But because impoverished masses are inevitably produced within civil society, and poverty is therefore no longer generated due to individual misdemeanors, this means that anyone in the state is latently poor. At the same time any poor—because the rabble makes itself and is not subordinated to any other objective condition—can become rabble. For the rabble is rather the product of a genuinely subjective operation, a subjective act. The direct consequence of this is that anyone in the state is latently poor and therefore latently rabble. More precisely one has to state that this logic only appears within the dialectical movement that consists in the form of "retroactive performativity,"[19] to employ Žižek's term. With the rabble the insight becomes possible that *anyone* in the state will have been latently rabble.

Here one finds a good example of "the conversion of necessity into contingency and vice versa" (HOPR, 117). The necessary production of the poor is converted into the contingent production of the rabble and its emergence in turn is converted into the retroactive insight that anyone in the state will necessarily have been latently rabble. Because of this logic of double latency the poverty-rabble becomes a universal rabble. One can also express this logic by reversing a Hegelian remark. If Hegel claims that "[t]he educated person, however, develops an inner life and wills that he himself shall be in everything he does" (Ibid., 110), one can state that the rabble is (or more precisely, will have been) in everything *without* doing anything. Although it also posits its supposedly merely particular position as a universal, it is able to refer to a universality that appears in this *logic of double latency* which is immanently produced behind the back of civil society. In a certain sense, to anticipate a formula which needs to be clarified in the following, one can claim that the poor rabble inserts an equality different from the one Hegel aims at when he claims that: "This single abstract determination of personality constitutes the actual *equality* of human beings" (HPM, 237). *Anyone at all is latently rabble* is the formula that will express this other equality.

The particularity of the rich, the luxury-rabble, is determined by the fact that, with its wealth, it transforms civil society not into a system of complete dependence, but a one-sided dependence. It postulates the absoluteness of a single and always isolated particularity as the universal and yet against it. It misunderstands this system as the system of his isolated needs and declares it as its own right to subsist without work and activity. Although everyone in the state is selfish, when understood as a bourgeois and not as a *citoyen*, he only can be it under the condition of universality to which he is constantly referred and bound. But to withdraw from the rational organization, i.e. to insist on one's egoistic interests outside the corporation and the estate means that the condition of possibility of the rich rabble is an arbitrary act of the will on the part of the individual to drop out of the universal mediation. *Anyone*—and this is decisive—who invokes his egoist interests and is outside of the estate becomes a gambler. *Any gambler who* is lucky in the game of chance decays to the luxury-rabble. Here one can see that first an arbitrary act of the will on the part of the individual is needed so that then the objective and external contingencies of the game can produce the rich rabble. This logic, which I will call the *logic of double contingency*, makes the rich rabble into a particular rabble. First subjective contingency is needed (the arbitrary decision to become gambler) and then objective contingency is needed (success in the contingent game). This double determination is the reason for the particularity of the luxury-rabble. The hypostasis of particularity and contingency into the real universal always particularizes the structure of the luxury-rabble. But how do universal and particular rabble relate to one another?

Chapter 6

Luxury-Rabble vs. Poverty-Rabble

[R]abble above, rabble below!

(Friedrich Nietzsche)[1]

Both the rich and the poor rabble are marked by a peculiar privation.[2] This privation is what both have in common, or, the common is what they are both lacking. However, one can remark already that the effects of the privation of the rich rabble have a different foundation and specificity to those of the poor one. In the following I will investigate these effects in detail. What should become clear is that under the name 'rabble' two different problems of Hegelian thought are hidden, and although they draw near to one another at certain points, they nevertheless remain separated by a deep rift. In the following it will become clear that the movement of privation only reaches its full radicality with the poor rabble and that this radicality consists among other things in the fact that he cannot be included in any category of knowledge (of objectivity, of the state and ultimately of Hegel's philosophy) nor be objectified. Hegel does not know anything about the rabble and he, by definition, cannot know anything except that it appears with the poor or better: it could appear. But at the same time it is never clear if it appears, will appear or already appeared. Therefore one cannot claim that the rabble is for Hegel "a sub-statist, numerically meaningless stratum."[3] One can rather claim that Hegel's *Philosophy of Right* from a certain moment on—the moment of his possible emergence—is constantly haunted by the rabble without being able to interrupt the logic of this infestation that traverses all of its domains. I will, by way of an immanent reconstruction, attempt to uncover something that in a certain sense remains inexplicable for Hegel, or rather, I will show how his descriptions of the rabble represent permanently failing attempts to comprehend and grasp the (poor) rabble. For the deduction of the these requires a clear differentiation of luxury- and poverty-rabble in order to provide for an adequate description of both, the structures of integration and of unbinding. Paradigmatically one can claim: the luxury-rabble loses honor, respect, customs, shyness of work, etc. because it was able to 'secure' winnings in the contingent game in which it arbitrarily decided to partake. Although its wealth is unstable, it appears to the rich rabble as so powerful that it understands itself as the only legitimate instance of right—beyond the state. The poor rabble, on the other hand, is, after an 'initial' loss—poverty—marked by a further and deepening loss. For from the specificity of the logic of privation from which there results the fundamental difference of the logical sequences:

1. '*Winnings—loss*' *(rich rabble) against* '*Loss—loss*' *(poor rabble)*. Because the poor rabble not only loses his property but in consequence everything that makes it a bourgeois in civil society. Its loss of shame, honor, etc. does not depend on a contingently accumulated and external wealth. Rather the deepening loss is a result of a genuinely *subjective operation*, as I will call it, and which Hegel calls "a disposition of mind . . . joined to poverty . . ." (HOPR, 221). In contrast, the genesis of the rich rabble essentially depends upon the exterior contingency of success in the game, although it creates the condition of this possibility himself by an arbitrary *subjective operation*. What results from the fact that both types of rabble are generated by a *subjective operation* is this:

2. the possibility of distinguishing between the *subjective operations* with reference to their logical position. The attitude that is joined to poverty is categorically different from the one that makes the gambler. Because the arbitrary and particular decision to posit oneself outside the estate and the corporation produces the conditions of possibility of the emergence of the rich rabble. The *subjective operation*, the subjective arbitrary decision, creates its conditions. But its emergence depends, following the logic of double contingency, on the exterior contingencies of the game, because "[w]hat is by nature contingent is subject to contingencies, and this fate is therefore itself a necessity" (Ibid., 306). In contrast, the conditions of possibility of the poor rabble are always already given by the economic dynamic, by the unavoidable production of poor masses that appear within civil society. On the one side we have a *subjective operation* generating the conditions of possibility, on the other we have a *subjective operation* that already relies upon an inevitable objective condition of possibility of the same operation. One can say that here the logical sequence '*subjective (arbitrary) operation—contingent winnings—loss*' (rich rabble) is opposed to the sequence '*loss—subjective operation—loss*' (poor rabble). Thus, there are two different reasons why the two types of rabble do not grant legitimacy to the existing institutions. This difference is reflected in:

3. the distinction between "*depravity/corruptness [Verdorbenheit]*" *and* "*outrage/ indignation [Empörung]*" (HPRV, 223) As soon as they emerge, both delegitimize each concrete and particular institution and any organized agency of the state by dissolving the organic unity of bourgeois and political life into a disparate crowd of individuals with particular interests. On one side, however, the declaration of illegitimacy is generated because the rich rabble posits itself, on the basis of its contingently won wealth, as absolute and paramount to all existing institutions. It hypostatizes itself and its wealth to become the

only valid right. In the lectures on the philosophy of right from 1821–2, the Hegelian notion of depravity precisely names this hypostatization.[4] It is one side of the rabble-like evil. For Hegel, evil in this context means that the will is heteronomously determined by contingency. As he had already clearly remarked in 1820, if a "particularity may take himself as the universal" and understands the participation in an estate only as a limitation, this is a "false idea . . ." (HOPR, 197). On the other side the indignation of the poor rabble with regard to the counternature of civil society is generated by a "ostensible feeling of right" (HPRV, 223). Indignation is outrage at the civil society and its movement. That only the poor rabble is indignant signifies that indignation can only be produced from the necessary product of the economic movement. It derives from the sentiment of an assumed wrong. Because the poor rabble declares the results of the counternatural movement of civil society to be a wrong that is happening to it. But because the rabble is in this way judging the movement of the existing order itself to be illegal, he interprets the state of right as a "state of lacking rights" (Ibid., 222). It thus relates to the objective circumstances in the mode of negation, and takes "the merely negative as a starting-point" (HOPR, 257) for its relation to the ethical community and is thus for Hegel the product of a specific "dissatisfaction that makes itself in this way" (HVORL4, 609), as an inner-subjective product of the privation of economic movement. By taking his particular judgment as the only valid standard with which to measure the objectivity of existing circumstances, the indignation of the poor rabble presents the other side of the rabble-like evil. Because the rabble also posits the contingency of its disposition of mind in a hypostatized way against the free will that realizes itself objectively in the ethical community. Poor and rich rabble share the judgment that the state of right for them amounts to a state of nature, an absolute lack of rights. This, however, happens because on the one side the luxury-rabble considers itself to be the all transcending strongest within this state, as real right, while on the other side, the poor rabble considers himself to be the weakest, as having absolutely no rights. Depravity as an expression of the hypostatization of one's own, isolated particularity to become the only absolute form of universality and indignation as the expression of an experienced deprivation of rights are the two sides of a coin whose name is "rabble." Depravity and indignation are Hegel's names for these two sides of a subjective position and conviction that is directed against the ethical community as such. This makes it clear that:

4. the loss of honor, shame and all the determinations which characterize the citizen in the state that is proper to them starts from the fact that both of them—albeit for different reasons—consider it their *right to unbind themselves from the (existing) right*. This is why one of the clearest definitions of the rabble that Hegel gives reads like this: "If man makes himself to be without rights and also keeps himself *unbound* from duties . . . then this is the rabble" (HPRV, 222, my emphasis). Rich and poor rabble unbind themselves because

of "a supposed feeling of right" (Ibid., 223) from the dialectic of rights and duties which operates as the central element of the ethical order. Because as Hegel states in his handwritten notes: "*Duties* are binding relations" (HGPR, 304). To renounce them means to *unbind* oneself from binding relations. The rabble in its two types is the result of an unbinding and retreats from the ethical-statist rules and offers of binding.[5] But it is again important to differentiate: If the rich rabble unbinds itself only to introduce a new binding order, which originates from its wealth, and is centered on itself and its fortune; if the poor rabble unbinds itself then it does this without any possibility of indicating a renewed or revised binding. One can remember in this context Hegel's remark that "the sanctity of marriage and honour . . . are the two moments around which the disorganization of civil society revolves" (HOPR, 226). Here it becomes clear that to stand outside of the corporation and the dialectics of rights and duties means to be some a sort of bastard of civil society. One loses the honor by not being bound to an estate or a corporation, and, with the same move, one also loses what is peculiar to marriage. Because Hegel writes that it is "our ethical duty . . . to enter into the married state" (Ibid., 164) and if the rabble unbinds itself from the totality of the dialectic of rights and duties, it even lacks this fundamental experience of an immediately ethical and social community. As a logical consequence for Hegel, the family is derived from marriage and he attempts to secure in this way the reproduction of the species.[6]

The rabble is in precisely this sense a-social. But Hegel also inscribes an essential historicity into marriage, as the introduction of marriage is alongside with the introduction of agriculture—which Hegel interprets as the introduction of private ownership—the second decisive moment which leads to the historical creation of the state. With marriage and agriculture finally "the nomadic life of the savage" (Ibid., 194) ends and is brought "back to the tranquility of private rights and the assured satisfaction of . . . needs" (Ibid.). Thus, "marriage is union [*Verbindung*]" (HGPR, 314), Hegel notes, and thereby implicitly marks in his own hand what the poor rabble lacks. It is the 'opposite' of union [*Verbindung*]: unbinding [*Entbindung*]. The consequences of this appear quite clearly when along with shame the need to own assured property is also lost. Of the "happiness through *each* other [*durch einander*]" (Ibid., 312), the only thing left is the nomadic con-fusion [*Durcheinander*] of the rabble who in the private right, which is the assured satisfaction of need is also unbound from this happiness. This is why one can claim that the rabble is unbound from the dialectical movement: unbound from it and at the same time by it. Its "attitude without rights" (HVORL 3, 703), which delineates the reason for the unbinding, leads it to claim the right to "subsist without honor and labor and activity" (Ibid.), and this leads it out of the mediating connections of rights and duties. To be able to subsist without labor and activity is:

5. the reason *why the poor rabble becomes lazy/foul [faul] and the rich rabble becomes wasteful / extravagant [verschwenderisch]*. I here read Hegel's distinction between "laziness and extravagance" (HOPR, 222) as the distinction between the two types of rabble. For both lose their habit of working. This loss leads on the one side to a merely consumptive attitude in the rich rabble which divests itself in extravagant luxury and which Hegel calls depravity; and it leads on the other side to a purely passive attitude of refusal whose ground is indignation. Both become idle, inactive and stick to a position which either claims to hold a power that transcends all institutions or delegitimizes them by indignantly referring to their impotence in view of the effects of the social dynamic. If one pushes the distinction between the two types a bit further, one can claim that the rich rabble relates to the poor like a 'god relates to an animal.' The rich rabble assigns the standpoint of the absolute to himself, of the absolute instance of right that transcends everything, a god-like position because it stands above everything (concrete, legal, institutional) due to the power that derives from wealth. Its idle depravity derives from this perspective from an idolization of its own particularity on the basis of his fortune. In contrast to this, Hegel assigns the position of an animal, which is fully deprived of any right and reduced to its interests and instincts, to the poor rabble. At the same time, the poor rabble cannot recognize in the ethical community anything but an agglomerate of interests and needs which due to their selfish nature lack any form of universality and legitimacy. It sees in it a mere game of instincts. The rich rabble, following this description, would be an idle and at the same (following his own self-understanding) omnipotent god. The poor rabble would be an incapable and thus idle animal. Both different types of idleness lead once again to the distinction between two logics of loss. This is because:

6. one has to note that both of the sides that are formally mediated in civil society—particularity and the universal—reflect back upon the two sorts of the rabble. The seemingly volatile distinction between indignation and depravity here becomes a decisive one. Because if the poor masses are necessarily generated by the dynamic of civil society, then the indignation about this poverty which is the ground for the forming of the poor rabble is generated contingently. This difference so far has taken the following form: 'subjective operation—contingent winnings' (rich rabble) vs. 'loss—subjective operation—loss' (poor rabble). With this the distinction between universal and particular rabble is also articulated. Here, one can now formalize two different logics that render the relation to necessity and contingency intelligible. With both of them different sorts of consequences are linked: both present chains of necessarily deducible and contingently supplementing and nondeducible coordinates. The different logic of the emergence, the different chains of contingent and necessary elements, determine their dissimilarity: while the logic of the emergence of the rich rabble follows the scheme 'contingent—contingent—necessary,' logic operates for the poor rabble following the

formula, 'necessary—contingent.' Contingently—through an arbitrary subjective operation—the conditions of possibility for the production of the rich rabble result; contingently it wins at the game; as a necessary consequence of this the rich rabble who is generated by the contingent winnings subordinates himself to the egoistical arbitrariness of his will and this drives its to prove it power externally. The formula of the rich rabble is: C–C–N.[7] Here it is productive to read this formula together with the previous one: 'Subjective attitude (interior, contingent in the sense of arbitrary)—contingent winnings (external, contingent)—loss (necessary).' It is important to think together both variants of the formula; in this way it becomes clear that, between the first and the second parts, a difference appears. The subjective operation that generates the existence of the gambler can be identified with particularity as such. The second contingency of the winnings is in contrast an external one. Therefore the third part, namely the necessary loss, is also marked by a split, being at the same time internally necessary (losing shame, honor, etc.) and externally necessary (being dependent upon wealth and to demonstrate it in the form of luxury). The exact logic of the emergence of the rich rabble therefore can be written in its abbreviated form as: $C_i–C_e–N_{i/e}$.[8]

The emergence of the poor rabble follows a different logic. It appears to be contingent as to whether the indignation about the necessary result of economic development, as the feeling of a privation of rights, emerges or not. If one again reads together the two formulas, for the poor rabble the following result can be given: 'Loss/poverty (necessary)—subjective operation (contingent).' Therein one can describe the necessary production of poor masses as an external necessity that derives from the objective, exterior movement of civil society (N_e). The logic of emergence therefore can be given the following form: $N_e–C_i$. Or to put it differently: depravity is a necessary result of the hypostasis of contingency (and of the side of particularity) in civil society; indignation is a contingent supplement to the necessary development of its unhindered effectivity. In the luxury-rabble civil society faces the countenance of the counternatural hypostasis of its own contingency ($C_i–C_e–N_{i/e}$); in the poverty-rabble, however, it faces the contingent indignation regarding the necessary product of its own counternature ($N_e–C_i$). Wherefrom one can derive:

7. a difference between *two concepts of possibility* that characterize the rich and the poor rabble. For, if there is at all a contingent power of wealth outside the institutions the rich rabble has to appear: his possibility is inseparable from its actuality; it stands and falls with it. As soon as through an exterior contingency wealth is concentrated in the hands of a private person, the rich rabble necessarily emerges. The possibility of the poor rabble depends on it making or not making itself, i.e. its possibility is and remains, awaiting its actualization which is introduced by a subjective act, the disposition of mind peculiar to him. This difference needs to be further differentiated:

the possibility of generating the rich rabble at first seems to be, following its principle, similarly general (or universal) as the one of poor rabble, because *any individual as individual* can become a successful gambler. However, the universality of the possibility of the poor rabble depends on objective conditions. The elaborated *logic of double contingency* conditions the possibility of the rich rabble. Its possibility is a mere possibility as long as it is not contingently realized (in the game). The possibility of the rich rabble always stands under the objective and external conditions to which the gambler has subordinated himself. It stands in "thoroughgoing dependence on arbitrariness and external contingency . . ." (HOPR, 182). The *happy few* depend on the externality of the *few happy moments*. The structure of the possibility of the poor rabble is in contrast determined by the logic of double latency so that with his appearance the retroactive insight arises to the effect that anyone can become poor and consequently anyone can become rabble. This logic makes it clear that the possibility of the poor rabble is not bound to any other condition, i.e. first and foremost not to any other external condition. Rather there is a permanent and universal possibility that the poor rabble is produced (poverty) and this production depends solely on a *subjective operation* (attitude). To speak in more dialectical terms: the single, isolated and particularized reality of the rich rabble will always have been relying upon a mere, purely contingent possibility, and the poor rabble on a necessary possibility that is constantly inscribed by the duration of civil society.

The reality of the rich rabble is grounded in a possibility that is always already marked by the *logic of double contingency* and always remains particular. The possibility of the rich rabble is in a double sense *a possibility of particularization*: 1. because it particularizes and isolates the one to whom the possibility belongs and refers him to mere contingency and 2. because it is as possibility itself particularized, always depending on the double contingency. This means: Not anyone can become a rich rabble. The reality of the luxury-rabble is grounded in a conditioned possibility of particularization that therefore remains particular even while seeming universal. The reality of the poverty-rabble, in contrast, is grounded in an unconditional possibility of universalization that remains universal even while seeming particular. Anyone can sink into poverty and can consequently become rabble; the possibility of the poverty-rabble does not know any (objective) conditions. The possibility as conditioned possibility of universal isolation and particularization or the possibility as unconditioned possibility of a singular universality, this is what fundamentally distinguishes luxury-rabble from poverty-rabble. Therefore one can claim that the generalization that retroactively results from the emergence of the rich rabble is nothing but a hypostasis of the mere particularity and its merely particular possibility. In contrast, the generalization that retroactively derives from the emergence of the poverty-rabble and follows the *logic of double latency* is a universal possibility.

A mere possibility of particularization differs from a necessary possibility of universalization.[9] But both can only be grasped retroactively because only then it does become clear that via the rich rabble there will have been a possibility of particularization in civil society, its "general principle is that of isolation."[10] Similarly, one can only retroactively determine that via the poverty-rabble there will have been a necessary and universal possibility that is granted to anyone (as latent rabble). This

8. makes it clear that the distinction between *conditioned and unconditional possibility* inscribes a difference into the forms of appearance that again fundamentally distinguishes between the degrees of privation and unbinding of the two types of the rabble. The rich rabble appears in and as luxury; the poor rabble appears in and as the poor. The rich rabble thus owns—in a twofold sense—a peculiar mode of appearing just because it has property. Indeed, the subsistence of the luxury-rabble is not permanently assured but for the *few happy moments* in which he is wealthy. Because the rich rabble only appears as long as it is rich, i.e. because it only appears at all as long as it is able to demonstrate his success externally, this condition constitutes his peculiar form of appearance. The rich rabble appears as long as he possesses and as long as it appears, it appears as proprietor. Therewith it is clear that the luxury-rabble for those happy moments in which it can call a contingent property its own, stands on the legal ground of the state. Because with this property it is still accessible by the state that can demand something from him—for example taxes. The rabble is therefore subject to Hegel's statement "that the state lays hold of someone only by that with respect to which he is capable of being held" (HGPR, 287). For the rich rabble this means that it can be lain hold of by his property. For, the luxury-rabble is in those moments in which it possesses a proprietor and as such can demand security for this property and has all the rights of a proprietor. But these rights are accompanied by duties—in relation to tax for example. It is precisely this which marks his paradoxical position: on one hand the rabble understands himself by virtue of property as an all-surmounting power, on the other side this power is a purely economical one which at the same time is still safeguarded by the right that remains effective in the state. That the rich rabble constantly undermines the security of its property, because it always newly puts it on the line, does not change the fact that it, although it falls out of the logic of recognition that instructs civil society and the state, is legally recognized as proprietor, at least for the *few happy moments* in which it is one.[11] It is this structure that constitutes the particular dangerousness and the peculiar counternature of the luxury-rabble: it undermines the structures of recognition and nonetheless can in the happy moments demand at least abstract, legal recognition. Here it becomes intelligible that the rich rabble is and can only be in a tamed in a way form that is not fully unbound from the state and its institutions. Because as long as it has possessions it remains as a person within the legal and statist sphere.[12] The

luxury-rabble is due to precisely this fact arguably the most radical hypostasis of the network of actions *contra naturam sui generis*, which is civil society. In contrast to this stands the poverty-rabble generated by the relation of deprivation that is necessarily dwelling in civil society. That it derives from a deepened loss means that its unbinding does not know any form of taming. For the rabble even lacks any mode of (exterior) appearance. If luxury is the specific form of appearance of the rich rabble and if it is an exterior demonstration of property which differentiates itself indeterminately, then one can claim that the poor rabble even lacks a peculiar appearance. Because already the poor lack due to the first, economic loss, property and all the advantages of civil society, the rabble now is a deepening of this primary loss. The clearest sign of this is probably that the rabble is indistinguishable from the poor. What characterizes the poor rabble is the attitude joined to poverty, which at the same time does not appear externally. What appears are solely the poor no matter if it is the poor rabble or not. There is no exterior criterion that would enable us to detect whether the poor is a poor rabble or a poor devil. The "minimal difference,"[13] which distinguishes both of them, that is marked by the attitude joined to poverty, generates no possibility of external differentiation.

Chapter 7

The Formula of Infinite Unbinding: "This is the Rabble," or Resentment-Rabble and Absolute Rabble

If man on any topic appeals to the nature and concept of the subject-matter, or at least to reasons, to intellectual universality, but to his feeling, the only thing to do it to let him alone, because he thereby spurns the community of rationality, withdraws into his isolated subjectivity, into particularity.

(G. W. F. Hegel)[1]

Whoever is of the rabble wants to live for free . . .

(Friedrich Nietzsche)[2]

So far I have described several scissions: civil society splits into those who find work and a place in an estate and those who are mere private persons; private persons split into poor and gamblers; the poor split into poor and poor rabble; the gamblers split into gamblers and rich rabble; the rabble splits into rich and poor rabble.[3] I have reconstructed the different logics of emergence of the types of the rabble and shown how they are related to different notions of possibility. The luxury-rabble relies on an always conditioned and merely particular possibility, the possibility of the poor rabble is necessary and universal, unconditional. The formulas of these emergences so far are: "inner contingency (subjective operation/attitude)—external contingency (contingent winnings)—external necessity (demonstration of wealth) / internal necessity (loss of shame, honor, etc.)" $(C_i - C_e - N_{i/e})$ = luxury-rabble; "external necessity (poverty)—internal contingency (subjective operation/attitude)"; $(N_e - C_i)$ = poverty-rabble. Therewith the formula of the poor rabble so far has one element less than that of the rich rabble. It is precisely the element that describes how for the rich, winning money is necessarily followed by a loss of shame and honor, etc. and a demonstration of wealth. One can claim that the third element marks in an abstract way the specificity of the loss. Necessarily, it is shown in the last step that the rich rabble will always have been a product of the absolute hypostasis of the contingent. That the reconstruction of the poor rabble so far ends with the second element is due to the fact that Hegel himself does not describe this moment of his genesis in any further detail. He, or so I want to claim, suspends the third element of the logic of emergence of the poor rabble because he interprets it solely as a "negative understanding" (HOPR, 258). Although Hegel describes the moment of emergence from the rabble's subjective attitude which supplements the necessarily present possibility but he does not specify what the loss of the poverty-rabble is. Hegel does not describe the last element of the logic of emergence of the poor rabble because for him it is the same as the second one. In this one can see the implication of what the poor rabble is lacking: it lacks the third element, which would enable to conceive adequately of his privation. In the following I will attempt to trace the so far lacking element of the formula of the poverty-rabble so as to be able to show in what way with it there ignites and unbinds a movement that Hegel himself does not make explicit, but that is nonetheless inscribed into his claims about the first two logical elements of the poor rabble. I will thereby show that Hegel did not himself proceed dialectically enough when speaking about the poor rabble. It is rather "as though the dialectic had become frightened of itself" (ATS, 80) as soon as it came too close to the poor rabble. The following remarks will therefore be an attempt to complete the logic of the poor rabble.

To start with this, it is necessary to deepen once again the differentiation of the two types of rabble. One central characteristic of the rabble that can be found in Hegel is his resentment.[4] I am aware of the fact that the notion of "resentment" cannot—to the best of my knowledge—be found explicitly in Hegel's oeuvre. In the following I want to develop a Hegelian theory of resentment from implicit hints that Hegel himself articulates. One of them lies in his usage of the word 'indignation' [*Empörung*]. For he employs it not just in an (affective) description of the attitude of the rabble but also in the sense of outrage, uprising or insurrection, as for example when he writes: "A rebellion in a province conquered in war is a different thing from a rising [*Empörung*] in a well-organized state" (HOPR, 275). In the following passage, he claims that the latter is a "crime against the state" (Ibid.). One can therefore first define resentment as that which is described in both rabble-formulas as inner contingency (C_i). It appears at a stage in which for Hegel the subjective operation, namely the attitude, contingently leads to the emergence of the rabble. For the rich rabble this means that its emergence begins with resentment. For the poor rabble this means that although it is a product of resentment, its resentment 1. relies on a necessarily given possibility of resenting and 2. that for Hegel it does not seem to be anything but resentment, i.e. indignation, dissatisfaction. From the formula of the rich rabble $(C_i - C_e - N_{i/e})$ it already became clear that the first stage consists in hypostatizing contingency in itself and that the other logical steps (from the contingent for itself to the necessary in and for itself) are products of the first hypostasis. The hitherto formula of the poor rabble $(N_e - C_i)$ indicates that its resentment is the (contingent) product of a necessary possibility. The rabble begins from a necessary in itself and comes to a contingent form of the for itself, that is resentment. But how to describe resentment more precisely? What relates and what distinguishes the two types of the rabble with regards to resentment?

Both are figures of resentment because both have a peculiar and contradictory attitude. One can say that for both their attitude leads to them "being unbound from the respect of others' rights" (HPRV, 222). They refuse not only to give others their recognition but also to make themselves addressable in terms of rights and duties for the others. Government appears to them only as an evil will; their "existence [. . .] corrodes the actual order" (HOPR, 252) and "as it were . . . hang[s]" political life "in mid-air" (Ibid., 292). Here it becomes clear the attitude is an essential point of crystallization of the rabble-problem. Because as Hegel states, "no one can break up this inner conviction of humanity, no violence can be done to it . . ." (Ibid., 110). It is, to quote Joachim Ritter, "that which allows no violent access to it."[5] Hegel consistently deduces that "morality and moral commands [which] concern the will in its most personal subjectivity and particularity . . . cannot be a matter for positive legislation" (Ibid., 202). But how can one understand resentment beside its rather affective components of dissatisfaction, depravity, indignation?

If one considers the decisive remark concerning the rabble from the *Philosophy of Right* things become clearer:

> The lowest subsistence level, that of a rabble of paupers, is fixed automatically [*machtsich von selbst*], but the minimum varies considerably in different countries. In England, even the very poorest believe that they have rights; this is different from what satisfies the poor in other countries. Poverty in itself does not turn people into a rabble; a rabble is created only when there is joined to poverty a disposition of mind, an inner indignation against the rich, against society, against the government, etc. A further consequence of this attitude is that through their dependence on chance people become frivolous and idle, . . . lacking sufficient honour to secure subsistence by their own labour and yet at the same time of claiming the right to receive subsistence. Against nature a human being can claim no right, but once society is established, poverty immediately takes the form of a wrong done to one class [*Klasse*] by another. (Ibid., 221)

The rabble indignantly and dissatisfiedly accuses society, government, etc. and declares the state of civil society and state order to be a state without right. This indignation is an expression of a deeper contradiction. For the rabble accuses existing circumstances of being without right *but he gains his idea of right from them*. It therefore adopts, without knowing it, the existing concept of right in order to be able to determine what has happened to it as a wrong. But that this is a wrong cannot be derived from given determinations of right. Rather, the poor is in a state of lack that he himself judges to be a wrong. "In this way his poverty becomes a wrong [*Unrecht*], an insult to his right, this produces a dissatisfaction that at the same time takes the form of right" (HVORL4, 609). Because, on the one hand, his lack is not recognized as a wrong by the existing right, and on the other he himself judges it to be an insult to his right, a wrong; he at the same time judges that the given state of right is not a state of right. As the right does not support his judgment about the wrong he experiences it loses for him the function of being a right, i.e. legality as such. This is the reason for his indignation. It is generated within the rabble when it judges its lack as a wrong and the existing right does not share this judgment. In the rabble the condition of possibility for the wrong and its condition of impossibility coincide. The poor rabble claims that a wrong has been done to it in civil society (poverty, lack); that this wrong is not considered to be one and does not get sublated makes civil society into a state of lack of right; from this the rabble follows a(nother) right which guarantees that the rabble will be provided for without laboring—and this is why the position of the rabble is contradictory for Hegel. Because a right to be without work opposes the (existing) rational and general concept of right.

If existing right operates by the objectification and realization of an always particular freedom then this can only be done by action and labor. Against the right of reason, which organizes civil society and the state, the rabble claims a right that suspends the mediation by work and activity. Since one's own activity is the foundation for the mediation within civil society of egoistic needs and interests with the universality of all interests, i.e. for the inscription of a universal into each of the isolated satisfactions of particular needs, the right which the rabble opposes to the existing right is one that is merely particular, particularized: it is valid for the rabble and for the rabble alone. To claim a right that is not only a right of the particular but that is merely particular as a right marks a central feature in the structure of the rabble's attitude. To claim a right that fundamentally does not fulfill the conditions of possibility of being a right—by being merely particular—by being a *right without right* is the basic structure of that which one can call *resentment* in Hegel. The term *right without right* names on one side the fact that the right which the rabble claims does not contain the necessary universality inscribed in the notion of right and therefore can be read as a right without legitimacy. But on the other side, by not having legitimacy, this 'notion' of right cannot claim a rational right against the existing right.

Furthermore a *right without right* is the point to which the rabble refers in order to indicate the wrong that has befallen it. The rabble "pretends" therefore to "subsist without labor and activity" (HVORL4, 703). This pretension is for Hegel a mere pretension that contradicts the notion of right despite being constantly referred back to it, as it is its enabling principle. If resentment refers to the structure of a *right without right* it becomes clear that not only one but both types of the rabble fall under this category. Although both are figures of resentment, they remain different:

Because for legitimating his wealth at all as 1. *his* wealth and 2. as his *wealth* the rich man, without knowing it, must refer to the category of property and therewith to the category of the rights-persona. He remains within the existing right. The rich rabble claims against the (existing) right a merely particular right (that of his wealth) which it takes to justify its existence and which assures it of a subsistence without work. This right of wealth is always already a true *right without right* that stands in contrast with the existing right; a merely contingent, particular resentment. In contrast, the poor rabble adherence to civil society that assures to anyone their subsistence through laboring. However, it produces impoverished masses that cannot ensure their subsistence. That the poor rabble is "lacking sufficient honour to secure subsistence by his own labour and yet at the same time of claiming the right to receive subsistence" (HOPR, 221) means for the poor rabble that he takes civil society at its word. Anyone has the right to subsist there through one's own work; the movement of civil society itself makes this impossible and poverty results; the poor rabble now clings onto the principle of civil society by addressing the same right that has deprived it of its right to declare this deprivation as a wrong. This wrong is neither recognized as one nor is it sublated. This leads to the declaration of a *right without right* that is adequate to his position as poor. The right the poor rabble declares is the right of poverty, of lack that Hegel sees as mere resentment. The rich rabble suspends the right by referring in a contradictory way to the superior, omnipotent right of its wealth—ultimately to the corruptibility of right—but remains as proprietor bound to the legal structures of ethical community. The poor rabble, however, refers only to the right of civil society and remains faithful to it although it has left it a long time ago. Both refer for different reasons to the existing right and oppose another right to it. That it is "lacking sufficient honour to secure subsistence by his own labour and yet at the same time claims the right to receive subsistence" means for the rich rabble to claim its wealth as the only valid right; this is why it thinks as a gambler that he could suspend the existing right and subsist without activity and work. Here the *logic of double contingency* is still valid. The rich rabble still remains as long as its property exists a rights-persona bound to the existing order.

Within the resentment-category the scission between rich and poor rabble is repeated.[6] Although both are determined by the contradictory structure of claiming a *right without right* one can easily distinguish two forms of this phenomenon. Also in resentment the *right without right* of poverty stands against that of wealth: a pretended right of lack opposing a pretended right of excess. The rich rabble declares a *right without right* because it makes contingency into the only form of right and with it the right into something contingent. This right necessarily relies on both an inner and an external dependence on contingency itself; this right is contingency and contingency is here (the) right.

If one remembers the logic of its emergence (C_i–C_e–$N_{i/e}$), one can precisely delineate the resentment of the rich rabble. One can see that in the first step, resentment is the subjective operation (C_i). If one now inscribes therein the general structure of resentment—to claim a right without right—it becomes clear that with the emergence of the rich rabble (with its last stage) one can remark that its resentment was always already been present from the beginning. This means that the claim of a right of wealth retroactively constitutes the rich rabble as that which it will always have been: a mere figure of resentment. The necessary loss of shame and honor that leads it to will the institution of a *right without right* in its dialectical genesis will always already have been nothing but the necessary result of a contingent and merely subjective resentment-attitude.

The poor rabble declares a *right without right* that also relies upon contingency. But this contingency is purely internal and adds up to a principal necessity. The poor lack something; this lack is considered to be a wrong; the lack is not considered to be a wrong by civil society and the state but is understood as a mere lack and therefore is not sublated. This enchainment generates indignation that includes a declaration of a *right without right*. Here one can see the deep structural undecidability of this place. For Hegel it is impossible to decide by means of the dialectical development whether one is here dealing with a lack or with a wrong. Because if the poor were in a state of lack he could not complain about it. Why? Because Hegel defines lack as follows: "If that which lacks something [*Mangel*] does not at the same time stand above its lack, the lack is not for it a lack. An animal is lacking from our point of view, not from its own" (HOPR, 33, trans. mod.). Lack is a category of the natural. The animal which is lacking something from our point of view does not have the consciousness of its own lack. If the lack that poverty presents were a lack in this natural sense, there would not be a possibility of complaining about it. Then the problem of the poor rabble would no longer be Hegel's problem. But the problem noted here does not reside in the domain of nature. Rather it resides in civil society, i.e. in a domain of cultural production. Poverty's lack is not naturally but culturally produced. Here, a further level of the problem becomes visible: at the stage of ethicality and civil society, any produced lack is *by definition* a wrong. But also this problem could receive a solution if Hegel could claim that poverty materializes due to individual failures or negligences. Then he could claim that poverty is the result of unlawful actions—a wrong committed by oneself against oneself. But here Hegel's insight reaches further, since civil society inevitably produces poverty.

The decisive consequence of this insight is that civil society itself constantly produces injustice. But Hegel cannot draw this consequence, since civil society is a part of the rational organization of the ethical, and even constitutes its peculiar "*world of appearance*" (Ibid., 180), and therefore cannot constitutively be a concatenation of injustices. The dilemma of the poor rabble's position is that it stands in the position of an artificially produced lack which cannot be recognized as such by Hegel. The Hegelian philosophy of right is here confronted with a problem of categorization, of indistinguishability. There is lack at a stage of the development of freedom where lack can only be a wrong and at the same time this wrong cannot be recognized, although it is constantly recognized as lack. As a result of this the position of the poor rabble is unique in Hegel's philosophy because it marks a point of indistinguishability and impossibility of categorization for which Hegel does not know any solution.[7] One has to clearly state what this means: the problem that the poor rabble displays exceeds Hegel's conceptual and philosophical categorization.

One can claim that the poor rabble draws contradictory consequences from Hegel's own insight into this indistinguishability and impossible categorization. As Peter Landau rightly remarks, "only if the individual is given the possibility to acquire rights in the world of things that are recognized by others is the universal capacity for rights more than an empty fiction."[8] Because civil society is constantly haunted by the impossibility of sustaining this possibility, the poor rabble is led to condemn the understanding of this capacity as an empty fiction without right. This leads it into resentment: to claim a right which is valid for itself and only for itself, a right to subsist without work. This is a right which no longer aims at acquiring rights in the world of things and this means it is a right which is detached from the "fundamental condition of . . . prosperity" (HOPR, 215) of any state: the possibility of free property. If one considers the logic of emergence of the poor rabble (N_e-C_i) two things become clear. Resentment appears as the contingent, subjective product of a necessary possibility and has to be understood in light of this fact. The right without right of the poor rabble is as particular and contingent as that of the rich rabble because it results from the subjective attitude that supplements the necessary condition. But this contingency is fundamentally different. Here one can see the scope of the distinction between the *logic of double contingency* and the *logic of double latency*.

One can state: *right without right* = resentment. But on one side this right is particularized by a *logic of double contingency* in a way that the luxury-rabble upholds the claim of a right to subsist without work *as long as* it actually subsists without work. As long as there is the rich rabble its *right without a right* is not only a counternatural claim but rather already actualized. It declares the right to subsist without work *because* he subsists without work. The right without right of the rich rabble is therefore twice particularized, following the *logic of double contingency*. It is doubly particular 1. in relation to the bearer of rights (the individual which he himself is) and 2. in relation to the period of validity and the genesis of right (that results from the external contingency of happy moments). It is a mere moment of the individual. The rich rabble appears therefore as that which he always already will have been: as resentment-rabble. Or better said: as soon as the rich rabble exists, the position of the gambler will never have been anything other than mere resentment. With this it is also stated that the loss of shame and honor that necessarily appears in the last of the three steps only indicates that honor and shame will always already have been lost with the gambler's existence. This necessity results necessarily from the last step. In short: the rich rabble is due to the logic of double contingency a rabble of a mere particular resentment: resentment-rabble.

The poor rabble, however, is the product of a more profound loss and displays the *logic of double latency*. This means on one side that the right to subsist without work that it claims is also a *right without right* and merely particular. But on the other side it does not rely on an already present assurance of its validity. The right the poor rabble claims is none that is already counternaturally actualized. It is rather the case that the poor rabble's right without right is claimed from a position that has lost even the security of subsistence. If the *logic of double latency* refers to the fact that anyone in the state is (or more precisely, will have been) latently rabble, then one can remark a fundamental difference from the resentment-structure of the rich rabble. The poor rabble's *right without a right* also knows the poor rabble only as a bearer of this right. But the *logic of double latency* shows that anyone in the state is latently rabble and therefore latently a 'bearer' of this particular right of the poor rabble. *The poor rabble declares therefore a right without a right that is valid only for him but nonetheless (latently) for anyone.* Or to put it differently: the poor rabble addresses a right as its right that is merely particular and nonetheless at the same time latently universal. The *right without right* of the rich rabble is a merely particular one; that belonging to the poor rabble is as a particular right itself universal. An interesting ambivalence should be clear here, for the complete mediation of particularity and universality for Hegel describes the essential trait of the sphere of ethicality.

The two types of the rabble are distinguished by the appearance on one side of a merely particular resentment, and on the other of a particular resentment which is latently the resentment of any citizen. Now, it becomes possible to indicate another scission: not only has the rabble split into rich and poor, but also, within the structural similarity—in resentment—something appears which surmounts the structure of the similarity. One can claim that with the formation of the rich rabble it necessarily becomes clear that it is *in and for itself* nothing but mere contingency. Following the logic of his emergence (C_i $-C_e-N_{i/e}$) it is *in itself* contingent, then *for itself* contingent and will therefore necessarily never have been anything but the hypostasis of contingency as such.

Here the question arises: what is the poor rabble *in and for itself*? I already indicated both the rich and the poor are guided by resentment and become shameless, honorless, etc. (C_i). They consequently throw off "the subjective bases of society" (HOPR, 222). But the luxury-rabble feels resentment against all social and collective institutions of civil society due to a momentary wealth, while the same does not go for the poverty-rabble. The luxury-rabble has something and loses (shame, honor, etc.) as a consequence of this having; the poverty-rabble has nothing and loses nonetheless even more. What this means can become clear when linked to the question of how the rabble unbinds himself from rights and duties. In doing this it unbinds itself from the first and fundamental imperative of the *Philosophy of Right*: "Hence the imperative of right is: 'Be a person and respect the others as persons'" (Ibid., 55). What is remarkable is the fact that this imperative takes the form of an imperative at all since this implies the possibility of not being a person and not respecting others as persons. And what this means is also clear: the rabble withdraws from this imperative by losing his respect for others and catapults itself in the same movement out of the status of a rights-persona. It loses its respect for the others because it is a resentment-figure that claims against the existing right a *right without right* and judges existing circumstances as being without right. As Hegel likes to claim, quoting Rousseau's *Social Contract*: "Not to be free is therefore a renunciation of a man's rights as a human being, and even of his duties" (HLHP3, 273). This delineates the horizon of what happens with the rabble. To withdraw from the imperative of right signifies losing the status of a person. If personality in its abstract form is understood as a free will giving itself external existence, i.e. as a will that in its most original form objectifies itself through property, the rabble is for Hegel the negation of personality.

It is imperative not to lose track of what this means for the distinction between luxury- and poverty-rabble. The luxury-rabble is ostensibly also without rights and duties just as the poor rabble is. But it can only unbind itself by declaring a *right without right* that originates in its wealth. Only because it remains bound to the existing right as a person, can it generate resentment at all, i.e. claim a *right without right*. The poor rabble in contrast is even unbound from the possibility of appearing externally. Only the poor rabble fundamentally loses even the possibility of accumulating property and therefore the possibility of giving itself an exterior existence in any way. *The luxury-rabble is only because it has; the poverty-rabble has nothing because it is (present).* For the luxury-rabble his property *as property* is subject to the same legal protection, i.e. jurisdiction, as anyone else's (property). "This world outside him" always "has its threads in him" so that he "consists of these threads" (HPM, 96) and at the same time this world assures him his counternatural maintenance and the validity of his *right without a right*. But the poor rabble loses even this minimal security and the form of fundamental integration because it forms itself from the penniless, the poor. If personality is in this initially abstract form the condition of legal capacity, this means at the same time that the poverty-rabble is not a person and also in a more radical way without rights. "If a human being makes himself, if man makes himself be without rights and also keeps himself *unbound* from duties . . . then this is the rabble" (HPRV, 222, my emphasis). This Hegelian judgment aims only and exclusively at the poverty-rabble because the rich rabble remains permanently bound to a form of personality, however residual, and receives from it the legal security of his property. Therewith it also unbinds itself from a fundamental duty that the rich rabble has unconsciously always fulfilled: "It is a duty to possess things as property, i.e. to be a person" (HPM, 218).

Only the poor rabble is fully unbound from right and duty because it is also unbound from the "freedom of the free as 'person' provided in right."[8] *Only the poor rabble is rabble in the full sense of the word* because it is the absolute unbinding from right and duty. Also this radical unbinding only goes for the poverty-rabble because it, being shy of work and without honor, without performing any actions does not enter into the external reality in which the luxury-rabble, by displaying "*external evidences*" (HOPR, 225) of its success, has always already taken his place. The poor rabble, however, remains stuck in his claim to a right without right and for Hegel it thus remains in a merely abstract interiority, in mere "negative understanding" (HOPR, 258). Consequently it negates its personality and presents the effective and real negation of the legal capacity: "*capitis diminutio*" (HOPR, 57) maxima. A pretended, ultimately particular unbinding is generated on one hand as the necessary product of a contingent wealth (luxury-rabble); a real and ultimately complete unbinding is on the other hand generated as the contingent and deepening product of a necessary and prior privation (poverty-rabble). The opposition of the two types of rabble is the opposition between a partial and a complete effect of unbinding. Here also a distinction within the temporal structure becomes visible. The temporality of the partial unbinding of the luxury-rabble follows a logic of the moment because 1. in each moment the given wealth can, due to the contingent game of civil society, be lost again and 2. in each moment there can be a harm done to his property, which leads to the immediate demand for legal security and therewith to the re-entry into a lawsuit. Therefore its *right without right* exists only as long as its wealth does; it is itself only as long as its fortune is. Its time, as the time of his (pretended) unbinding is the time of the *kairos*. By contrast, the temporality of the real unbinding of the poverty-rabble follows a *logic of eternity*, because at no time can the poor rabble re-enter legal and statist contexts, if the possibility of accumulating property has also been lost. Only for the poor rabble can it be said that *its time is eternity because only the poverty-rabble presents the paradigm of absolute and complete unbinding.*

This movement is remarkably described in Hegel's posthumously published lectures under the title of "Pauperization as a chance for the capitalist" (HVORL4, 609). But Hegel claims already in the *Philosophy of Right* that the "creation of a *rabble of paupers* . . . brings with it . . . conditions which greatly facilitate the concentration of disproportionate wealth in a few hands" (HOPR, 221). On the one hand, the poor rabble encourages an increased concentration of wealth in the hands of the few. The more the poor insists on his *right without right* and thereby even loses the possibility of accumulating property for eternity, the more property is acquired on the other side. Due to his resentment, the rabble also loses his rectitude, because there is no "conformity with the duties of the circumstances to which he belongs . . ." (HOPR, 192, trans. mod.). The mere 'presence' of the poor rabble intensifies this logic. The concentration leads to a reciprocal disproportion at the other end. The wealth concentrated in such a way once again gains what it should lose in the corporation, namely the "pride or envy" (HOPR, 226) it can inspire. In short: the 'presence' of the poor rabble reciprocally produces the presence and subsistence of the rich: *reciprocal becoming-rabble*. The hands of the few in which the wealth is concentrated therefore are no longer the non-upright hands that always already know wealth only as the wealth of the few and derive from it the *right without right* of the few. With the emergence of the rabble the movement of civil society becomes more and more rabble-like. Civil society becomes the society of the resentment-rabble in which poor and rich rabble unbind themselves in different ways from the ethical community by claiming their *right without right*. Both stick less and less to customs and more and more "cling to" themselves and are led into the "emptiness of fancies" (HA, 711) about what they can claim *de jure*.

Excursus: The Rabble as Social Pathology? On Axel Honneth

Can the resentment-rabble be described as a "social pathology" (HPIF, 40) in the sense intended by Axel Honneth? Honneth's reconstruction is an attempt to conceive of Hegel's Philosophy of Right as the outline of a social ontology, and to develop from it a theory of justice which is valid for any social community. So: what to do with Hegel's rabble, Mr. Honneth? The pretension of his theory is to describe all figures of negativity that appear on the different stages of the dialectical unfolding of the idea of freedom in Hegel—the criminal, the ironist—as social pathologies. It is remarkable that in his re-actualization of Hegel he speaks not once about the rabble. Therefore I will show why the rabble is a problem that is also not soluble by means of Honneth's reconstruction. Is the rabble a social pathology?

To use Honneth's terminology, it comes, "to a halt in his 'ethical' everyday life" (Ibid., 40) and out of this "moment of crisis" (Ibid.) the rationality of the normative guidelines of the already institutionalized social practices breaks up. This leads the rabble, if one follows Honneth, either to retreat to the mere consciousness of being a bearer of rights and to a pathological "fixation on legal freedom" (Ibid., 35) that renders it incapable of participating in social life. It would so actualize "the possibility of withdrawal behind all norms" inherent to formal right "within the sphere of ethical life . . ." (Ibid., 36). This would bring it to "a painful condition of unfulfilment and indeterminacy" (Ibid., 45). Or the resentment-rabble would distance itself from all existing social norms and get lost in something that is always included in the moral standpoint: the tendency of "losing oneself in a bottomless pit of self-questioning" (Ibid., 41) which would bring him to not act at all any-more and to the point of "suffering from indeterminacy" (Ibid., 23). Hence Honneth has to claim that the unbinding and privation of the resentment-rabble is an effect that results from a totalization of either the formally legal or the moral standpoint into the only standpoint that has universal validity. Both standpoints of freedom are necessarily passed through in order to reach an understanding of individual freedom and freely assured self-realization, i.e. to subjective consciousness. This means that any free action is the result of a rational self-determination of a rights-persona that understands himself as such. But both standpoints, if totalized as the only valid determinations of freedom, become problematic in their application to social reality.

If one follows Honneth in this diagnosis, one has to judge that the resentment-rabble is the problematic result of a totalizing extension of a moral and/or legal conception of freedom into the totality of existing practices. Then the 'suffering from indeterminacy' which the resentment-rabble presumably experiences would be the result of a "conceptual confusion" which has "become the foundation of practical attitudes in life . . ." (Ibid., 45).[10] To go against this, Honneth sees limited means; what helps is "a constructive therapeutic critique that stimulates a liberating self-reflection" (Ibid.). However, if one looks closely at the Hegelian text one can see a slightly different solution to the rabble-problem. If one shares Honneth's reading the rabble can be conceived of as a figure of what Hegel calls "erring conscience [*irrendes Gewissen*]" (HGPR, 257). This position Hegel defines as follows: "I only take what I find in my con-science; no other source . . ." He also claims that with it comes a loss of "abso-lute honor." But he proposes for the confusion of practical attitudes in life a different solution to Honneth. The rabble so understood would be:

> like a disgraceful animal whose nature is nothing but evil, destructive, to be beaten to death,—or at least to be ejected from society—those it does not need.—You should not need me; I am for myself, my own end—Good, so be it—but for you—to be *needed*, i.e. to stand in legal, ethical community . . . requires trust . . . If I would have to assume they are erring conscience, recognize only that as a right which they find only in their subjective con-science, so that therein is the opposite of everything which is legal, ethical, I would be in a worse situation than being amongst robbers because of them I know they are robbers . . . (HGPR, 258)

For Hegel it is unambiguous that at least the application of the conception of freedom that follows from the moral standpoint is not only problematic, it is simply destructive. An effect easily detectable in the intensifying movement which is produced by the declaration of the poor rabble's *right without right*. These destructive effects—that cannot only be understood as resulting from a "romantic individualism" or "precritical religion" (HPIF, 42)—attack the consistency of ethical community. Accordingly the Hegelian means is not the stimulation which refers to the existing intersubjective relations and makes it reasonable that they present the necessary preconditions of each free (and thereby communicative) self-realization. He has rather seen that there cannot be any constructive means by which to oppose the erring conscience that I here read as the Honnethian-Hegelian paradigm of the rabble-problem. He who has lost his honor is from this perspective no better than a disgraceful animal; as an animal which, due to his animality, causes permanent damage and has to be met with exclusion and finally extermination. Hegel knows: there is no path stimulating self-reflection that leads to the rabble who will have been forever unbound from ethical community and nonetheless persists as a threat within it. That Honneth comes to a different solution is a result of the fact that his reconstruction of Hegel's argument misses one essential point. Since he diagnoses social pathologies from a critical perspective and for them therapeutic operations exists, he neglects to consider something that is of huge importance for the rabble from a Hegelian standpoint: evil.

Evil is defined by Hegel as the complete handing over of the subject to contingency (of his drives and desires). This handing over he describes as a deficient, because heteronomous, determination of one's own freedom: "The natural . . . when it is drawn into the orbit of the will which is free and knows that it is free, acquires the character of not being free and is therefore evil" (HOPR, 138). In this heteronomous determination of the will the individual does not set *an* arbitrary content over against *an* existing universal but contingency *as such* against universality *as such*: subjectivity becomes the incorporation of chance. As a consequence, "*subjectivity* . . . then is *eo ipso for itself*, it retains its separate individuality, and is itself this arbitrary will" (Ibid., 136). That this form of subjectivity takes sides with arbitrariness against universality is a consequence that Honneth misses. This "diremption [. . .] distinguishes human being from unreasoning animal" (Ibid.), although Hegel is clear that only human beings are capable of good and bad. However, in a certain sense—as the later investigation of the notion of habit will show—the rabble is for Hegel—as "innocent people"—"worse than evil" (HGPR, 263). But it should be clear here that the quoted passage is explicit: the rabble degenerates into an animal because he is evil. For Hegel it is the incarnation of arbitrariness—the hypostasis of heteronomous determination—and offers no resonating space for the voice that wants to constructively stimulate the universal in him. The human being which made himself into an unreasoning animal is 'to be beaten to death,' he has become killable life.[11] Hegel goes farther than Honneth because he considers the threat of a radical unbinding from any universal, that he calls evil, and the range of its effects to be untreatable. One can claim that Honneth develops a theory of justice that has no place for the Hegelian conception of evil, of the evil rabble. Honneth only knows totalizations of wrong and one-sided conceptions of freedom that can be treated because they are simply pathological.[12] With this Honneth seems to rashly identify civil society exclusively with the standpoint of morality and therefore to forget the deprivation of right and its consequences that occur in the singularity of the rabble-problem. He discusses social pathologies only with regard to the subject and not as pathologies of the social itself, which take place in the dynamic interdependence of subjective position and objective conditions. Although he notes that Hegel sees in civil society certain "tendencies of social disintegration", he (falsely) believes on the one hand that Hegel would only counter them with the corporation (without also invoking the police, etc.). On the other hand, he precisely cannot conceive of these disintegrating tendencies in their specificity, that is, he only discerns in them the effect of a social pathology that presents itself in a purely subjective manner and is the result of the totalization of either the moral or the legal standpoint—this would be valid, if at all, only for the luxury-rabble. The only rabble that Honneth can think and know is the rich rabble. He fails to discuss the disintegrating tendency as a possible (subjective and objective) result of the economic movement itself and to link it with the problem which is the most radical product of this disintegration: the poverty-rabble. Honneth's theory is a Hegelian theory of justice, which although it might be able to problematize luxury as a genuinely subjective product, does not do justice to the necessary production of poverty and thereby to the poor rabble. Honneth's theory of justice is a theory with no place for the poor.

I here want to return to the question of the third element in the logic of the emergence of the poverty-rabble. Both types of rabble share the resentment structure of claiming a *right without a right*. But their scission repeats itself on different levels: a merely particular resentment against a particular-universal one; a particular unbinding of rights and duties against a complete one; a peculiar way of appearing in luxury against the loss of the form of appearance. Against this background I want to take seriously the claim that Hegel does take the determination of the rabble to its logical conclusion. If the rabble is defined only as far as the subjective attitude which contingently supplements the necessarily present possibility, then Hegel compresses on the second logical stage of the formula I have developed so far (N_e-C_i) the attitude and the peculiar form of privation that the rabble is marked by. He identifies attitude and privation, conviction and deepening loss. If one can read the formula of the rich rabble ($C_i-C_e-N_{i/e}$) as the dialectical movement from a contingent in itself via a contingent for itself to a necessary in and for itself, again the question arises: what is the poor rabble in and for itself?

One can claim that the 'presence' of the rabble disrupts even the logical movement of the *Philosophy of Right*. The rabble mobizes [*verpöbeln*] the consistency of Hegel's own logical deduction. Hegel seems to mark the fact that the rabble even lacks the in and for itself of the dialectical movement. The rabble thereby remains in abstract interiority and mere "negative understanding" (HOPR, 258) and the dialectics falters in the contingent for itself of the attitude. To speak with Adorno: when Hegel speaks about the rabble "when he meets with something contrary, things are not that dialectical."[13] For the differentiation into mere particular (rich rabble) and particular-universal resentment (poor rabble) delineates that the poor rabble will not always have been mere resentment. Even in resentment and its inner-particular constitution something appears that is not a merely particular resentment. Since the *right without right* of the poor rabble is the impossible right of anyone and does not know any limiting condition. But how can the poor rabble be universal as a particularity?

If one remembers the peculiar form of unbinding that the poor rabble displays, an answer to this question seems possible. Against the particular unbinding of the rich rabble the poor rabble introduces an absolute one. That which appears via the *logic of double latency* as universal is nothing but this absolute unbinding. The universal in the particularity of the poor rabble is the unbinding, the privation peculiar to it, and this consequence Hegel rightly and in the name of the right attempts to avoid in defining the poor rabble. But even the last element of the poor rabble's logic of emergence is followed by an external necessity (N_e), although we have yet to determine it more precisely: the poor rabble lacks even the specific way of appearing. Rather a necessary consequence is that due to his resentment-stance, i.e. due to its refusal to work, it does not appear externally at all. Only the poor appear and the poor rabble is and remains indistinguishable from them. But with this the rabble unbinds himself completely from the logic of recognition, thus: "If man makes himself be without rights and also keeps himself *unbound* from duties . . . then this is the rabble" (HPRV, 222, my emphasis). At the same time its subjective attitude is determined to be unbound from any form of shame, honor, habit, etc. As a consequence one can deduce that the poor rabble also has no interior determinations. The abstract interiority that Hegel reproaches the poor rabble for does not have any determination. Hegel neither knows why the rabble appears (it makes itself) nor whether it has emerged or will emerge (because only the poor appear). Therefore, Hegel calls the indignation an essential reason of his genesis. But that Hegel uses 'indignation' as a category of affects and instincts and—although this is etymologically false—in the sense of revolt, rebellion, points toward a substantial ambivalence. For the indignation of the rabble, although it seems to be merely and abstractly interior, contains the additional component that the rabble produces effects which attack the state and ethical community. This becomes clear when Hegel writes: "A rebellion in a province conquered in war is a different thing from a rising [*Empörung*] in a well-organized state. It is not against their prince that the conquered are in rebellion, and they are committing no crime against the state . . ." (HOPR,

275). This passage implicitly indicates that within an existing statist association, indignation about and against the state is the greatest crime. At the same
time the rabble does not appear in the form of a criminal because it does not
appear at all. The problem of the rabble's indignation is thereby made clearer:
the rabble is affectively indignant about the state and the existing order. This
leads it into resentment, claiming a right without a right, which presents one
moment of an absolute and complete movement of unbinding and in the last
instance leads from an 'indignation about' to an 'indignation against.' In this
way one can resume Hegel's twofold usage of indignation in the following
way: *The true rebellion of the rabble is the unbinding.* Therefore, following the *logic
of double latency,* a further scission becomes thinkable. It becomes possible to
think that from the state of (objective) lack in which the poor resides, a deepening (subjective) privation and unbinding is generated, such that it becomes
clear retroactively that this privation will have been the peculiar (objective and
subjective) universal of the poor rabble and therewith of anyone. The truly
universal, which appears in the deepening privation of the poor rabble and
makes the *logic of double latency* thinkable, is that anyone in the state (logically)
prior to any concrete determination will have been nothing, or better: *Nothing
but rabble.*

Therefore one can derive from the poor rabble as resentment-rabble another
consequence which delineates the in and for itself of the rabble. A rabble that
is dialectically unbound even from the subjective-interior limitation of the
stage of the for itself, i.e. of resentment. Hence the in and for itself of the
poor rabble is what I want to call the *absolute rabble.*[14] The reply to the question about the in and for itself of the rabble—about the third element of its
logic of emergence—leads to this consequence determined by the dialectical
logic. The last element does not describe a necessarily produced state of lack
(poverty) nor an (external) lack of something (labor, capital, representation,
etc.), nor does it involve a further loss which would come in through the attitude that supplements poverty and which could be described solely as an inner
lack (of shame, honor, habit, etc.). Rather, one can deduce from the logic of
double latency that the last element of the poor rabble's logic of emergence is
about lack as such, about unbinding or privation in and for itself. This is not to
say that the resentment-rabble, which delineates the dialectical stage in which
Hegel ends with the determination of the rabble, would as such be the *absolute
rabble.* But from it, thanks to the retroactive insight that anyone in the state is
latently rabble, arises the thinkability[15] of a more radical unbinding. The in
and for itself, the third stage of the poor rabble refers to the thinkability of an
absolute unbinding, of a privation absolutely purified of all determinations. It
refers to the *absolute rabble* and the in and for itself of privation; what Marx will
call "absolute poverty" (MEPM, 107). Here it becomes clear why Hegel com-
pounds the last stage of the logic of the poor rabble together with the second.
He tends to describe the *privation in and for itself* as privation *of* the in and for

itself, i.e. as a loss of the third stage which would make it impossible to think of privation as the most fundamental universal. Now the formula of the logic of emergence of the poor rabble can be completed ('N_e–C_i–$N_{i/e}$').

The necessary possibility of poverty delineates the condition of a contingently supplementing attitude, of a *subjective operation* which allows us to infer that the whole movement will have been nothing but the movement of privation, loss or absolute poverty as such. The universal which marks his particularity is absolute privation, absolute poverty, complete void of determinations, radical un-differentiation. It will therefore be, will always already have been, as this Nothing, the universal which latently marks anyone. The universal of the unbinding of the rabble is the void (of determinations, etc.) itself. The particularity as any "particularity by itself is measureless excess, and the forms of this excess are themselves measureless" (HOPR, 183). But the rabble-particularity is marked by the fact that it is in and for itself, as the "nomadic life" (Ibid., 194), the absolute void of determination that will always already have determined anyone. 'N_e–C_i–$N_{i/e}$' is the formula of the emergence of an absolute privation, of the complete void of determinations whose name is *absolute rabble*. Only now does it become apparent that anyone is and remains (latently) *absolute rabble* because anyone will always already have been it.[16] 'N_e–C_i–$N_{i/e}$' is the formula of an infinite loss and of its far-reaching consequences. And "then this is *the [absolute]* rabble" (HPRV, 222, my emphasis). This (hypo-)thesis can only be verified in comprehending the unbindings within the logic of the *Philosophy of Right*. For only when one demonstrates what the rabble is deduced from can one show in what way the absolute rabble is a fundamental problem for Hegel which at the same time can still be thought. I want to claim in the following that this absolute privation and absolute unbinding is not a purely abstract, speculative construction which would not bring about effects within the reality of the state and would, as mere abstract interiority, be simply insignificant. It is not a logic that would construct an "empty striving towards the (abstract) infinite" (HOPR, 148); it is not about falling back into the position of mere negative understanding. For the *absolute rabble* is 'present.' It is there, although for Hegel it is deduced from legitimate existence (in civil society, state, history, etc.). In the following I will follow this peculiar 'presence' of unbinding, this absolute privation of the absolute rabble and its effects for the structure of the *Philosophy of Right* to show, on one side that the name 'rabble' in Hegel is a synonym for unbinding and privation and to answer, on the other side, a question that Hegel poses in a different context: "But how can something be present and yet not exist?" (HPN, 155).

Chapter 8

The Lost Habit: Elements of a Hegelian Theory of Laziness/Foulness

But idle thinking cannot be at all.

(G. W. F. Hegel)[1]

An essential element of the problem of the rabble is, as Hegel remarks, that it becomes "shy of work" (HOPR, 221, trans. mod.) because "it lacks . . . the honor to secure subsistence by his own labor . . ." (Ibid.). Hegel marks the problem resulting from this even more clearly in his later lectures when he notes that in the rabble generally "the habit of laboring, the need for industriousness disappears . . ." (HVORL4, 609). One may encapsulate Hegel's diagnosis by saying that the rabble loses the habit of being active. This loss means at first glance that the rabble does not endeavor to find work in civil society and withdraws from its mediating relations. If one keeps in mind that the (rational) activity names the decisive feature of spirit that for Hegel enters the world and history with the reformation, then to lose the habit of working means not only to renounce social labor but moreover any form of activity and therefore to stand against the mediating movement of spirit itself. The rabble is not merely unemployed; it loses, as I want to claim, in a more fundamental respect the habit[2] of being active and thereby poses a problem that has far-reaching consequences in Hegel's philosophy.

Hegel remarks in the *Philosophy of Right* that "*practical education* [*Bildung*], acquired through working, consists first in the self-perpetuating need for something to do and the habit of simply being busy . . ." (HOPR, 191). Once this foundation is built it can be further specified. Practical education through work produces the habit of working—of this practice. Here it is already clear that it is this product of practical education that the rabble loses when he loses the habit. The evaporation of the results of practical education, i.e. of the habit to partake of activity as such, refers to an effect of de-education or un-education. These are essentially linked to the practice that gets lost, which is a formative practice, and what is formed are *habits*. For if one takes into account another fundamental remark from Hegel's *Philosophy of Right*, then education is always "*learning* and *getting used* to something through discipline . . ." (HGPR, 249). Education means to get used to, develop habits, and education is thereby always mediated via formative activity. "[P]ractical education is precisely education in the habit of being busy" (HOPR, 191). It consists in the production of habit, the habit of this (educating) activity. I only touch on the Hegelian notion of education because the cited passages can be instructive in helping to understand the relationship between activity and habit. Education I take to be the connection of practical activity, for example work, and the formation of the habit *of* such practical activity. Activity and habit are therefore from the beginning closely related. Active education forms habit and more precisely the habit of activity, of busyness as such. But this, as it might seem, merely temporal determination (first there is activity, then the habit of it) already contains the logical structure and the universal of their relation. One can see that in this sense habit also plays a central role in the statist community. Only through the production of "the habit of simply being busy" can there be "a habit, produced by this discipline, of objective activity and universally applicable skills" (Ibid.). Only through activity is there the formation of habits, and this education consists in a fundamental sense in the formation of the habit of activity *in general*. Only as a consequence of this habit-forming, a habit can be generated which enables us to work objectively, i.e. in mediating relations with others and following the laws of objective world. All this is needed in order to develop skills that allow one to assume a place in an estate or a corporation. Habit in Hegel does not only have the function of educating the subject, it is also essential for the objective constitution of (ethical) institutions.

Therefore Hegel can declare that the first human nature is transformed "into a second, spiritual nature, and makes this spiritual level *habitual* to them . . . To this extent, habit is part of ethical life . . ." (HOPR, 159).[3] It thereby belongs to the stability and perpetuated constitution of the state. That something becomes habitual means for Hegel that it becomes second nature. In this context, this means that objective activity, work, becomes habitual and thereby the second nature of man. To understand what it can mean to lose this second nature—can there be a return to a first nature?—it is necessary to conceive of the notion of habit in more precise terms.

In the anthropology, the first systematic part of subjective spirit, which deals with the formation of the soul—the spirit in its immediate and natural state—one can find, in Hegel's *Encyclopedia*, a definition of habit. He there determines it in an ambivalent way: it is, on one hand, "the mechanism of self-feeling" (HPM, 131), which is supposed to mean that habit leads to a deadening of the intensity of the activity, to a mechanization and ultimately to forms of unconsciousness and lack of interest. The intensity and vitality of an activity of life is lost in the moment at which it becomes habitual, becomes a pure mechanical "repetition"—a repetition without consciousness of repetition. In this way, man appears as "unfree" in habit because he is "no longer interested, engaged, or dependent with respect to" (Ibid.) its sensations. Habit appears in this first perspective as the converse of freedom. In this first functional determination it is: "(a) The *immediate* sensation as negated, as indifferent." Thereby it is "[h]ardening against external sensations" and "protecting us from misfortune . . ." (Ibid., 132). From this it follows that: "(b) Indifference towards satisfaction; desires, urges are dulled by habit" and thereby it achieves a rational liberation from them which is to be distinguished from an irrational renunciation and asceticism.[4] Finally "habit as *dexterity*" is produced. Therefore one can claim that "habit is a form that embraces all kinds and stages of mind's activity" (Ibid.), for example standing, seeing and ultimately thinking. To act at all in the existing objective world—and dexterity names the general manner of such an action—one has to be habituated to the laws which such an action is subordinated to. This is valid, as Hegel articulates in the *Philosophy of Right*: "since action is an alteration which is to take place in an actual world and so seeks recognition," it therefore must be "in general accord with what has validity there" (HOPR, 128).

One has to be habituated to the objective circumstances in order to be recognized. Therefore men who are habituated in the sense of acquiring dexterity are "those who . . . can do what others do" (Ibid., 186). For only habit can "supply the individual activity with participation and recognition [in the objective world]," i.e. give it an objective form and a valid content. With this threefold determination of habit—as hardening, indifference, and dexterity—is already indicated that it is not reducible only to mechanical repetition. It internally and necessarily changes into another form. By deadening the intensity of an activity it leads to the possibility to perform different activities at once. Thereby it increases the degree of universality of the activity. It is its peculiar ambivalence that it is not only the converse of freedom but at the same time the condition of freedom. There is, and this is how one can conceive of Hegel's repeated and insistent emphasis on this point, no freedom at all without habit. This can be made clear by referring to an example from the *Encyclopedia*: writing.[5] To learn writing one initially needs to rehearse certain procedures and techniques, to learn the rules of the practice, and one has to be in a state in which there is a blind and mechanical application of the rules. Initially "we must direct our attention to every individual detail, to a vast number of mediations" (HPM, 136); only by becoming habituated to the rules and by rehearsing is it possible to become "*free* from them" (Ibid., 131) and to realize one's own freedom in writing. This ambivalent structure of habit not only plays a decisive role when it comes to activities like writing, but for any activity. Habit intensifies the vitality of each and every individual— and consequently also universal—life. To be able to generate this increase, there is a constant necessity for unconscious repetition as one part of habit. No wonder Hegel can claim that "we are ethical[ly] unconscious of ourselves" (HOPR, 154, trans. mod.).

Against this background he can insist that habit describes a fundamental process of "embodiment" (HPM, 132). Embodiment means that it is only through habit that man is capable of transforming his body into a versatile instrument of the soul. As Alain has already remarked concerning Hegel:

> Here the body is no longer a foreign being, reacting belligerently against me; rather it is pervaded by soul and has become soul's instrument and means; yet at the same time, in habit the corporeal self is understood as it truly is; body is rendered something mobile and fluid, able to express directly the inner movements of thought without needing to involve thereby the role of consciousness or reflection . . .[6]

Here it becomes clear that habit does not describe a singular state but rather takes its necessary place at each stage in the development of the activities of spirit. In this way, only with the marital bond can there be "unity with someone . . . i.e. habit" (HGPR, 328). Because only in this "*ethical* root of the state . . . [does] a substantial unity . . . of subjective particularity and objective universality" (HOPR, 226) becomes habitual. In love, the habit of the sensed substantial unity with another human being also structurally implies the habit of intersubjectivity tout court. This brings along with it the desire for unity with someone without whom "I would feel defective and incomplete" because only in relation to him can "I find myself in another person . . ." (Ibid., 162). Without this habit, one of the roots of the state is lost, the root of sociality.

Habit also transforms the bodily organization, the sensations, and needs. If practical education consists "in the self-perpetuating need" (Ibid., 191), then it becomes clear in what way the natural organization of man is changed by labor. Also, on a more universal level, the constitution of an estate—and of the corporation—in the state depends on the integration which transforms the dexterity of each individual formed by habit into the mediated universality of all who are equipped with it. Through habit a need for others is generated. The estate is a sort of "institutional place where one satisfies one's own need collectively in a *habitual* and stylized manner."[7] Practical education—that is, i.e. activity—produces the habit—of laboring and as dexterity—whose more universal form materializes in an estate. Thus, on this more universal stage the habit of collectively satisfying one's needs is generated. The linkage of a repetitive aspect becoming mechanical on the one hand and the realization of freedom in an increasingly universal way on the other is an integral and essential component of the constant birth and the perpetual growth of the ethical from out of the free will. In this way, in the universal activity in the estate, a necessary relation to others is produced which at the same time is concretely determined by the individual estate and becomes habitual.[8]

No activity without habit (of activity) and without habit no (more universal) activity. This is the dialectical formula for the notion of habit itself. Applied to the context of ethicality one can already conclude the following: without the habit (of work) there would be no ethicality and no universality. Only through stable mechanical repetition does it become possible to introduce differences which increase the degree of the realization of freedom. Habit in this sense describes a productive and producing relation of *difference and repetition;* wherein mere repetition and productive repetition determine themselves as being involved in a reciprocal dialectic. As can be shown, Hegel's notion of habit always fulfills the same function: the forming of a new and more universal nature. This means that activities have come to be repeated in a merely mechanical, unconscious way so that they necessarily appear to me as belonging to my self-feeling—for example that standing and breathing belong to me, and this habit, this "soul of custom" (Ibid., 159), enables me to perform more universal activities. Since in this way the natural organization is changed, Hegel can always conceive of the respective degrees of habit in terms of second nature[9] and refer to the fact that in it any subject has the possibility of owning itself in a universal—and not only an isolated—manner.[10] Habit names at one and the same time the mechanical character of self-feeling and the "vitality and persistence of subjectivity."[11]

That the ethical "appears as a general mode of conduct, i.e. as *custom [Sitte]*" and that thereby the "habitual practice of ethical living" is "put in the place of the initial, purely natural will" (HOPR, 159) means that custom appears to the particular individual as his own—second—nature. The individuals reproduce it mechanically—which also implies that they cannot conceive of their own nature without it—and through it alone can they realize their freedom in a stable way. Only through customs becoming habitual does a particular and always singular realization of freedom become thinkable for Hegel. The range of this determination becomes even clearer if one takes into consideration the fact that ethicality is at the same time the sublation of the first two parts of the *Philosophy of Right*—"the pre-political existence of man,"[12] of abstract right and morality. As it describes the development of the notion of freedom, it initially begins as one-sidedly objective in the guise of abstract right, and continues one-sidedly subjective as pure moral consciousness—the mere subjective 'right' of morality. Habit here means that man gets used to the mediation of the two one-sided positions: the mere external right of existing laws and the mere internal right of subjective convictions are reshaped in the mediating process of habit and in this way man is constantly reborn in a second nature.[13]

If the realization of freedom is subjectively attested in acting and in the respective works of the individuals, as well as objectively in the laws, then ethicality is the habit of mediating the two. Man's nature no longer appears to him either as the dominance of heterogeneous drives to which he is subordinated or as the dominance of external laws which oppose to this natural unfreedom a secondary unfreedom of prohibitions. Rather in habit the objectivity of effective laws and the subjectivity of one's own conviction regarding how to realize one's own freedom are mediated with one another. More precisely: only via the mechanical repetition of the objective laws that stabilizes ethicality can there be—in different singular forms—creative realizations of one's own freedom. Habit is always the habit of the individual that in the state mechanically reproduces the same by way of his universal activity—organized in the estate and the corporation—and thereby—and only thereby—is it able to realize his freedom in a radically particular form and to satisfy his needs that have become social[14] "The formation of habit refers at the same time to an interiorization of ethicality."[15] If any individual educated by habit "will[s] that he himself shall be in everything he does" (HOPR, 110) because it is only in this way that he can realize *his* own freedom, what can it mean to lose a habit? One can understand Hegel here in two ways: on the one hand in the sense of an (already concretized) habit of concrete labor in civil society, on the other in the sense of a (structural) habit of activity as such which concerns the whole education of the subject and has thereby mediated the constitution of ethicality. To lose the habit of working presupposes that the idleness that results from it refers to a complete loss of habit or of activity. But is it at all possible to lose habit in such a way that one is essentially inactive? Is such a loss of habit at all thinkable for Hegel?

To answer these questions I will follow one decisive consequence that for Hegel is implied in the loss of the habit (of work). As he explicitly claims, without the habit of activity "there is laziness/foulness [*Faulheit*]" (HVORL4, 609) and laziness is one of the sources of the "creation of a penurious rabble" (HOPR, 222). That laziness is one of the sources of the rabble means not only that it is one of *two* sources, along with extravagance, but also that laziness is merely *one* of two, which is to say, only the objective, external source but not the subjective, internal one. Laziness *and* attitude are needed. If one reads the cited passage against the background of the discussion of habit the importance of this will swiftly become apparent because it describes what happens if the ethical, mediating process of subjective and objective sides, i.e. habit, is lost: there is laziness/foulness. Laziness and the loss of the habit of working are—on both of the described levels—structurally homologous. Therefore, in order to understand the loss of habit, one should ask: How does Hegel define laziness/foulness?

In the following I will uncover *elements of a Hegelian theory of laziness/foulness.*[16] In the *Philosophy of Right* Hegel writes of laziness/foulness [*Faulheit*], rotting [*Verfaulen*], decay [*Fäulnis*]—all of these notions taken literally refer to the same semantic field that is indicated by the German word *faul* which means lazy but also rotten. The first important passage reads like this: "the body is the reality, while the soul is the concept; but soul and body ought to be adequate to one another. Therefore a corpse is still an existent, but its existence is no true existence; the concept has left it; and for this reason a dead body putrefies [*verfault*]" (Ibid., 42). If the body is no longer adequate to the soul, or more abstractly, if the reality is not adequate to the concept, then this inadequate relationship produces the fouling, putrefaction of reality. A dead man is still— and this 'still' is decisive—an existence, but only as long as the no longer true relationship between concept and reality leads to the putrefaction of the dead body. Putrefaction, *Verfaulen*, is therefore defined as a process that is inaugurated as the result of an inadequate relationship between concept and reality. Any untrue and conceptless existence putrefies and becomes a putrefying existence. This first definition of *Verfaulen* can be applied to the rabble. That it is not adequate to the concept of the free will—in its different organizations as citizen, bourgeois, moral conscious, etc.—is the reason, following the Hegelian logic, that it putrefies, that it becomes and is foul, lazy, *faul*. It is the untrue, conceptless existence in the state. It seems as if the rabble putrefies, *verfault*, but laziness, *Faulheit*, is one of his very sources and not an effect produced by his emergence. This means that it is not first the rabble that putrefies. If laziness, *Faulheit*, is one of the sources of the rabble this means that the nonadequacy of concept and reality has already to be present before his emergence. Laziness is already given with the poor. But one can also conclude that if poverty is a social product then this laziness, *Faulheit*, is also one. It becomes clear for the question of the loss of habit that the poor is reduced to one of the two determinations of habit. What does that mean?

That poverty is socially produced means that it "is inevitable that many people not of a criminal disposition are cut off from the green tree of morality"[17] and excluded from any possibility of social, practical activity. If the twofold determination of habit is to deaden the intensity of an activity and of the life related to it and therefore also to be the condition of possibility for the realization of freedom on a universal level, this means that the poor are cut off from one of the two sides. They lose all the advantages of civil society but at the same time the needs that became habitual—and were acquired in civil society— persist. Thus the poor are left with only the merely mechanic repetition. They repeat without realizing their freedom. They get used to the mere repetition of their own needs. Habit becomes positive. But if this mechanical side of habit is bound to notions of devitalization, the poor is reduced to a devitalized life, a life without intensity. This is the reason for the nonadequacy of concept and reality in his case and therefore he becomes lazy, he putrefies, *verfault*.

Following this logic, for the poor goes: "Life does not live"[18] and, one can add, therefore it putrefies. The application of this logic to the relationship between rabble and poverty produces an unambiguous result: the production of poverty causes a nonadequacy of concept—free will—and reality (poverty), and this initiates a process of putrefaction, *Verfaulen*, at whose 'end' stands the putrefied, fouled rabble. Hegel remarks already in his early Heidelberg lectures that poverty "usually brings in its train . . . idleness . . ."[19] He develops elsewhere the way in which such a nonadequacy of concept and reality comes about and what results from it. It happens, according to his example, when organs are cut off from the organism and therefore from their own concept. Cut off, they are in a nonadequate relation to their concept. As Hegel paradigmatically formulates: "the hand, when separated from the body, putrefies . . ." (HPN, 18). In this context it is also interesting to read that "a hand, if severed, loses its independent subsistence; it does not remain what it was in the organism; its mobility, agility, shape, colour, etc., are changed; indeed it decomposes [*Fäulnis*] and its whole existence perishes altogether. It was sustained in existence only as a member of an organism, and had reality only as continually brought back into the ideal unity" (HA1, 121, trans. mod.).

The nonadequacy of reality and concept dissolves the reality which without a concept is nothing but mere reality, without participating in the necessarily organic unity of the idea. Put differently: decomposition, *Fäulnis*, and putrefaction, *Verfaulen*—Hegel uses the two terms synonymously—occur as soon as reality is as cut off from its concept as the hand is from the organism in Hegel's example. This means that the poor who becomes lazy, foul and begins to perish becomes rabble. The poor's existence is in an inadequate relation to his concept. This relationship itself reflects this lack and the poor finds himself—by not being represented in and by it—cut off from the organism of the state and his ideal unity. This (necessarily) happens because he even loses the residual form of activity which could be sustained by begging and withdraws into a *right without right*. This process is accompanied by a similar transformation of his mobility, agility, shape. All determinations of the poor change. If all determinations of the existence of the poor perish, one might say that the poor simply croaks and disappears, although this seems to be the only immediate consequence. But the poor whose determinations are fully transformed, the poor who enter into decomposition, *Fäulnis*, and whose whole existence is dissolving are the rabble if the attitude belonging to him adds up. Initially the poor seems to die a political and representative death by being reduced to the mechanical repetitive side of habit. This is why he is dissolving socially. Following the political death is the second, social, real death and the poor should be sublated by the movement of history. But the dissolved poor who has croaked delineate the structural place in which the rabble can emerge. In this way one can draw the consequence that Hegel has dissolved the existence of what I have named the *absolute rabble*. The *absolute rabble* is the complete negation of all determinations—even that of existence. The way in which one arrives at it is by way of the processes of putrefaction and decomposition.

Hence the process of putrefaction ultimately signifies: the complete dissolution of all determinations and with it of the entire existence. One can claim that the rabble is a putrefied existence—and in this sense not even a mere existence. But one should not take the logic of putrefaction, as described by Hegel, to be the sole reason for the emergence of the rabble. It is not only the result of an objective putrefying process which starts with the poor. Rather one has to stress that the notion of laziness, *Faulheit*, has to have a different status when it comes to the rabble or the poor. If the rabble only emerges 'after' the putrefaction, the laziness of the rabble has to have a different determination than the one delineated so far. It will be my aim in the following to distinguish between the putrefying (poor) and the putrefied (rabble), between the foulness of the poor and the foulness of the rabble. For the rabble, although dissolved, does not simply disappear, rather it insists in a problematic or a rotten way in Hegel's philosophy. The completely dissolved poor is the rabble: the rabble is a completely dissolved existence. It has an existence which is not one. But this dissolution of the whole existence does not lead to the disappearance of the rabble problem; rather it seems initially to constitute it in a peculiar way. For the rabble, even when dissolved, is 'present,' there—one might say that it is present as 'inexistent.' The rabble in-exists.[20]

Already a superficial observation is sufficient to indicate that it is no contingent matter that Hegel takes the detached organ as the paradigm of putrefaction. Rather, this paradigm clarifies a specific point in the inadequate relation between concept and reality. What the example clarifies is that the hand can persist only as an element of the rationally organized organism and only in this way can it assume functions and tasks in the organism. The implications of this paradigm are far-reaching. For the hand is characterized as the specifically human organ. The "hand [is] that magnificent tool which no animal possesses" (HOPR, 68) and because "no animal has such a flexible tool for external activity" the hand is the "*tool of tools*" that "is suited to an endless multitude of expressions of the will" (HPM, 110).

The hand is *the* tool of man because it materializes paradigmatically both the potential infinity of expressions of the will and at the first stage it is the instrument of the conscious realization of freedom. For this realization always appears as self-realizing activity. The hand is also capable of grasping things; performing complex gestures such as taking hold of something in such a way as to make it into a tool—delineating in a basal form the structure of labor. The hand is a tool because it allows man to relate to objects in the objective world through labor. Therefore Hyppolite is fully justified in writing that "the hand is the organ of labor, but it can also be considered as presenting within itself the structure of labor, the individual traits that correspond to innate dispositions or acquired habits."[21] The hand presents the bodily quasi-atom of the mediation of subject and object, of particular and universal, of the primary nature of the individual and the second nature of the—practically educated—ethical community. This is why besides the erect Gestalt, to human expression belongs "the formation of the hand especially, as the absolute tool" (HPM, 109), since it makes possible what remains impossible for any animal. "Through the use of the tool man breaks off his living relation to living nature and places a relation oriented to his goals in its place."[22] The hand makes man into man because it allows him to relate to the objective world in a different, and namely a practical way. It is the paradigmatic organ of practical activity. Through the hand the world becomes in a fundamental way the place of the expression of human will and thereby the site of his practical intervention. It is the organ that distinguishes man from the animal already in his bodily constitution because it enables him to *express* his will in a basal form and thereby it reflects the historico-practical process of the education of man. From this, it becomes clear that not only do the notions of man and of the human organism determine the notion of the hand but that the notion of the hand also determines the notion of man and of his organic determination. The individual organ determines the organism just as much as it becomes in this determination an element of the organism that determines it. The hand is Hegel's preferred organ because it participates in a specifically human expression. It is a paradigm of the human.

But if the hand is cut off from the body, this organically related relationship of determination is lost. The hand loses its relation to the will, the world and the possibility of expression and activity. It loses the organism and because this organism will always have been a human organism it loses man as such. If it loses the relation to the human organism, it loses in a certain sense itself. It is impossible for it to be a medium of expression because it is detached from the free will which enables it to do so. Only as the organ of an organism can the hand as hand realize actions [*Hand*lungen].[23] The concept of the hand implies the possibility of human activity. A detached hand is a hand without will and possibilities of acting, a hand without man, or: an inhuman hand. A detached hand that therefore became inhuman has only an external, i.e. inessential reality and does not stand in an adequate relationship to its concept. For this reason its whole existence is dissolved and it putrefies. The Hegelian paradigm of the detached hand explains the problem of organic separation on different levels: it—literally—refers to a state of disorganization, to a state of dehumanization, of un-conceptuality and in-essentiality. Here it again becomes clear that the detachment of an organ from an organism always has two aspects: the organ is first detached from the organism and then from its own concept. It is (conceptually) no longer an organ. This conclusion explains the dialectical volte-face that the concept, for example the concept of an organ, is always rationally organized. Even the concept of putrefaction is itself organic, since it describes the sublation of the inadequacy of reality and concept. It negates therewith the negation which the inadequacy implies and transposes it into an organic state. The putrefaction as the negation of negation (of an inadequacy) defines the organic movement which is already implied in the notion of putrefaction. But what does the detachment of an organ signify for the organism? A passage from the *Philosophy of Right* in which Hegel presents an analogy between the human and the political organism is interesting in this context: "But the ugliest person, or a criminal, or an invalid, or a cripple, is still always a living human being. The affirmative, life, subsists despite such defects, and it is this affirmative factor which is our theme here" (HOPR, 234). What happens to the detached organ does not befall the organism from which it was detached. The organism remains one, even as crippled. A crippled state in which poverty exists is still adequate to its concept.

If the detached organ negates its own concept, which is necessarily implied in the organism, then the crippled, faulty organism by no means negates the concept. Thus it becomes again clear that only the inadequacy of reality to its concept describes a negation. The state does not start to putrefy when organs detached from it begin to putrefy. For decomposition and putrefaction name processes of transition, inaugurated by an inadequate relationship between reality and concept, at whose end stands the dissolution of the conceptless reality. For the discussion of the rabble this means that the inadequacy of concept and reality which prevails in poverty produces decomposition, *Fäulnis*, and actuates a process of putrefaction, *Verfaulen*, whose most radical result is the rabble. The rabble is that which emerges from putrefaction. The rabble is following this logic the fully decomposed poor[24]; the poor whose existence is totally dissolved. The poor is the severed hand of society[25] whose existence dissolves.

One can note that the rabble names a *Ver-Wesen*[26] in a double sense. Being without a concept means to putrefy, to decompose, and the putrefaction, *Verwesen*, is only an expression of what already is in reality: the detachment from the concept, i.e. concept- and essencelessness. The putrefaction, *Verwesen*, *as a process* is the result of this essencelessness; but the putrefaction, *as state* of the inadequacy between concept and reality also names the essencelessness of reality as *Ver-Wesen*. *Ver-Wesen* names the couple of process and state, of essence-less reality and putrefaction of it. Since the hand gains a persistent autonomy only if it is, as an organ, a member of an organism, the particular free will can only realize itself if it is, as organic part, in a rational relationship with the state—and this means with itself and its own concept. A biological as well as a political organ without organism is a conceptless and thereby essenceless organ; a dissolving and putrefying organ; one that is consumed by decomposition and putrefaction—because it is already a *Ver-Wesen*. There is initially "worthless [*faule*] existence" (HPH, 36) which then dissolves even as existence. What consequences can be drawn from this?

Hegel describes organic life in his *Encyclopedia* as a perpetual self-restoration "in the process of its own destruction." Organic life has to assert itself over against the objective world which it faces at first externally and with which it has to quarrel. Any organic life is "in conflict with air" and "a wound, for example, only becomes dangerous through exposure to air" (HPN, 109). Therein it is again habit that delineates the decisive moment in which this conflict becomes part of self-feeling and is repeated mechanically, and is at the same time the condition of possibility for the realization of one's freedom. One learns to breathe, which makes out of the constant conflict with air a moment of practical education and is able to quarrel with the world on a more universal level and realize one's freedom therein. The capacity of active—and herein lies the emphasis—self-restoration distinguishes organic life from the inorganic. Organic life knows practical education and therefore it also knows the habits that are involved in it. It is able to restore itself recurrently. It is able to recreate itself in dissolution.[27] The inorganic however "which cannot withstand the struggle must fall into decay [*verfaulen*] . . ." (HPN, 109). This passage is the only one in Hegel's oeuvre where he states a direct connection between the inorganic and decay, *verfaulen*, and this is important for the question being discussed here. If one relates this passage to those I have previously been discussing one may conclude that the inorganic decays by definition. This reading is valid if one understands the inorganic as that which does not accord with any organic organization and whose reality is detached from its own organic concept. The inorganic can (initially) have consistency and existence but it cannot be active and this means that it cannot have life because life is determined by its being active. The inorganic names, in this reading, the fundamental structure of an inadequacy between concept and reality.[28] The inorganic is therefore that which previously stood in an organic relation from which it was subsequently detached. One can conclude that the inorganic is septic, i.e. engendering putrefaction, *Fäulnis*. If there is something inorganic, it engenders putrefaction and this is only an expression of the inorganic. The septic is the inorganic; the inorganic is the septic.

Such an extrapolated determination of the inorganic clarifies why for Hegel the organ detached from the body, the hand, is the paradigm of decay. It became a conceptless organ because it became inorganic, i.e. it lost its activity, its life, its membership of the organism. The organ detached from the organic organization within an organism arouses putrefaction and it putrefies because it became an *un-organ*. The prefix 'in' of the 'inorganic' therein delineates the negation of the organic relation which can only be sublated by the negation of this negation. The existence of the inorganic as of the *un-organ* has to be dissolved in order to sublate the negation of the necessary organic organization, the disorganization. Also the poor has become, like the rabble, by falling out of the political-organic order of the state, an *un-organ*. Here also it is clear that Hegel's definition of the inorganic is also valid for the political body. For the organic structuring of the concept itself produces this equation. Hegel can therefore constantly use this analogy. When a—political or individual—body—does not perpetually restore itself in constant activity, structurally it comes close to the inorganic which is not able to self-reproduce. This perspective now allows us to understand one remark from the *Philosophy of Right* in which a connection between putrefaction and habit is formulated.

Hegel states there that it is only because war breaks into history from time to time that "the ethical health of peoples is preserved in their indifference towards the stabilization of finite determinacies; just as the blowing of the wind preserves the sea from stagnation [*Fäulnis*]." Putrefaction would be unavoidable if "a prolonged calm" or a "perpetual peace" (HOPR, 307) were to be installed. This is not at all a merely metaphorical discourse but also a structural one. Metaphorically war is similar to the wind that preserves the statist sea of processes of putrefaction and decay but it also refers to a moment of historical activity that stands against this political putrefaction. Hegel here thematizes the problem of the positivity of habit in terms of putrefaction and decay, dissolution.[29] This means that habit can lead to a "being posited, fixated and at the same time, to solidification."[30] This can happen when there is a hypostatization of one side of habit, mechanical repetition if the increase in universality of the realizations of freedom is subordinated to merely mechanical reproduction. Mere repetition leads to death and consequently putrefaction enters. Habit can become positive in the way that it "blinds us to that on which our whole existence depends" (HOPR, 241). This can lead to the fact that "the fullness and zest that originally characterizes the aim of life are out of question . . . it is an existence without intellect or vitality . . . as a political nullity and tedium" (HPH, 75).

Here Hegel explicitly shares the diagnosis of this reduction of habit to just one of its facets also for the poor: they become a political nullity and therefore they are left to rot. Not only does the detachment of an organ from an organism arouse putrefaction but also the organism can turn into a dead existence if it entrusts itself to the mechanical side of habit. This danger is implied in this side of habit and marks the index of a specific form of temporality that is linked to habit. For if habit becomes positive there is a "life dissolved in decay" (HPN, 264). Due to the organic organization of the concept what goes for the human organism also goes for the political: "when he has once come to feel completely at home in life, when he has become spiritually and physically dull, and when the opposition between subjective consciousness and spiritual activity has disappeared" (HOPR, 160) it collapses. As the individual human organism has a specific time—youth, adolescence, maturity, old age—the political-statist organism also follows this logic of historical development. Therefore "by the habit of mental life, as well as by the dulling of activity of his physical organism man becomes an old man" who "lives without any definite interests . . . and the future seems to promise nothing new at all . . ." (HPM, 61).

As soon as the realization of freedom becomes in a certain sense objective—as soon as the given possibilities have realized themselves[31]—the activity of realization blunts and the merely mechanical, unconscious repetition takes priority. Then the higher *habit of life* is needed to sublate this negation. When this status is reached in the development of ethical life via the mechanical repetition of the given and at the same time via the loss of creative vitality, on the political level an additional moment is needed in order to convert the unlively political existence into dissolution and to sublate it into the organic proceeding of the historical movement. For what happens to detached organs in the process of putrefaction? One needs a (historical) executive assistants.[32] War is needed. It is the necessary *habit of history* which converts political nullities into dissolution and therewith performs a process whose end was already decided. "A people can only die a violent death when it has become naturally dead in itself" (HPH, 75). Hence the political life haunted by putrefaction, as well as the inorganic in general, is not able to persist with the active restoration in the struggle with externality and crosses over into (historical) dissolution. Mere repetition produces inorganicity and its expression is the septic. This can also clarify Hegel's remark which relates to the becoming-positive of habit: "The human being also dies from habit . . . for the human being is active only insofar as he has not attained his end and wants to produce and assert himself in the effort to attain it" (HOPR, 159–60). If the human being only mechanically repeats what becomes his habit there is a devitalization of life which leads to death, to the becoming-inorganic of life, at whose end stand putrefaction and decomposition. Both begin due to the inadequacy of concept and reality. It can find its ground either in a counternatural detachment—of an organ from an organism—or it can be a product of habit as pure mechanical repetition which names the reason for the naturality of death. The *danger of the inorganic* is a decisive moment for the problem of idleness or laziness. Hence Hegel formulates a clear maxim for the political body: "no one of its moments should appear as inorganic aggregate" (Ibid., 291, trans. mod.). That this maxim is not an imperative—indicated by the word 'should'—is clear as a result of the fact that it cannot be universalized. As Gans rightly remarks: "States are individuals with a slightly longer life but which also fall in the end, destroyed in the struggle with world history. They are rivers that pour into the ocean of history, the last objective of the real world."[33]

Each state has its time. Every state will revert into a political nullity whose existence will be dissolved by the habit of history. Remembering the dialectical determining relationship—the organ determines the organism as the organism determines the organ[34]—one can foresee a further moment. As Hegel already clearly remarks in 1802: "[T]he ethical life of the individual is one pulse-beat of the whole system, and is itself the whole system."[35] An organ not having this organic bond with the organism does not produce a problem, because as it is detached from the organism and its concept it putrefies. But if *in* the political body something inorganic appears, an *un-organ*, then it is at the same time detached as it is still a part of it. It is decisive to distinguish the detachment from society that poverty implies from the detachment from all determinations that the rabble implies: poverty stands in an inorganic relation to the state and its concept, because it is involuntarily reduced by the bourgeois economic dynamics to the mechanically repeating side of habit. This induces a process of putrefaction which dissolves all the determinations of existence of the poor. The rabble as *un-organ* emerges at the end of this process. The rabble is a putrefied existence, i.e. it is no existence. At the same time the *logic of double latency* has shown that with the rabble there emerges the insight that it is latently present in all elements 'prior to' the process of putrefaction. What is valid for the inorganic in the logic I have been discussing is also valid for the poor as un-organ: it putrefies and dissolves. Thereby the implied negation is negated and sublated. Poverty means that an *un*-organic relationship, a relation between the negation of one's own concept and the organism exists. *Rabble means that there is an inorganic as well as an organic relation to the concept.* For the rabble emerges at a stage where the negation of the organic relationship should itself be negated and sublated. This doubling delineates the terminological usage that I will make in the following of the notion of the *un-organ*.[36] Either the organ is within the body and is determining the organism or it is detached; it is thereby no longer an organ and therefore does not determine the organism. The *un-organ* marks the position of a *peculiar 'negation'* of an organ which is, at the same time, positively there and determines the organism from the inside and cannot be a simply negation of the organic as such because otherwise it would be posited outside the organism. The *un-organ* is both: internal and external, a detached and *un-organic* part. It is neither not organic (as poverty or the severed hand) nor organic (as normal, bound organs). Rather it is *un-organic* (as the rabble). The detached organ that insists in the organism still determines the organism, and in a harmful way. An inorganic ensemble in the political body is detached from it and harms it at the same time as being an inorganic part of it. Therefore Hegel can conclude that "a power or activity in the state must never appear and act in a formless, inorganic shape, i.e. on the principle of plurality and number" (HPM, 244).

Otherwise, the political body faces the threat of becoming inorganic and ultimately of entering into its dissolution. Since "[w]hat disorganizes the unity of the logical-rational, equally disorganizes actuality" (Ibid., 241). In the *Philosophy of Right* the content of this formulation becomes a concrete guise when Hegel diagnoses: "the sanctity of marriage and honour . . . are the two moments around which the disorganization of civil society revolves" (HOPR, 226). Civil society—explicitly not the state—is threatened in these two moments with disorganization, becoming inorganic. This means: civil society is due to its logic of needs itself driven to produce disorganization, which is compensated for by marriage and the corporation and the honor of its individual members. The corporation and marriage designate the institutions which sublate the menaces of the civil-social dynamic and convey them into the ethicality of the state. Without it the state, that Hegel also calls "the nervous system," in which family appears as "sensibility" and civil society as "irritability" (HOPR, 239) would be an inorganic ensemble. But poverty is a product of civil society and gives rise to a problem that cannot be compensated for by marriage or corporation.

The rabble designates at least for civil society the danger of the inorganic ensemble, of disorganization. It produces as *un-organ* which can no longer be drawn back into the ethical by marriage or the corporation effects amidst civil society. Amidst civil society an inorganic *Ver-wesen* takes place that at the same time cannot be dispelled by the institutions which should return "the *ethical* . . . to civil society as something immanent" and which name the place of the dialectical transition to the state. The rabble appears precisely there as *un-organ*, as *Ver-Wesen*. If these institutions are suspended in their effectivity, "my particular end" is not "identified with the universal," and thereby "the state is left in the air" (Ibid., 240). Against putrefaction only rational activity is of any avail, an activity whose institutional place is delineated by the corporation. Only rational activity is capable of interrupting the processes of destruction by mediating between individual well-being and the universal. A constant restoration in dissolution. Therefore Hegel can call the estate whose participation leads to the corporation a "mediating organ . . ." (Ibid., 289). The participation in an estate, which the poor and the rabble lack, cares for the fact that it is in the state "[m]uch the same thing . . . as in the organic body . . . There is only life at all points and nothing withstands it. Separated from that life, every point dies" (Ibid., 264). The rabble cannot be inscribed into any organic relation with statist institutions—except when it becomes a criminal. But it is "[t]he nature of an organism . . . that unless each of its parts is brought into identity with the others, unless each of them is prevented from achieving independence, the whole must perish." This is why when it comes to political organisms it is adequate to use the "the fable of the belly and the other members" (Ibid., 242) and why the *un-organic* rabble marks an untamable difficulty. For not to be related organically to the state and its other members means not to be "taken up into the totality" (Ibid., 290) and as Hegel clearly states: "Thus subjective particularity was not incorporated into the organization of society as a whole; it was not reconciled in the whole, and therefore . . . it shows itself there as something hostile, as a corruption of the social order" (Ibid., 196). It is the origin of the danger of a "mass or an aggregate . . . in opposition to the organized state" (Ibid., 290); a danger for the political organism *in* the organism itself. But might it not be the case that the rabble, because it is a *Ver-Wesen*, an *un-organ*, perishes altogether in its existence and finds its sublation in the dialectical movement? Would it not be befallen by the "countercharge"[37] (Ibid., 289) which—following Hegel—necessarily results from his standpoint?

I want to follow up on the thesis that the putrefaction and decomposition (of the poor) lead to the full dissolution of existence, but that the laziness/ idleness of the rabble describes a state which is in a way yet to be determined and which takes place *'after'*—and at the same time logically *'before'*—this process of dissolution. The idleness of the rabble describes a 'state' which concerns 'something' whose existence is fully dissolved but which is and remains permanently present as dissolved. If the putrefaction describes *the* objective process of the genesis of the rabble—idleness as one of its sources—then the attitude which supplements poverty marks his *subjective genesis.* Only by relating both components can one reconstruct the idleness-problem. Hegel himself addresses this when he asks: "But how can something be present and yet not exist?" (HPN, 155)[38]

Initially poverty appears as the inadequacy of concept and reality which Hegel, referring to the logic of putrefaction, calls misery [*Elend*]. "If the body does not match the soul, it is a poor sort of thing [*etwas Elendes*]" (HOPR, 17). Misery names this inadequacy. The misery that is poverty refers to a fundamental nonconformity of concept and reality. The logic of misery can be grasped as a specifying supplement to the logic of poverty and putrefaction. One can conclude that poverty necessarily leads to misery because the body of the poor does not match the active soul; because for them activity is made impossible. Indigence is therefore always also a (bodily) effect of idleness. To pass off this indigence, however, as something sacred was characteristic of the rotten structures of the Church in mediaeval times before the Reformation. In the church "Pauperism, laziness, inactivity was regarded as nobler: and the Immoral thus received the stamp of consecration" (HPH, 380). Hegel by contrast insists, referring to the Reformation, that it is a matter of individual's honorability to gain subsistence through work. For "activity and mobility are precisely what manifest the higher ideality of life" (HA1, 131), as he has it in the *Aesthetics*. But if the rabble is marked by the attempt to claim a *right without right* that posits it beyond the rational context of activities, then it can be understood analogously to the living thing of which Hegel claims that it "displeases because of its drowsy activity; it drags itself painfully along and its whole manner of life displays its incapacity for quick movement and activity" (Ibid., 130ff.): the *sloth.* If the whole habitus of the sloth refers to the incapacity to move and act and due to its drowsy activity, one can take this as a further guide in our reading of the rabble-problem. The sloth can thus be considered to be a twofold paradigm: it is an animal and thus privative with regard to human being (it does not experience its own limitedness, which derives from the external determination of his will by his instincts, and his needs) and amongst the animals it presents the one which displeases due to its lethargy. It is in this sense also privative with regard to animals. The sloth can be read as a figure of privation.

The rabble is lazy because in poverty there is an inadequacy which makes them putrefy. The poor as "idlers" (HPH, 423) become rabble at the end of the putrefaction when the peculiar attitude of the rabble joins in. If the rabble is now a fully putrefied existence, this means that it does not even displease because of its drowsy activity but rather by not being active at all and due to the fact of having lost all determinations of the existing. The rabble loses the habit of being active and this means that it is the completely sluggish, the *absolute inert*, the fully putrefied and dissolved existence. The inertia of the rabble is more radical than the drowsiness of the sloth. The problem here has the following logic: in the movement of civil society a lack is produced. This lack is initially fully external, an objective lack. The poor lose all external property, but at the same time poverty is not a result of individual misdeeds. This external lack means that there is a negation: a negation of property and of the possibility of entering into the mediating context of civil society. Thereby the negation is deepened to encompass the organic bond and the organic integration. Poverty is negation inasmuch as it is always also an inadequate relation of concept and reality: a negation of the necessary and ideal organic structuring of the concept. Therefore the poor putrefy and dissolve; after dying a political death—which posits them outside representation, they ultimately die—a social, an existential—death. Astonishingly, the rabble emerges '*after*' *the putrefaction*. Rabble is the name for that which is present of negativity—which has theoretically already disappeared—'after' the negation of the negation.

It emerges at a stage where theoretically the negation of the negation of poverty has (or should have) taken place and this negation converted into the 'positivity' of sublation. One can conclude that the rabble marks a place in which a peculiar positivity of negativity appears—a present, insisting in-existence. This positivity follows from the Hegelian logic of the rabble although Hegel constantly insists that the rabble marks the "negative outlook generally" (HOPR, 289) and can be understood as being purely privative or as a mere abstract negation of determinations. For Hegel one can say that "this indeterminacy is itself only a negation in contrast with the determinate . . ." (Ibid., 31). He recoils—as I want to claim—from his own insight.[39] For with the rabble there appears a *different concept of indeterminacy* which cannot be conceived of in the form of the negation of a determination, of the determinate. If one can claim that the Hegelian concept of determination is always 'to be determined as something', this is because for him—to quote Spinoza—*omnis determinatio est negatio*.[40] This means also that "any determination is finitization" which in turn "means 'must-end,' to-pass-over-oneself, but not into nothing, rather according to a determinate negation into the higher, concrete universal . . ."[41] After the negation of negation there is with the rabble something present that is not negation or 'something,' nor is it sublated. Rather there is a passing-over-oneself into the void of determinations. This passage marks a second type of laziness—the laziness of the rabble.[42]

But which laziness comes after the putrefaction and the full dissolution of existence? A laziness which cannot be the idleness of something that exists any longer. Here one finds concentrated all of the elements that have formed a part of our investigation up to this point. For the question arises as to what the subjective, inner correlate of the external, objective inadequacy of concept and reality is. Initially it might appear that the rabble falls under the definition that Hegel gives of the inert will:

A will which resolves nothing is no actual will; a characterless human being never reaches a decision. . . However 'beautiful' such a disposition may be, it is nevertheless dead. . . Only by resolving can a human being step into actuality, however bitter this may be to him. Inertia lacks the will to abandon the inward brooding which allows it to retain everything as possibility. But possibility is not yet actuality. (HOPR, 37)[43]

Inertia—the inertia of the will—is still—although only present as possibility—part of the freedom of subject. For it lies in the freedom of the subject "to slip into the standpoint of . . . untruth, and laziness [*Trägheit*] . . . and stick to it knowingly" (HPR1, 90). The inertia is inertia of the free will which abstracts from all reality because it considers any determination to be an abandonment of his freedom. Hegel's criticism is clear: the abstraction from reality and the persistence in the standpoint of pure possibility makes the inert will incapable of action. The inert will is a free will which limits itself to the mere possibility of freedom and in it becomes unfree will, for his persistence in the pure possibility makes him *determined as undetermined*. The possibility of the inert will which conceives of itself as absolute is therefore a *possibility without the possibility* of realization. The "inert entity" is the "extreme of [the] abstract being-in-itself" (HPS, 312) of the will. Inertia means abstraction. This is why to the inert will corresponds the dead disposition which dislikes "the transition from undifferentiated indeterminacy to the *differentiation, determination* and *positing* of a determination as a content and object" (HOPR, 30). Does this judgment not also fit the rabble? An inert will would be inadequate to the concept of free will and would putrefy. But the poor does not himself decide to be poor; he is not the pre-reformatory, supposedly sacred poor to whom asceticism and property-lessness is the highest good. Poverty in civil society is defined in such a way that the poor lose all advantages, and all possibilities of realizing their freedom, but at the same time the needs of civil society persist. *They want to but they cannot.* One can conclude that due to this impossibility the poor ultimately becomes internally inert as well; his will reflects the external prevention of realization.

If inertia would present an (internal) analogue of the will to (external) poverty, then this would mean that civil society produces the impossibility of being socially active. The economic movement of civil society produces inertia—first externally, then internally—and then causes the bourgeois to complain about it. Poverty is—following this intuition—initially an objective and externally produced inertia that is then reflected in the inert will of the poor. The will of the poor is therefore not by definition the inert will. Rather it is a will which due to the externally produced poverty (=inertia) has no possibility of activity left and for this reason becomes or is inert. This is because the inert will is, due to its own abstraction of all determinations, self-inflictedly a limited will, but things stand differently with regard to poverty. The inert will of poverty is produced by the objective impossibility of differentiation, determination, and positing that comes into being by non-self-inflicted poverty. His exemption from all external determination is not a persistence in the pure and absolute inner possibility. Rather it is itself a determination which is externally produced—by the economic movement. The inert will of the poor which persists in abstract interiority is always already a will that is externally determined by poverty and only as a result of this does it fall back into internal inertia. At the same time one has to stress that the inadequacy of concept and reality in poverty—which can be conceived of as an inert will—makes all determinations of existence disappear. This is also to say that even the (inert) will dissolves in the process of putrefaction. The rabble is the result of this and therefore one can claim that all its determinations of existence are dissolved, even the will, or at least the free will. Eric Weil is among those who have recognized the range of this problem and he rightly remarks that the rabble "does not *will*, he cannot *will*; for, and this is equivalent to saying that it is without reason."[44] But the determinations of existence in the Hegelian state imply the realization of freedom which has its origin and foundation in the free will. If one defines poverty as inertia of the will, the analysis leads to the following constellation: the rabble appears logically 'after' the inertia of the will, as a product of the dissolution that results from inertia. If even this determination of existence dissolves, then what determined this existence in the first place also dissolves: the free will, which was in inertia inadequate to its concept. The rabble does not persist in the position of a mere possibility without actuality; rather, even this possibility of realization has dissolved. *The rabble is the impossibility of the Hegelian concept of the free will.* The rabble is thus not the inert will, for the inert will is also a determination of an existence, of the inert and dead disposition. Therefore one can claim that the rabble is more inert than the inert will, since even the will gets dissolved in the process of putrefaction.

If the inert will still has the possibility of realizing freedom, one can say that the rabble marks the position in which only *an impossibility of realizing freedom* takes place. But what is inertia without a will? Here again it is instructive to glance at the *Encyclopedia*: "*In itself*, matter is inert, i.e. matter as its Notion, opposed to its reality" (HPN, 48). This means that matter may in fact fill space but is at the same time determined by a "quite indeterminate difference" which "is not yet a difference of matter as such" (Ibid., 47). Matter stands in a position structurally analogous to the inert will. This analogy may be made if one first points out that matter as the inert will both precede all determinations, i.e. both of them are negations of determination and are therefore determined as undetermined. If the inert will is transformed into a resolute will, which derives from a decision of the will itself (and is implied in the *decision* to abstract from all determinations), matter only appears in space when it passes into determinate formations of bodies. This delineation of matter can serve as a paradigmatic and heuristic point from which to continue the investigation.[45]

Matter *in itself* is inert because it fills space prior to all determination in an indeterminate way and indicates only the possibility of the appearance of bodies in space. But it persists in this possibility since no determination results from it, no positing of difference. This passage is remarkable when applied to the rabble-problem.[46] The rabble does not have any determination of existence anymore and thus cannot have any determinate difference in itself. With the putrefaction of all determinations the possibility of difference and distinction also putrefies. There is in this sense no difference of the rabble in itself and it therefore distinguishes itself exclusively by its constitutive indeterminacy and not due to a determination which it receives from everything else.[47] This also means that the rabble cannot name the matter *in itself* because it no longer contains the possibility of realization since it appears at a logical place where the *in-and-for-itself*, i.e. the negation of negation has already taken place. The rabble appears when the abstract in itself (of a free will without determinations) of the mere possibility of determination is already converted—by a first negation—into determination and realization (in civil society). But if on this level of realization an inadequacy of reality and concept appears (poverty), this negation is sublated through negation. The rabble appears on the level of the in and for itself but as the peculiar—absolute—negation of all determinations. At the same time it is clear that everyone is latently poor and therefore latently rabble and therefore, the rabble seems to mark something which lies in a peculiar way 'prior' to the singular and universal realizations of freedom—although this peculiar, logical 'priority' can only be revealed retroactively. The rabble therefore seems to fill the ethical space of the state in a peculiar way—as matter for Hegel fundamentally fills space.[48] If the rabble in this curiously analogous way seems to indicate the *matter of ethical space* then this matter would be one which only appears as matter at all '*after*' the realization; a matter *in and for itself* without determinations; a matter which is present—one could write: pre-sent—without being existent.

Consequently, the rabble would not only be the inert matter *in itself*, but the matter of ethicality *in and for itself*. The rabble would be a matter which does not exist 'before' and cannot exist 'after' and the determination. For any existence would inscribe determinations into it, but the existence itself would remain indeterminate—it would rather present itself only within the process of determination. The rabble, a peculiar matter of ethical space, appears 'after' the determination in *retrospect* as the logical 'before' of determinations. But one needs to be precise here: the inert will marks an indeterminacy as the negation of all determinations (a will poor of determinations); but any single determination of the will—in a process which finally creates civil society and the state—leads in its mediated universal (economical) movement to the unavoidable production of poverty, which is the external negation of property and of the possibility of participation in the rational mediating context of work; the processes that necessarily carry out this negation (putrefaction,

dissolving) lead to the sublation of the state (the negation of the existence of
the poor); finally, the rabble appears without external determinations by making itself through the attitude which supplements poverty.

One can understand this account as providing the dialectical-logical genesis
of "absolute poverty"(MEPM, 107).[49] The inert will would be poverty in itself;
the external poverty would be poverty for itself; the rabble poverty in and for
itself. Or: inertia in itself is matter; *inertia for itself is poverty; inertia in and for
itself is the rabble.* The in and for itself which is the rabble is split.[50] The rabble as
the matter of ethicality is both: an effect and also the logical *a priori* of the ethical space. He only emerges in the process of determination and as an effect of
determination ('after') the ethical and as soon as it emerges it brings with it
the insight that it will always have been a part of every element of ethical space
('before'). So: is the rabble the matter of the ethical space?

If the matter filling space always finds itself parceled out in multiple "whole
or single bodies" that unify everything to form individual and in each case
"different quanta" (HPN, 47) constitutes unities that appear in space, does
this mean that this is also valid for the peculiar, inert rabble-matter? If one
takes a step back from this question to consider once again what has become
clear so far, one will come closer to an answer. The problem that poses itself
here is that this peculiar matter has to be without determinations, and must
constitute the ethical space as absolute void but without being dialectically
determined as indeterminate or *not yet* determined matter. If the rabble thus has
no existence anymore, this also means that its *in-organic* presence is bodiless
and does not have any appearance proper to him. The rabble never appears
as such, never as himself, but always only in the poor, as the poor, and the *logic
of double latency* has shown that he is therewith latently included everywhere
without appearing. The rabble is in this sense an *un-organ*, which one can at
the same time delineate as an *organ without a body*.[51] I use *organ without body*
synonymously with *un-organ* to emphasize its double bodylessness: first, the
organ is detached from the body to which it belongs as an organ according to
its concept, and secondly this organ does not itself have a body, no external
appearance proper to it. It appears as detached, even from the determination
of the body. If this peculiar *organ without body* that the rabble is, is also marked
by its inertia and can be conceived of as the peculiar matter of the ethical
space, how does this logic relate to the one Hegel describes in respect of the
relationship of physical bodies in space?

If matter fills space, then it is always already unified into unities that are,
while themselves material, the first appearance and existence of matter. This
individual body, as the "immediate one" (HPN, 49) of the matter, is embodied so as to form a unity, but, like matter itself, it does not have a movement
proper to it but enters into it thanks to a collision with another body. Bodies
are localized matter, i.e. they are unities of matter necessarily appearing in a
place. Bodies are matter which begins to differ from itself and that appears.

The collision marks a point of encounter between two bodies in a "struggle for one and the same place" (Ibid., 50). By encountering themselves in a place, a collision between one body and the other is generated. This determination is already enough to mark a fundamental point. Namely that there is motion for an individual body only as a result of its collision with others. Motion is no absolute but a fundamentally relative notion. It is deduced from the fact that "there is not empty space . . . No matter how hard and brittle the matter is imagined to be . . ."(Ibid.).[52] Because there is no empty space there are always collisions between two bodies that repel one another. This means: there always already is motion, for there is always already a collision of bodies, and motion is "to be in one place, and at the same time to be in another place . . ." (Ibid.). Motion is incessantly and constitutively relative. But why should this determination of motion be helpful here? Dieter Wandschneider has articulated one consequence of this conception which is interesting here:

> The surprising result of the equivalence of cinematic relativity and inert corporeality opens, if I am not mistaken, a perspective on the possibility of non-relative movement. Purely formally, this equivalence also means that a "non-body"—whatever that may be—is one that can in any case no longer have a relative movement—a strange thought, to be sure.[53]

He formulates a consequence which results from thinking inertia and bodilessness together. That this thought seems strange to Wandschneider is due to a twofold difficulty. An absolute movement—a movement which is no longer describable in terms of motion—would be the movement of a non-body which he cannot specify more precisely. But it has become clear that the rabble can be understood as an non-body, namely as an *organ without a body*, as an organ that does not have a body and which is detached from the body whose organ it should be due to its concept. If the rabble, being such an organ, were to move, his movement would hence be absolute and not relative. What does this mean?

Initially it means that this motion would not find an end. It would be infinite motion. At the same time it would not be a movement of one body in one direction, but rather of a non-body in infinitely multiple directions. It would not be limited to one place, rather it would be explosive. If the relativity of motion depends on the localization of the body, then a delocalized, unlocalizable movement seems thinkable. The *logic of double latency* has shown that latently anybody in the state is rabble and as a consequence the rabble is present in all elements of the state. Hence it would be in this 'latent way of being' everywhere and absolute, never unambiguously localizable and not bound to any place. Once in motion, once emerged, this non-body appears retroactively anywhere. As soon as in the historical specificity and particularity of civil society the rabble emerges from the poor, it becomes clear that it will always already have been latently everywhere. Once in motion the rabble is absolute (in motion). Therefore in the movement of society itself something is produced (poverty) which presents the condition of possibility of the absolute motion of a non-body (rabble). If this possibility is combined with the process of putrefaction and with the rabble-attitude, an absolute, infinite and explosive movement is generated. A movement of dissolving turns into a multidirectional, explosive movement. The rabble, as soon as it emerges, is thus always explosive.[54] The emergence of the rabble as a matter of ethicality always means a rabble-explosion. And one can see that an absolute and infinite motion has to be one that lasts forever, i.e. is eternal. This consequence can be made intelligible when we take account of the fact that the rabble loses habit. If habit always means a habit of activity, to lose the habit means to not be active anymore, to not move. But if habit contains by its becoming-positive the moment of finitude of (the active, moving) life, one can understand which form of absoluteness enters the picture here. For habit introduces temporality into life; man dies out of habit. From this it follows that the rabble does not die. It does not die since it should by rights already be dead and dissolved; after the negation that is poverty it should have been negated and sublated.

The rabble emerges in a peculiar interstice between life and death; of a life after death, or better: of a life of the dead.[55] In this sense it not only names an *organ without a body*, an *un-organ*, but also the place of 'something' *un-dead*. For it can not fall under the positive judgment that the rabble is dead, because then it would putrefy due to the inadequacy of concept and reality. It is already a result of the putrefaction of poverty. But nor can one judge negatively and claim that it is not dead, since this would mean that one could rewrite this judgment into a positive one: it is alive. Therefore only one possibility remains and that is that it falls under a—Kantian—infinite judgment: that it lives as dead, the it is *un-dead*. One can see why the temporality of the peculiar interstice is eternity. *Eternity is the time of the rabble*. For once emerged there is no possibility that it could return from his dissolution back into existence, into time. Its bodiless, *un-organic*, *un-dead*, inert, idle presence is eternal. The rabble is *un-dead* in the accentuation of his temporal dimension; it is an *un-organ* in the accentuation of the inadequacy of the relation between reality and concept; it is a *Ver-Wesen* in the accentuation of the absolute dissolving of all determinations. In the following I consider this definition to be inherent to the notion of the *organ without body*. The rabble as an *organ without body* is *un-dead*; its time is eternity; it is an *un-organ* because it is detached from its organic relations and has in itself no body; finally, the reason for its twofold bodilessness is that it is the result of a process that has made all of its determinations rot.

Now it is clear: what produces it and lets it latently appear everywhere— the reason for its temporality—is—as soon as there is poverty—its attitude. The rabble constitutes itself only when poverty and the process of putrefaction are supplemented by its peculiar attitude. For the origin of the rabble cannot be explained only with reference to the relative economical movement. It produces itself—from poverty, is itself (and at the same time not without poverty) the reason for its absolute motion. But does this self-making imply a moment of freedom? Does this not imply an act of determination which breaks with the aforementioned indeterminacy? These questions point in the direction already indicated by Hegel's notion of habit: if habit mediates objectivity and subjectivity in the production of a second nature, the loss of habit means, objectively, putrefaction. But what does it mean subjectively? This is a question of will and attitude. Also, a neuralgic point is stressed here. For it first has to be investigated more precisely how the rabble-attitude is constituted if the rabble only emerges after the loss of all determinations of existence, and, secondly, the discussion of the concept of attitude seems to mark the place for an objection to the investigations thus far. This objection in its most fundamental form runs as follows: the rabble is a problem of civil society but not of the Hegelian state. This would mean that Hegel's sentence "a beginning of inequality in civil society" is multiplied "infinitely" (HPRV, 221) and it concerns civil society but never the state. Or one could say: the rabble is not Hegel's problem. Hegel could then say that when poverty is produced and the rabble emerges, 'so much the worse for the facts.'

I will show in the following that this objection cannot be sustained. I will demonstrate that the problem of the failed sublation which poses itself in the transition from poverty to the rabble and with the peculiar presence of a positivity of negativity 'after' sublation, is repeated in the transition from civil society to its institutions and the state. The state is not confronted with the rabble-problem in the form of a problem of inequality within civil society, but in the 'form' of a fundamental problem of inconsistency which follows the *logic of double latency*. To prove this it is necessary to explicate the concept of attitude. I will show that not only do the institutions which are understood as the objective substantiality of the state produce ethicality as something immanent within civil society, but also, the dialectical genesis of attitude—of the subjective substantiality of the state—fails to convert the rabble-problem into a statist sublation. Only by doing so will we be able to grasp why it is that the "the most horrible rabble that even fantasy cannot imagine" (Ibid., 223)—also Hegel's fantasy—presents a problem which remains unsolvable in Hegel's philosophy.

Chapter 9

Without Attitude? Rabble and State

Great revolutions which strike the eye at a glance must have been preceded by a still and secret revolution in the spirit of the age, a revolution not visible to every eye, especially imperceptible to contemporaries, and as hard to discern as to describe in words.

(G. W. F. Hegel)[1]

One has to investigate the rabble-attitude in order to understand how the rabble is able to make itself. If everything is dissolved, how can the rabble make itself? Hegel's first answer is that its auto-genesis is largely dependent on the attitude that supplement poverty. Therefore a reconstruction of Hegel's notion of attitude is essential. So, how does Hegel define the notion of attitude? A fundamental definition of the disposition of mind which appears in the ethicality of the state reads:

> The political *disposition*, patriotism pure and simple, is certainty based on *truth*—mere subjective certainty is not the outcome of truth but is only opinion—and volition which has become *habitual*. As such, it is simply a product of the institutions subsisting in the state, since rationality is *actually* present in the state . . . This disposition is, in general, *trust* (which may pass over into a greater or lesser degree of educated insight), or the consciousness that my interest, both substantial and particular, is contained and preserved in another's (i.e. in the state's) interest and end, i.e. in the other's relation to me as an individual. In this way, this very other is immediately not an other in my eyes, and in being conscious of this fact, I am free. (HOPR, 240)[2]

Attitude is defined as 1. certainty based on truth; 2. volition which has become habitual as result of statist institutions; 3. trust which consists in the belief that my interest in the realization and self-determination of my freedom comes into its own as it defines the state. This in turn means that 4. the state does not appear to me as other but I recognize myself as free within it and that only in this way does my freedom become fully real, i.e. objective. In this complex linkage of different moment Hegel marks a fundamental point: attitude is not merely a form of subjective opinion or a variant of subjective conviction. For attitude understood as certainty based on truth and habitualized volition is first and foremost a result of statist institutions and thus always already more than subjective and arbitrary *doxa*. This is decisive because attitude cannot be understood merely subjectively, moralistically but at the same time it concerns in a fundamental way the (inner core of the) subject—as subject within the state. Therefore here it is necessary to reconstruct how Hegel thinks the relationship of the subject to the state as essentially a place *within* the subject, in his attitude.

The attitude is thus to be consistently distinguished from opinion. If it were to be a mere subjective opinion about what and how one's own good should be conceived—independently of the state and its institutions—Hegel would here still be at the stage of morality, i.e. the free will for itself which knows that its freedom only relates to itself. If abstract right, the first being-there of the free will, did not know subjects, but only persons, i.e. merely potential agents without interests, the stage of morality concerns and treats first the motives, needs and interests of the subjects. Morality for Hegel deals with the relationship which the subject has to his actions. For it describes a "determinacy of the will, in so far as it is interior to the will in general, and thus includes the purpose and intention, as well as moral evil" (HPM, 224). The subject becomes conscious of the infinity of his free will—i.e. that this will is already free because it can abstract from all determinations and determine itself—and consequently it experiences the demand to recognize nothing in its will which is not justified by it. This is "the obstinacy which does honour to humanity" (HOPR, 16), as Hegel writes. In this way the will relates to itself in an internal form and in the perspective of intention and purpose to its own actions. This means initially that morality is the stage of the free will for itself, which relates itself consciously to itself and its actions. But this knowledge is not yet mediated with reality. Morality signifies that the "right of the subjective will is that whatever it is to recognize as valid shall be seen by it as *good*, and that an action, as its aim entering into external objectivity, shall be imputed to it . . . in accordance with its *knowledge* of the value which the action has in this objectivity" (Ibid., 127).

The free will for itself knows itself as free and demands the right to know and recognize itself in all his actions as free will. But political attitude is situated on a logically higher stage. In it subjective knowledge (certainty) and truth, reality and freedom have to enter into mediation. Ethicality, which logically lies before while at the same time succeeding morality in the order of development in the *Philosophy of Right*, sublates the mere for-itself of the will and mediates it with the objectivity of the necessarily existing ethical community. This is why Hegel can claim that political disposition, patriotism, is a result of existing state institutions and at the same time can be understood as subjective certainty based on truth. Therefore he can assert a sharp distinction between opinion and true political attitude: "If . . . this disposition is looked upon as that which may begin of itself and arise from subjective ideas and thoughts, it is being confused with opinion, because so regarded it is deprived of its true ground, objective reality" (Ibid., 241). If the free will for itself is supposed to be the sole ground of reality it misunderstands that it could never realize itself without an already existing objective reality—and its laws. Here one finds a clear definition of *doxa* in the Hegelian sense. It consists in the misconception of a subject who thinks himself able to begin by himself alone—and this is already quite telling for Hegel's characterization of the rabble as self-making. Opinion in this sense also stands for a denial of reality and implies a denial of the reality of the ethical institutions in which any subject is always already integrated. Therefore morality only presents formal conscience, formal certainty and not true certainty.[3] For it marks a reflection on the infinity of the freedom of the will which is at the same time lacking objectivity. Ethicality now concerns the free will in and for itself, i.e. the free will of the subject in a mediating relationship to the objectivity of laws and institutions. The attitude names the structural place where "*effective* ethicality" appears, for in it it becomes clear "that any individual knows of the identity between his deepest interest and that of the whole."[4] Attitude concerns the subject in a way that names the relation of subjective will and knowledge to the state.

In the attitude the mediation of the individual subject with the whole of the state and its institutions presents itself as the truth *in* the subject and as the truth *of* the subject. For "the State really rests on thought, and its existence depends on the attitudes of men, for it is a spiritual and not a physical kingdom" (HLHP1, 439, trans. mod.). It is important to remark that the word 'spiritual' here should be understood "in terms of obtained capacities and practices of which one can say that natural organisms have created and authorized them."[5] as a habit which has been adapted to the existing circumstances but at the same time as subjective knowledge, true certainty, i.e. as knowledge of oneself and of one's own habit. In this knowledge the subject is conscious of the active-repeating production and of the habit which is produced by this activity. Or as Nancy expressed this relationship—in a different context: "I know the truth outside myself [in ethicality], and I know that I am the truth outside myself [the habit of my activity which it produces]. Me, the truth, I know that I cannot confuse myself with any 'self'."[6]

Neither enables this relationship that I think I could commence all be myself—the truth of myself persists in itself—nor that I have been the victim of a simple interiorization in the particular realization of my freedom—my particularity as subordinated to the state. I know that I by acting externalize my action, posit it under the laws of the objective world and that my action therefore does not only count for me but also for others. This mediation is generated by attitude. Neither is one dealing here with a subject that commences all by itself nor with one that takes to the existing objective circumstances.[7] Formal conscience in contrast persists structurally in the position that from the perspective of the subject any action can be either good or bad—as the ironist has it—and is pleased by the (subjective) arbitrariness of this determination. But true conscience consists in the insight of reasons,[8] in a subjective knowledge that is directed toward the necessity inherent in the existing without giving up "the right of the subject to find his *satisfaction* in the action" (HOPR, 120). Only an interest, a need that seems worth realizing can be an effective reason for the subjective realization of freedom. Therefore the purely formal and abstract aspect has to be overcome. The ethical attitude, i.e. the true certainty is thus grounded in and on morality but overcomes it necessarily. It present the "innermost moment or aspects . . . of self-consciousness" (HPR 2, 442) and consists at the same time "in sticking steadfastly to what is right, and abstaining from all attempts to move or shake it, or derive it" (HPS, 262). Political attitude, patriotism, marks the point in which in the inner core of the subject the habit of volition appears, a habit that is directed toward the maintenance and stability of the existing circumstances in which the subject can only understand itself as free.

The arising of such a habit in the subject is not independent of the subject's educational process—from his upbringing within the family to the voluntary choice of a profession in civil society which leads to the estate, right up to the state—since the constant regeneration and perpetuated production of the statist community is not thinkable without the multiplicity of singular individuals. The attitude as a subjective, ethical phenomenon (of free will) consists in the certainty based on truth and in the habitualized volition which guarantees at one and the same time the freedom of the individual and the basis of the autonomy of the universal. The attitude is not a mere emotion but nevertheless contains certain dimensions of it.[9] Bringing to mind once again the structure of ethicality in the *Philosophy of Right*—family, civil society, state—it becomes clear that attitude as certainty and habit must also be developed according to these stages. in the following pages I shall reconstruct the genesis of attitude in terms of these stages in order to conceive of its constitution in a more precise way. I will thereby proceed from the family, via civil society, to the state. Since each of these stages is interdependent, it will be impossible to avoid certain anticipations and certain recourses.

Already in the family, ethical duties may be found which do not find their ground in a contract or promise or purely external rules. They are rather bound to the self-understanding of each individual as a "member" of this "*immediate substantiality*" (HOPR, 162), i.e. for example to the position of the father, mother or child. Each member of the family is therefore no longer purely abstract for itself as a person, i.e. as a bearer of rights, but rather stands in a necessarily objective (and always already reciprocal) relation to others. But the attitude is in the family in a certain sense still too natural because the "feeling of its own unity" (Ibid.), that is family, does know objective requirements which appear to its members as duties. But the realizations of freedom,[10] rights and duties which result from it appear only in the form of an emotion, love between its members. The family is in this sense a form of immediately institutionalized ethical community—therefore Hegel reads it along with the introduction of private property as the primordial founding instance of all states. "This is why we may see the family as the state in embryonic form."[11] In it the "unity between human beings . . . is felt—i.e. lived in the subjectivity as this, habit . . ." (HGPR, 328). The unity with others becomes habitual in the subject, i.e. second nature, so that he cannot think of himself without others, in other words, without sociality. In this way Hegel also defines the attitude of love: "The first moment in love is that I do not wish to be a self-subsistent and independent person and that, if I were, then I would feel defective and incomplete. The second moment is that I find myself in another person, that I count for something in the other, while the other in turn comes to count for something in me" (HOPR, 162).

I do not count for myself any longer but I count in another. Therefore I count in a more objective way—than I could being alone—and I thereby have the habit to only experience myself as complete when I am not *just* myself. In this sense one can recall Adorno's remark: "What is merely identical with itself is without happiness."[12] The insight is already Hegel's. The happiness of love in the family is not to be merely identical with itself but rather to stand in a constitutive relation with others, a relation which has become second nature. However one needs to leave this embryonic state of ethicality and the immediacy of the loving sentiment, which is still bound to the arbitrariness of the feeling subject, must become objective and rational. The emotion is too mutable to found a stable ethical community in it which would encompass more than just the members of the family. Hegel makes this point clear when he writes that one cannot claim a right against sentiment, for this would be equal to a right to have rights and he concludes that the sentiment offers insufficient ground for ethicality.[13] He attempts to demonstrate that the feeling of love is lacking due to "the initial contingency of its existence" (HOPR, 175)—a problem which informs his entire discussion of divorce[14]—rationality, necessity and stability. We may say of love what Hegel says about premodern ethicality: "The ancients did not know anything about conscience . . ." (HGPR, 302), in the same way, the family does not know anything about conscience and ethicality and yet it already senses it. It is a mere premonition of true ethicality: emotional ethicality. The lack proper to emotion indicates why the family dissolves and its children have to become members of civil society. Only at this stage can free self-determination—in the free choice of a profession, which is anchored in the principle of subjectivity (morality)—be found.

One can note that attitude marks in the statist constitution precisely the moment which takes the specificity of modernity into account. In it, the "principle of subjectivity" is the principle of the state, i.e. the individual, and it culminates "in the self-sufficient extreme" (HOPR, 235) realization of freedom acquiring its right.[15] Modernity, for Hegel, is the modernity of the subject which autonomously posits aims for its actions. This indicates why attitude is decisive. The attitude assures the objectivity of the statist principle: the free subject. For the true ethical attitude reflects—in its form as well as in its content—the truth of the constitutive principle of every modern state: the self-determining free will as realized. Therefore Hegel had to show that attitude is not a product of institutions and right alone because "the laws of the state therefore cannot possibly seek to reach as far as a person's disposition . . ." (HOPR, 98). It is impossible to induce in a purely external way a conviction in the subject—not even with violence. Even the family, due to its naturality, is external to the subject since the individual feels himself to be within it, but does not know himself to be there. Only when every moment of mere subjective conviction is suspended can it be said that "ethical life is a subjective disposition, but one imbued with what is right in itself" (Ibid., 152). Only when the ethical as such becomes the second nature of any individual does anyone realize his freedom and at the same time produce the state in his realizations. Only in this way can the state, despite the (potential) infinity of individual interests realizing themselves within it, remain a stable reality.

With this it is clear that the state has to be distinguished from civil society. In it there exists a formal universality of interests and needs via the mediation of egoistic activities. But it is clear that in it there may be the habit of this formally universal activity but its rationality is only unconsciously present in the individuals, as the automatism of a blind repetitive satisfaction of egoist interests. The universal mediating context remains unknown. The formal universality is not knowledge, it is not the certainty of the individual. For civil society knows the universal only as an *unconscious universal* of habit. But the ethical attitude needs both moments—habit and certainty—which means that state and civil society—already with regard to the subject—need to be distinguished. Only in this way it is thinkable that the principle of the modern state—self-determining subjectivity—and its reality—the objectively realized freedom of the subject—coincide. Then attitude appears in the subject as knowledge, as a reflection of being used to the universal. Rosenzweig rightly remarks that Hegel for this reason rejects any use of the notion of patriotism which only recognizes actions which are exceptions to the ordinary ethical life—as subjective sacrifices for the social totality (RHS, 133). The habit of activity in ethical institutions cannot mean that the subject is introjected something to form a sacrificial consciousness. For "The spheres of right and morality cannot exist independently [*für sich*]; they must have the ethical as their support and foundation . . . Right exists only as a branch of a whole or like the plant which twines itself round a tree that is firmly rooted in and for itself" (HOPR, 153).

Without the ethical as existing mediator which mediates right with subjectivity and morality with objectivity, neither objective right nor subjective morality is stable. Organic structuring and stability can be gained for a community only

in the state. That the ethical is the foundation—i.e. that it lies logically prior
to the stages of abstract right and morality—once again clarifies the fact that
the *Philosophy of Right* should not be read exclusively as a phenomenological
story of the realization of the free will.[16] The ethical is logically presupposed as
an element in which morality and right assume their proper place. It presents
the foundation because, due to their inherent abstractness, neither right nor
morality are stable or effective: morality is abstract and unstable as a result of
the pure subjectivity, i.e. arbitrariness, of its determinations and abstract right,
as a result of its inflexible objectivity and due to the inflexibility of its initial
positing, does not know subjective free self-determination. The ethical disposition is the mediation of both. Therefore patriotism is, as ethical attitude and
as principle of the state, the actually constitutive moment of equality in the
state—and not merely legal or moral equality. As Rosenzweig penetratingly
remarks: "This equality of attitude is now the unique equality which Hegel
recognizes for the state." The equality of citizens—which here refers to the
'citoyen'—means an "equality of attitude" (RHS, 133–4), as an equality of
self-feeling, as the being-one-in-difference of all individuals in the state. For
Hegel, true equality only exists in the state and only as ethical. Therefore, attitude is decisive as *the* moment of equality as it describes the equality of subjects
internally and through their actions. "Hereby a universality is founded which
makes human life and living together possible."[17] Every subject knows itself—
out of habit—in the production of itself and the state as realizing its freedom.
It knows and wills itself as subject in the state and therewith wills the state as it
wills itself—it wills itself as statist. In attitude, as habitualized volition and true
certainty, the will directs itself onto itself as free and in a rational-universal
way *by* mediating itself with the state. This is why one can claim that the true
ethical attitude is the place where the free will wills itself in its freedom. A will
habitualized to the active determination knows itself in it as realized and is a
will which reflects itself as such and which is certain of itself in this habit: a free
will which wills itself as free will.[18]

But how to mediate something picked out (subjectively) arbitrarily and a
necessarily stable ethical content? This mediation cannot introduce a hierar-
chy either of the subject or of the object. To clarify this, Hegel marks that the
family also appears as a person because it owns property and stands as a rival
over against other people in civil society. Also this natural ethicality appears
as *one* constituted interest among others and is in comparison with others only
one personal interest of many. But to realize the free will of the individual in
the certainty of its freedom and in a habitualized volition one has to surpass
this formal universality. For "true conscience is the disposition to will what is
good *in and for itself*. It therefore has fixed principles and these are for it determinations and duties that are objective for themselves" (HOPR, 132). The
attitude as habitualized volition therefore also implies the habit of duty: a volition that is directed toward the stability of that which is in a way that I myself

have produced it in the realization of my freedom and which enables me constantly to to do so. Duty is a way of perpetuating freedom. Duty means that the individual is no longer in an immediate unity with that which he should do, as he was in the family, but in a relation of reflection, of reflective distance. The political attitude as certainty thus relates to the habitualized volition and presents a sort of *habit of habit*—and this reflexive habit is what Hegel calls the ethical attitude. One gets used to others in the family, and then in civil society one becomes accustomed to providing for one's subsistence by laboring and one thereby enters into an active mediating context with others which do the same. Thereby this activity generalizes itself—still unconsciously—by seeing that my satisfaction is assured only by the secured dutiful production of the satisfaction of all others. By not only perceiving the acquired habit as my unconscious second nature but also by knowing it as my duty—my duty is therefore nothing external to me but belongs to my nature—a habit of habit forms in which I know myself as free. No forming of attitude without ethicalization, no ethicalization without the formation of attitude.

Attitude thus signifies the point in which the will has both its reality in the ethical and in the self-consciousness of the individual. This is why Hegel can claim that "ethical life is a subjective disposition" and "the truth of the concept of freedom . . ." (Ibid., 152) the self-feeling and self-understanding of any subject conceives of itself as a subject only in the state and considers this necessary to his own nature. This nature appears for any individual as the realization of his own freedom and as the knowledge of this realization it is the knowledge of the reality of freedom and of the rationality of one's own habits.

The attitude is the "subjective substantiality" (Ibid., 240) of the state or as Marx rightly recalls: "political sentiment is the subjective, and the political constitution is the objective substance of the state" (MCH, 7). For the individual "knowing the universal as his moving end realized the universal. And as a result, it has its being there in him because without him it would be a mere abstractum" (HVORL 3, 496). *The state is nothing without the subjects; the subjects are nothing without the state.* The state is the only true form of life of the ethical and thus the actual rational form of human life because it is the "rational in and for itself . . ." (HOPR, 228). This objective rationality is reflected into the attitude. This is why the essential political content of the state consists in the political constitution and the political attitude. In the patriotic attitude one can see, due to the constitutive aspect of habit, the stability of an ethical form of life which in its structure, rationality and spirituality differs from the life form of animals: "Like the elephant has a different life than the wolf, he, the ethical man has this life" (HPRV, 152). Nevertheless one has to note at the same time that attitude is not a mere habitus. For "the animal does not come into conflict with what it should do, man has to know what he should do and to educate himself" (HVORL 3, 495). The life of ethical man is necessarily a life in a state in which he posits the state as form and content of the realization of his freedom and knows of this determination.

The state is the rational nature of free man and attitude is the rational habit and true certainty of this rationality. Therefore political attitude delineates the structural moment in which the fulfillment of duties appears as completely mediated with the performance and realization of his freedom. This is why Hegel can claim that "virtue [*Tugend*] is the ethical order . . . solely as the individual's simple conformity with the duties of the circumstances to which he belongs, it is rectitude . . ." (HOPR, 157) this virtue as attitude is the double of habit and certainty marks an important implication. If conformity is the decisive feature of subjective virtue in ethicality, this means that there is a privileged place for the formation of habit in the form of the virtue of rectitude. For rectitude means "that an individual fills its place, this is the main thing, that it honors its place, although the individual is only by external circumstances, by pure external necessity posited there. It has to sublate this form, has to stand there with freedom because I should stand, I will to stand there" (HVORL 4, 524). In civil society the place in which the individual wants to stand as it is supposed to stand is, as Hegel has demonstrated, the estate and the corporation. One has to recall here that the individual voluntarily—but due to the external need of providing for his own subsistence autonomously—chooses an estate. In it the individual gets used to itself as a realized free will and to the duties that accompany it.[19] Its honor is to will to stand as it is supposed to stand. In the estate, the individual according to its own skills that are also forms of habit provides for his own well-being in mediation with the others from the same estate. In the estate, collective standing becomes habitualized. Thereby, the mediating movement causes one to realize not only the rights of one's own interest but also the duty to constantly produce alongside this the satisfaction of the needs of the others. This is why the ethical attitude is also a virtue as a habitualized consciousness of duty. As Hegel formulates this in his *Encyclopedia*: "The moral duty in general is, in me as free subject, at the same time a right of my subjective will, of my disposition . . . In ethical life these two sides have their absolute unity, though here too duty and right return to one another and join together, as is the way of necessity, through *mediation*" (HPM, 218).

'Virtue' initially means to be used to an activity which is subordinated to the exigency of conformity with the circumstances and becomes second nature. Civil society thereby provides a formula in which the individual follows his own interests and therein at the same time maintains the whole. This leads to the consequence that patriotism as political attitude is essentially reliant on honor and rectitude. For both describe the conformity of actions with the political regulations and institutions—with what Hegel calls the political constitution[20]—of the state. Attitude as the subjective constitution of the state is thereby already conditioned by the institutions. The estate in precisely this sense is a "mediating organ" since it stands "between the government in general . . . and the people broken up into political spheres . . ." (HOPR, 289). It mediates object and subject as well as subject and object. The integration into and the participation in one estate becomes—in the world of the appearance of the ethical—the necessary condition of the ethical connections. Now it also becomes clear why the content of political attitude appears as trust. This trust names the "fundamental sense of order which everyone possesses" which "holds the state together . . ." (Ibid., 241). It constitutes a fundamental sense that 1. everyone possesses and 2. is a sense of order. Trust names thus a subjective belief in the rationality of objective statist circumstances which has become habitualized. This is why "the disposition is, in general, *trust* . . . or my conscious interest, both substantial and particular is contained and preserved in another's . . ." (Ibid., 240).[21]

Through trust there is a feeling of integration and identity with the ethical substance in all individuals: the substance is no longer alien, external to the subject but he is convinced that he can only be free in it. The interest—initially self-seeking then generalized via the estates—of a subject has become the interest of the substance itself.[22] But one has to emphasize here that civil society does not realize this structure completely. Although the corporation—and in a certain sense any estate—can derive a collective interest—in the sense of an association of many interests—out of the egoistic isolated interest, the end of the corporation always remains a "restricted and finite" (HOPR, 227) one, because at the same time the gathering of individual interests is constantly referred back to what it consists of. *Associated* individual interests remain associated *individual interests*. David James rightly remarks that the "corporation represents an enlightened form of self-interest."[23] At the same time, one has to note that

the spirit of the corporation . . . is now inwardly converted into the spirit of the state, since it finds in the state the means of maintaining its particular ends. This is the secret of the patriotism of the citizens in the sense that they know the state as their substance, because it is the state that maintains their particular spheres of interest together with the justification, authority, and welfare of these. The spirit of the corporation immediately entails the rooting of the particular in the universal, and for this reason it is in this corporate spirit that the depth and strength of disposition which the state possesses resides. (HOPR, 279)

The corporation roots the particular in the universal and vice versa. For in it a reversal takes place: the particular interest and end of the individual becomes *immediately* identical with the maintaining and providing for the universal. Therefore Hegel attempts to demonstrate that the corporation is not situated at the stage of the estates. It is rather the case that in it a form of universality transgressing the estate, a self-knowing universality is anticipated which produces—with the help of the other institutions of governance, public judicature—an attitude which contains not merely honor and rectitude but rather true certainty and complete habitualized volition. Thus the bourgeois does not become a *citoyen* by simply egoistically following his interests. Otherwise Hegel would be a spokesperson—albeit advanced—of a liberal or instrumental conception of reason. Also the common pursuit of the individual interest is a way—even if reflected—of pursuing the individual interests and the dialectical movement which should lead to the intertwinement of individual freedom. The stability of the laws cannot merge to be a mere addition of mere egoistic interests.

This is precisely why Hegel does not rely on an automatism of the *invisible hand* for the deduction of ethicality and its attitude. This would not be sufficient to speak of the genesis of the political attitude but would only generate a thinking of formally mediated universality. Here Hegel goes farther than Adam Smith.[24] One can say that Smith's thought devotes itself exclusively to considering individual interests and is unable to attain the level of universality. It precisely cannot be interest which drives out ethicality and its attitude. The corporation names the place in which the particular interest is and becomes more than itself. Only if the individual knows the assurance of himself to be identical with the maintaining of the universal and if he knows that the universal maintains him, only then can one speak of a rooting of the particular in the universal. The corporation presents hence a universal reflected in itself: 1. in relation to each member and its free will; 2. in relation to other corporations; 3. in relation to the institutions of the state. Through the common property it has the objectivity which assures the persistence of the corporation and the provision concerning its members. It is neither simply the emotion of the individual—neither mere habit—nor just the objective validity of the right—the mere knowledge of its validity—which leads to the political attitude. Therefore the corporation is immediately the rooting of the particular in the universal, the latter being both self-feeling and a knowledge of the stability of the institution. The attitude as habitualized volition and true certainty no longer corresponds to the register of the emotion in its initial sense. But how to conceive of an emotion which is not subordinated to arbitrariness?

Attitude is not logically inferior to emotion. Rather it—since the state is also logically prior to the stages of right and morality—names a relationship which is even *more immediate*. Attitude is "closer to identity than even the relation to faith or trust" (HOPR, 155). It is therefore fundamentally different from the "religious peasant's belief in nature or god."[25] Political attitude signifies rather a *habit of oneself as another*—in the self-certain form which has eradicated the arbitrariness of mere emotion and subjective opinion. Political attitude names an emotion—a self-feeling—that is no longer an emotion—which is to say, arbitrary. It is an emotion which is more than just an emotion, namely: truth and certainty. Attitude is a *true emotion*, not an authentic emotion, rather as a sort of objective emotion in the subject: *an emotion of truth and at the same time a truth of emotion,* an emotion which never deceives and has its foothold in ehticality by being, as fundamental feeling of order. Or as Hegel writes concerning the linkage of truth and emotion: "The patriotic disposition acquires its specifically determined *content* from the various aspects of the organism of the state . . . Hence these different aspects are the *various powers* of the state with their functions and spheres of action, by means of which the universal continually engenders itself, and engenders itself in a necessary way . . . This organism is the *political constitution*". (HOPR, 242). The content of the attitude is organically structured[26] because it is itself a part of the organic structuring of the state. Attitude, developing from family, civil society and finally corporation, and the state, takes its content from the stages of this educational process. This means that on the one hand it reflects the moments of its formative process in its content—it contains all these dimensions—and on the other hand it thereby takes up the persistence of the whole of ethical community—it contains therefore the rationality and reality of the state. Attitude is in this sense trans-individual and transcends even civil society.[27] It fulfills the task of collectivizing the individual by reflecting—knowingly and reproductively—in its content the organic structuring of the ethical institutions. The political attitude is always subjective and collective.

Let me summarize the investigations of habit and attitude: habit produces a permanence of the subjective will by producing a second nature; it creates a persistence of the will which is directed toward the ethical whole and its perpetuated production: this is the first part of political attitude; certainty passes through a parallel process: initially it appears in the unstable form of emotion, by only knowing myself as complete when mediated with the other; it passes over into the honor of the estates and rectitude in which I know the obtainment of my own interests as the obtainment of my own subsistence. I alter it in the corporation to become certain that only the persistence of the existing institutions and the state can maintain the particularity of the interests—as the universal entitlement of all particular interests; certainty thus develops from emotion by way of the subject's moral self-determination of its own good to truth. Thereby one can only think of the true ethical attitude as a result of the organic integration and binding in and to the ethical community. It is in this way alone that "the person ceases in this disposition to be an accident of substance" and "without reflective choice the person fulfills his duty as his own and as something that is and in this necessity he has himself and his actual freedom" (HPM, 228). What Hegel here describes as a reversal from accident into substance marks exactly the point which is produced by habit and certainty. The individual remains an accident of substance as long as it does not reproduce it habitually and know itself in it as actually free. This transition from substance to subject—one can claim that it is the subject as substance[28]—delineates the determination of the attitude's content as organic, the state has become a *collective subject*. Thereby the emphasis lies as much on the collective, which is the habitualized reproduction of the whole and its persistence, as on the subject, which knows itself as realized in the whole and so produces itself and the whole by its activity. The persistence of the collective-subject is the persistence of its production which became habit and the certainty of the subject. This is the actual climax of Hegel's notion of attitude.

One has to clearly articulate its radicality: the ethical attitude contains a knowledge of the unconscious which is always necessarily present—the formal universality which operates automatically—of the ethical whole itself. If the self-feeling produced by habit describes an automatic and unconscious repetition, then the concept of attitude marks that the individual has something in the form of knowledge which it unconsciously thinks of as belonging to itself. Political attitude means that I know what I perform unconsciously as my truth and only this knowledge posits me in a true relationship with the ethical community. For this knowledge of the unconscious performance conserves the unconscious and is still a knowledge of it. But what can 'unconscious' mean here? If in every individual, not only do the automatisms of habit remain unconscious, but also the totality of all habits in the state—i.e. of all individuals—then this knowledge of the habit(s) is a knowledge of the unconscious in different regards. Attitude is a knowledge and certainty of others (and oneself) as an other with an unconscious.

This means that 1. I am certain that I am always already dependent on the other, on intersubjective relations, which determine me (the other *in me* which appears as my habit—in my own unconscious automatisms—and the other external to me as the others with whom I always stand in relation and against whom I have an "answerability to my-neighbour-with-an-unconscious"[29] and also as the Other that always already determines me—for example my family, a constitutive "I was not there"[30])—this is certainty of myself as / in an other; 2. this certainty consist in the trust that the other is not only something external which confronts me and against my will determines me, but as the other within me it is also dependent upon this structure that marks me (others constitute themselves through me as I constitute myself through them, by becoming other); 3. from this I gain the certainty based on truth that the other is an other with (the same) unconscious so that he also refers in his realizations of his free acts of will to something that transcends him, just as I do. In this way, the mutual relationship itself always already and necessarily transcends the pure subjective conviction of this relation (morality) and its pure objective stability and givenness (right). *Where once there was id, thanks to the attitude, now there is ego, but without abolishing the id, rather sublating it into a knowledge about the id.* This is the complex relationship which is effective in the ethical attitude and it is therefore important to remember that: "The unconscious [. . .] forms

the locus of psychic activity whereby a human being becomes a 'subject' by
metabolizing its existential dependency on institutions that are in turn sustained by acts of foundation, preservation and augmentation. And by 'institution' I mean all sites that endow us with social recognition and intelligibility,
that produce and regulate symbolic identities."[31]

Christophe Menke has in his reconstruction of the connection of multiplicity and beauty in Hegel's conception of the drama convincingly distinguished
two form of multiplicities which surely are only valid for the premodern understanding of ethicality but can nevertheless be helpful for the investigation:

> The common ethical substance consists of a *multiplicity of values*; this is why
> the ethical-beautiful integration of the individual subjects into community
> proceeds in a way that is oriented by the different values. Likewise, the other
> moment of ethicality, that of individual subjectivity consists of a *multiplic-
> ity of individuals*; this is why the ethical-beautiful integration of community
> with its members proceeds through different individuals. Due to this double
> multiplicity the 'unseparated' association with community can happen from
> both directions within irreducibly multiple and different ways.[32]

Menke's comment clarifies that any of the many different individuals is able
to orient itself toward different values and that any of the values may be
assigned to a multiplicity of different individuals. In this way there is an
internal multiplication of the description of the relations. What Hegel still
wants to grasp in the ethical attitude—specifically in its modern form—is
the knowledge—a knowledge of the unconscious—and the habit of one's
own orientation at values and at one's own particularity and also the knowledge and habit of the multiplicity of values and individuals. The following
investigation will be guided by the hypothesis that the rabble is a (modern)
multiplicity which can be put neither on the side of the values nor on the
side of the individuals—nor can it be the mutual multiplication of both.
This is to say that Hegel's definition of modernity as a "world which . . . does
not exclude multiplicity and difference but withstands it"[33] can be reconstructed, but linked the same time it reveals that linked to the rabble is a
problem which lies beyond the impossibility of totalizing this multiplicity and difference and withstanding the impossibility of its unifying reconciliation. Not only is modernity for Hegel distinguished by its attempt to
withstand this conflict which is a conflict of multiplicity and unity; Hegel's
modernity is also marked by the fact that in the place where it attempts to
confront the question "which agitates and torments modern society especially" (HOPR, 221)—the question of poverty—it is confronted with a different problem: the problem of a negativity without relation, an "unemployed
negativity"[34] and this means with a *new concept of indeterminacy* (an indeterminacy in and for itself).

Starting from this reconstruction of the decisive elements of attitude one can now return to the question of the rabble-attitude. Hegel gives his most important characterization of this attitude in the following remark:

> The lowest subsistence level, that of a rabble of paupers, makes itself . . . Poverty in itself does not turn people into a rabble; a rabble is created only when there is joined to poverty a disposition of mind, an inner indignation against the rich, against society, against the government, etc. . . . In this way there is born in the rabble the evil of lacking sufficient honour to secure subsistence by its own labour and yet at the same time of claiming the right to receive subsistence [a right without right]. (HOPR, 221, trans. mod.)

The rabble makes itself. This judgment seems to indicate that the rabble for Hegel falls under what has been shown to be the definition of *doxa*. The rabble opposes the truth of ethical community and its reality with a mere opinion. The rabble-attitude which has as its content only indignation against all possible instances and institutions—the 'etc.' in the passage quoted above—seems to describe a merely moral attitude which opposes itself to all concrete institutions and denies them their justification. Indignation would then be the content of the rabble-attitude. But is Hegel's judgment really valid for the rabble? As Marx rightly remarked, in a passage where he implicitly refers to the discussion of poverty and the rabble in Hegel, this indignation is one "to which it is necessarily driven by the contradiction between its human *nature* and its condition of life, which is the outright, resolute and comprehensive negation of that nature."[35] Indignation is an expression of a contradiction.[36] I have shown that this contradiction enters because in poverty there is an inadequate relation between concept (free will) and reality (poverty). This contradiction is already the result of another contradiction, which civil society itself produces, namely that anyone should subsist by means of their own labor in it but which makes it impossible for anyone to be able to subsist by himself. This double contradiction[37] leads to the dissolving of all determinations of existence which Hegel described as putrefaction. Hegel's critique of the rabble-position seems clear: it is a mere particularity that arbitrarily posits a self-determined end—as the content of the merely moral attitude—against the universal. Here one can start to answer what the in and for itself of poverty, what the rabble as not only the completely putrefied *organ without body* is objectively, but what it is subjectively.

If Hegel claims that the concrete content of the ethical attitude is composed of the organic structuring of the state, then one can note that the content of the rabble-attitude—because it is an *organ without body*—cannot accord with this organic structuring. The detachment of the organ from the body means for the content of the rabble-attitude that it is not organic, not a social one. For if it de-legitimizes any institution of the state, it not only—following his own entitlement—dissolves their persistence but at the same time their rationality and therewith the organic structure of the constitution of the ethical community itself. The delineation of the rabble-attitude as indignation means that its content is a purely negative one. It is a content which decomposes everything and dissolves it as something which should not be. Starting from this one cannot generate customs or a social community. Indignation in this sense would be a further inadequacy of concept and reality and therefore it is for Hegel a position of untruth. Such a particularity is therefore evil: the mere for itself is "evil in the case of the will . . ." (HOPR, 77). The rabble becomes evil because it is only for itself, does not know of the necessity to generalize oneself and gets into contradictions. Therewith the rabble negates the ethical as such and also sociality as such: due to its attitude it is always a-social. At the same time the only thing that appears within the rabble-attitude is an infinite movement of negation from which nothing escapes. If already the poor does not participate in any estate and falls out of the political structures of the state, the rabble is marked by an attitude which became "hostile and contrary" (Ibid., 173) whose gaze does not see any organic ethical-statist community but only illegitimacy.

If one can claim that marriage can be divorced, because it is based on merely arbitrary emotions, as Hegel continues, this does not go for the "state, because it is based on the law" (HVORL 3, 554). The rabble however tends even to dissolve the state into an unlawful association by indignantly doubting the legitimacy of the law and its institutions. Because it lacks the decisive organic building blocks of the ethical attitude, the rabble also lacks the ethical attitude. The dissolving movement which concerns all determinations of existence also seems to concern all determinations of attitude. This is why Hegel can describe the rabble-attitude in the *Philosophy of Right* in the following terms: "To take the merely negative as a starting-point and to make the willing of evil and the mistrust of such willing the primary factor, and then on the basis of this presupposition slyly to construct dikes whose efficiency simply necessitates corresponding dislikes over against them, is characteristic in thought of the negative understanding and in disposition of the outlook of the rabble" (Ibid., 258).

This passage is astonishing because Hegel draws a parallel between the rabble-attitude and the negative understanding. Because, as I have proved, following Hegel's own definition, the rabble cannot take this position. Already the poor does not come into the negative relation, of concept and reality, by his own fault. Accordingly the inert will of the poor is nothing but an internalization of the objective impossibility to act, which civil society produces. Therewith Hegel's delineation of the rabble as making itself by its attitude is imprecise. One can only concede to Hegel—with regard to his judgment that the rabble makes itself—if one takes into account that the *condition* of this self-making, poverty, is a necessary consequence of civil society. The contingency

which appears in the emergence of the rabble is not, as Hegel claims, merely
contingent. The condition of the radical contingency of the emergence of
the rabble is necessarily present. Indignation as a constant feature of its attitude is the necessary content of a contingent attitude which is directed toward
the necessity of its own possibility. Therefore the rabble cannot be counted
as a form of negative understanding, for the decisive definition of the latter is the contingent-arbitrary abstraction from all concrete determinations.
In consequence, the rabble, being the particular stage which comes 'after'
poverty—and this means that it sublates and dissolves it—and also appearing contingently from poverty, does not fall back into a position of negative
understanding or moral evil. Rather it emerges as already dissolved existence,
as negation of negation (of poverty) in a place in which the inadequacy should
be overcome. There is the negation of negation but nevertheless the rabble is
as the in and for itself of poverty present after this sublation; as *organ without
body*, as *absolute rabble*.

Against Hegel's own definition the rabble does not take the merely negative
as a starting point, rather it *is* the negative as such—and this in a form which
is not merely possible but rather impossible. If Hegel refers the rabble back to
negative understanding and moral evil he attempts to tame that which, following the logic of his own description, resists this taming. The rabble is, as
Hegel suggests, no figure of negative understanding, of moral evil, a mere subjective figure which arbitrarily withdraws from the objectivity of the existing
circumstances. Rather the objectivity of the existing laws necessarily produce
something (poverty) which stands on the edge of the objective community, at
the "edge of the void" (BBE, 175) and only there is the rabble able to make
itself. The rabble is indignant about the possibility of his its presence and it is
therefore not merely subjective, no fanatical figure. The rabble is not a figure
which falls into abstract, subjective imagination, but it is first and foremost a
figure which refers to its own objective conditions of possibility and *subjectivizes*
them. The rabble is a materialist figure.[38]

At the same time it is important to determine more precisely one effect of
the contingency of the supplementing attitude, of indignation. This contingency is on one side in its possibility necessarily inscribed into civil society
and overturns the state on the level of attitude, but this means on the other
side that the emergence of attitude cannot be described as following laws of a
necessary and rational development, of history, of freedom. The *emergence of
the rabble is not deducible*. At the same time the dissolving of all determinations
describes an excess of the negative, an excess of inconsistency over the movement itself and this in the *position of the subject*. Civil society cannot include
everything that it produces; the state constitutively contains (as a part) 'something' which does not belong to it.

Hegel thus commits an error of categorization with regards to the rabble. He
is confronted with a problem that cannot be grasped in the available categories,

because with the rabble there appears the radical problem of determining something which constitutively, i.e. in and for itself is undetermined and is at the same time not a mere negation of determination. Hegel describes this indeterminacy hastily as the mere negation of all determinations and therewith as indeterminacy, that is negatively still dialectically determined. This is why he understands it as negation: as a negation of the ethical that signifies a reversion into mere morality; as the negation of morality which appears as a negation of the universal and an insistence on the particular, i.e. as evil will; as negation of the determinations of the will which stands against the realization of freedom, i.e. appears as abstract, negative understanding. But none of these characterizations are suitable for the rabble—or more precisely: they are only valid if one leaves the rabble's objective (and material) condition of possibility out of the picture. The rabble appears, against Hegel's reading but still according to Hegel's own deduction, as the *negative in and for itself*: not the negative as the subjective starting point and therewith as the place of a subject (of negative understanding and indignation) which would remain merely for itself, but rather the negative as such which marks the site at which, if one might say so, a *rabble-subject* could form itself. If the rabble loses all determinations and—as assumed so far—therewith also the will, this determination of the rabble as subject in the Hegelian sense cannot be uphold. The greatness of Hegel consists in marking that the rabble designates the place of a *possible subject*. But the only appearance that accords to it is the disappearing because it does not have any determinations of existence nor any way of appearance proper to it. For Hegel it is therefore nothing but semblance, for semblance "we call a *being* that is directly and in its own self a *non-being*, a surface show" (HPS, 87). With the notion of semblance and appearance Hegel means the existence of a thing that makes his existence different from his essence.[39] In this sense one can conceive of the putrefaction happening to the poor as dissolving the semblance of an irrational existence. But the rabble appears after the dissolving of the semblance and cannot designate an immediate non-being.

It marks—as one needs to state *against* Hegel—the irruption of inconsistency into the consistent structures of the ethical; it is only generated in the moving relations of the ethical community but falls out of these relations. It is obvious that indignation, the content of the rabble-attitude, is not a mere moral indignation, but rather it reflects the dissolving which already objectively marked the position of the rabble and continues it in 'interior' reflection. In the rabble-attitude one cannot find stability, sociality, for the determination of the ends of this indignation do not exclude the rabble itself; its attitude can also be directed against himself: the rabble splits, and does not know any unity. Therefore indignation is necessarily indignation about the condition of its own possibility. In this sense the attitude of the rabble is not an attitude which corresponds to the Hegelian concept of the ethical attitude as habitualized volition or true certainty. The rabble-attitude is according to its peculiar logic without attitude because it 1. does not include habit or habitualized volition, because it 2. has lost the necessary ethical self-feeling, and 3. is driven into the status of an a-social particularity. One can claim that the rabble indignantly looks at the ethical community and does not see anything but an "aggregate"; its gaze sees the people as mere *"vulgus,* not [as] *populus . . ."* (HPM, 215).[40] For it does not recognize any deeper ethical unity in the existing circumstances but only the same dissolving that is happening to it. It sees in the ethical nothing but an aggregation because it itself is the product of a dissolution whose condition the ethical community unavoidably produces. It sees everywhere the actuality of its own possibility. The rabble sees what is enabled in the civic movement anywhere as actual possibility. That for the rabble the people appears only as *vulgus,* as vulgar, means that it sees everywhere what it itself has become: a dissolution of all determinations. The vulgus is "the people *dissolved into a heap"* [41]—the people which has lost the unity which the ethical produced among its multiple parts in an organic way. Because the rabble only beholds a dissolved people, it corresponds to the scission which already marks him etymologically. For the German word *'Pöbel'* derives from the French *'peuple'* which refers back to the Latin *'populus.'* But it already gains its pejorative connotation in Middle High German. The rabble is already etymologically derived from the people as *populus* but names the rabble precisely as a "nasty mass with a despicable connotation . . . beyond the honors of labor"[42]; the people as *vulgus.*[43] From the ethical relations of the *populus* the rabble as *vulgus* appears, which beholds only *vulgus* everywhere. The rabble names precisely the scission of the people into *populus* and *vulgus,* because it sees precisely this matter as the peculiar matter of the ethical space. This insight is mediated by the *logic of double latency* which makes anyone in the state latently rabble. If the rabble decomposes the rationality and organic structuring of the state with its attitude, then it can only do so by suspending within its attitude the unity that exists between the individual and the state. The rabble sees everywhere only *vulgus* instead of *populus,* pure multiplicity instead of ethical unity, infinite scission instead of organic structuring. For the rabble, there is, following a word of Machiavelli, "only rabble in the world."[44] Its attitude is itself a vulgar attitude. The rabble seeing only *vulgus* determines itself therefore as part of the inorganic, unstructured multiplicity of the *vulgus.*[45]

Therefore the rabble is much more vulgar—in the sense of *vulgus*—than Hegel thinks, for its attitude reflects its own complete dissolution. And this dissolution expands, it is contagious. That the inorganic arises somewhere *in* the political body means not only that this inorganic being putrefies and dissolves its existence but also that according to the *logic of double latency* the putrefaction and the inorganic spreads, appears everywhere as the which it will always already have been. With the rabble comes the related insight that everything can become rabble-like, that the whole organically structured ethical community is always already confronted with the latent threat of becoming rabble-like, or even more: that the ethical will always only have been the fragile uniformly organized rabble. It is in this sense, "the deadening for all rational concepts, structuring and liveliness."[46] With him Nietzsche's insight is verified: "There is hidden rabble in you as well."[47]

The fully putrefied rabble produces the threat of decay in the state. For if one conceives of the rabble as 1. an *organ without a body* which 2. remains in the body from which it is detached, one can claim that the attitude describes the relation of this organ to the body. Here 1. that what remains in the body does not have any determination (of existence) and 2. its relation to this body is exclusively defined as negation from the perspective of the (political) body, of the organism. For the negation which conceives of the undetermined as still determined in a dialectical way, still describes in this sense a (proto-)organic relation. But this cannot go for the rabble. By itself the rabble is undetermined in a *non-dialectical way*. Because Hegel neither knows if there is, has been or will be the rabble, his description represents the attempt to give it a determination *tout court*: The rabble would then be the negation of the organic structuring as mere for itself of the will. The rabble is in this sense always already the "the most horrible rabble that even fantasy cannot imagine" (HPRV, 223) because it also reflects its objective dissolution internally. Fantasy cannot imagine it because the rabble-attitude consists in the claim that the social bond which encompasses the organic ethicality of the state is itself nothing but an always fragile fantasy. The limit of fantasy is its own abolition.[48]

By way of the emergence of the rabble ethicality decomposes into the under-lying rabble-matter, into a *pure and therefore un-organic multiplicity*. 'Rabble' is the name of something present and material, or more precisely, a real aboli-tion which denounces the ethicality and sociality of community as a mere fantasy, and a fragile one at that. Therefore the rabble is so horrible that even fantasy cannot imagine it: the rabble is no imagining and has nothing fantas-tical about it, rather it assumes a position which suspends any fantasy of the ethical and social—one can say that through him it becomes clear that the social is secondary. It is present, material and at the same without determina-tions and threatens to sever the substantial bond by his peculiar a-sociality and to unmask it as mere fantasy. It threatens to dissolve the relations of the state and to the state which find their decisive and condensed place in the atti-tude of the subject. But what does it mean that the rabble subjectively reflects its objective dissolution?

It means on one side that the name 'rabble' refers to something that can be described as a *state of dissolution*, the absolute putrefaction in which all deter-minations are dissolved: this is the rabble as the *matter of ethical space*. At the same time the rabble-attitude presents on the other side a *process, an activity of dissolution* which Hegel describes as indignation: this is the rabble as an *organ without a body*. The rabble is in this way always already passive, externally deter-mined by the necessary condition of possibility of its emergence (poverty). But there is a complete state of dissolution (objectively) only when this process of unbinding is converted into the activity of dissolution (subjectively), in short: when it is subjectivized. But then activity no longer means to perform possible actions and to realize one's freedom in this way, but activity in this sense means that to *subjectively appropriate the impossibility* to act which the poor confronted already (objectively and) externally and to direct one's volition toward it. This happens in indignation which leads to the claim of a *right without right*. The willing of this objective impossibility also indicates that this impossibility lies at *the ground of the ethical*. This affirmation is the impossible action. To act neither purely passively nor purely actively but rather starting to will from an impossibility, suspends the pre-given distinction of activity and passivity, of action and active resistance. And this is precisely the point through which the rabble makes itself.[49]

Thereby on the one hand, objectively, the complete dissolution of all determinations of existence takes place and on the other, the peculiar negativity subjectively presents itself and persists without an existing relation—without being the negation of something. Initially it seems as if the rabble judges that everything that is can be decomposed. However this judgment is not the last word. For the rabble is in itself—as the matter of the ethical realm—the state of complete dissolution and his attitude yields the following consequences: 1. anyone is—according to the *logic of double latency*—latently poor and therefore latently rabble and 2. that the rabble is latently contained everywhere and has at the same time no determination—i.e. is an un-organic part of any element of the state. Therefore Hegel is at the same time right and not right. If he delineates the rabble as evil and one can understand the contradiction of the evil will in a way that derives from the necessary universal demand which is inherent to any particularity which wants to remain for itself, then he is right. But he is not right insofar as he does not see that the rabble, precisely by being without determination, names a particularity but at the same time a particularity which due to the *logic of double latency* is in itself universal. The contradiction which is supposed to take place in the rabble is not a contradiction which Hegel could resolve. The rabble has the status of a particularity that is immediately universal, not by an act that realizes freedom and this means, not through 'labor.' It affirms the impossibility of being universal beyond action and rational activity—and in fact without doing *something* in any actual sense. Through the fact that the dissolving of all determinations of the rabble latently concerns anyone, it is in this particular indeterminacy generalizable, universalizable. If one links together the questions of the emergence of the rabble and that of his universality one can claim: the rabble is universally implied, it is a singular universal. The *logic of double latency* describes one dimension of this implication. But as the rabble as matter of the ethical space remains forever in this implicit dimension; there is no direct access to the rabble, no knowledge about his existence. That it makes itself is Hegel's description of this subjective side of the peculiar emergence of matter, of this object of pure implication.[50] Although the Hegelian description of the rabble-attitude as morally evil and structurally analogous to negative understanding cannot be upheld, he has marked a decisive dimension with it—and this represents his greatness. The rabble remains implicit as long as this implication does not come to light through a subject.

The decisive aspect of the determination of the rabble-attitude is that Hegel clearly sees that the contingent intervention of a subject, a subjective operation is needed to produce this peculiar and always necessary implicit dimension. If Hegel makes the rabble *in toto* into an irrational contingency, he loses what he already exposed before: the place at which through a subjective intervention the implicit dimension can be as necessary as the implication itself. The contingency only concerns the eruption but not the position of the rabble as such. Hegel is right to mark the contingency of the rabble-attitude but he is not right in interpreting this contingency in a way that the rabble as such is merely contingent. One has to claim *with* Hegel that the dimension of contingency is decisive and further that it is linked with an activity of the subject. But one has to claim *against* Hegel that this cannot mean that the rabble would just be a mere contingent irregularity which would not have any necessity. This is for that reason that to which the contingency of the indignation refers is a necessary implication which only becomes retroactively clear in its necessity through the contingent genesis of the rabble. Therefore through its attitude, which in truth is not an attitude stricto sensu because it is nothing but the dissolution (of that which exists), the rabble refers to an equality which is caused by an organically formed structuring of an attitude and could be described as knowledge about the other (and oneself as other) with an unconscious. Rather it is an equality which in a peculiar way lies 'before' the Hegelian equality although it only becomes visible 'after'—or in the process—of the production of ethical equality through attitude, as an interruption of the structures of the state and of attitude.

The access of the implied 'before' is always retroactive and starts from a moment of rupture with the organic-statist structures. The temporality which the rabble describes through its attitude is the *future anterior*.[51] As soon as it contingently makes itself it becomes clear, in the sense of the *logic of double latency*, what necessarily will have been implied 'before' its emergence—the rabble as matter of the ethical space. In this passage of Hegel's system of philosophy –objective spirit—he deals with the historical specificity of social-ethical living together, with politics and confronts something that he neither can fully explain with reference to the *specificity* of social dynamics nor the specificity of *historical* dynamics. Encapsulating the problem one can say: under historical conditions and in the economic movement of modern civil society something can emerge that 1. cannot be (fully) derived from these conditions and this movement and 2. that yields the insight that it will always already have been implied and possible 'before' these conditions. What has emerged in the interruption of the structures and of the world of appearance of the ethical is the matter of ethicality itself which at the same time can only come forward because of a subjective intervention, a subjective operation. In Hegel's state, with the rabble there emerges an equality which breaks with the determinate and determining structures because it will have been 'before' the equality of attitude belonging to the ethical community and (latently) includes anyone due to its constitutive indeterminacy. From and in the historical movement something erupts which cannot be understood out of the necessary movement of history, but is rather an interruption of radical contingency into it. From and in history something a-historical emerges because the matter of the ethical breaks into history as that which will have lied 'before' the ethical and the state; something that is, or better: will have been eternal. What in and from the dialectical movement is produced is something transhistorical. Or to put it differently: one can learn from Hegel's marking of the place of the rabble what it means to think *stasis*. Only through the dialectical movement is something produced which can be retroactively understood as logically prior to it and without which it would not be thinkable.[52] To take up a formulation by Marcuse, if the "possible is only that which can be derived from the very content of the real,"[53] then the rabble is something that withdraws from such a derivation. The emergence of the rabble cannot be derived from the historical movement of civil society or the state because it relies only on a radical subjective contingency. It marks the point in which the derivation rails, falters and something underivable, contingent comes into play: the rabble marks a point of impossibility (of deductive derivation).

Hegel wrote in his *Aesthetics*—speaking about the transition from the romantic to the novel—that to not remain in the mere subjective for itself one "needs to punch a hole in the [existing] order of things, to change the world" (HVAE2, 219); here, this remark gains a different meaning. For it is not so much that the rabble does punch a hole in the existing order but rather it is itself the *hole in the order*. It is the hole in which all determinations dissolve; a hole in the structure of the state. In this context another of Hegel's words, this time of the early Hegel, can be taken up and it can be claimed that all institutions in the state and the state itself get "struck on the head like being struck by an invisible hand"—by the *organ without body*—and they "do not know what is happening."[54]

If the rabble-attitude marks the point in which the dissolution whose conditions are constantly produced in the state are reflected back onto it and this precisely from a place of which the state is unable to know anything, then it becomes clear that this is not only a problem of civil society. For in it the bond with the state is torn apart and this in a way that an immanent universality of the particular position of the rabble opens up which is *more universal than the state*. The interrupting emergence of the rabble cannot be sublated in any

Hegelian way anymore because it breaks with the statist equality of attitude and posits a fundamental equality without determinations, an equality of the pure undetermined multiplicity against it. The negativity that the completely putrefied, *absolute rabble* is, cannot be negated, but itself tantalizes everything and dissolves it. The rabble is an ethical problem *because* it is the peculiar matter of the ethical space. It is a problem of the state *because* it is more universal and questions *for all* and in an *in-different* way the relations to the state by enabling the insight into a fundamental equality which lies beyond statist ethicality. However this does not refer to a position of absolute externality, rather the rabble 'appears' only in a place which is constantly produced by the movement of civil society in itself. The rabble emerges at a local place, at the edge of society, as particularity which is at the same time more universal than the statist ethicality. From the relations of civil society, the state and its institutions something emerges that cannot be derived from its relations. This is the reason why Hegel claims the rabble makes itself. The possibility of this results necessarily, but its realization appears at the same time always seems impossible because the possibility of the emergence of the rabble marks the place in which there is the impossibility of action and realization—for "it becomes impossible for poverty to bring something in front of itself."[55] The emergence of the rabble is therefore at the same time externally possible and impossible or more precisely: it is necessary and impossible. But to pursue the question as to the way in which this dissolution takes place in, from and with the rabble, one has to follow another question which allows to investigate the status of impossibility: How is it possible for the rabble to fall out of right? How can he unbind himself from the statist relations of right and duty?

Chapter 10

Without Right, Without Duty—Rabble,
Right without Right, or Un-Right

"Justice" is a philosophical word—at least if we leave aside, as one should, its juridical signification, which is entirely the preserve of the police and the magistracy.

(Alain Badiou)[1]

Has the rabble to stay . . . He is a fact but no right.

(Eduard Gans)[2]

"[E]ssentially it holds good that whoever has no rights has no duties, and vice versa" (HPM, 218). This is how Hegel summarizes his previous explanations in paragraph 486 of his *Encyclopedia*. He resumes there *ex negativo* what he had previously delineated, namely that rights and duties are always in a relationship of mutual conditioning and have to be understood reciprocally. But how is this reciprocity established such that it makes it possible to already anticipate what it signifies to fully fall out of this mutually binding relation? It means not to count as a person, for, as already mentioned, the fundamental imperative of the *Philosophy of Right* demands: "Hence the imperative of right is: 'Be a person and respect the others as persons'" (HOPR, 55). How is this commandment justified? The starting point of right[3] is the free will and the "system of right" presents for Hegel "the realm of freedom made actual . . ." (Ibid., 26). This is to say that freedom should not be understood merely negatively, as a capacity to resist inclinations and desires, as "freedom *not to act*,"[4] but necessarily as freedom becoming actual. Right is "spirit making itself actual . . ." (HGPR, 81). From here it becomes intelligible why the imperative even takes the form of an imperative. For without realization, freedom is not freedom and the form of this realization is right: *realized freedom is juridified freedom.*

Therefore it is necessary, if one is to be at all able to realize freedom as one's own, to be as a person and respect all others as person, as figures of realized freedom. This imperative as the central imperative of right is at the same time an *imperative of freedom.* For if a will is disrespectfully directed against another, it is at the same time directed against the entitlement of realizing one's own freedom which also determines itself; it is ultimately directed against itself. Here a moment of "reflexivity"[5] comes into play. Reflexivity names the constitutive relation of the legal subject to itself, the legal subject who knows himself as both a legal subject and a bearer of duties. This reflexive relation of the subject to itself whose most original form is described in Hegel as free will forms "the universal legal capacity of man as man" which at the same time is "the elementary concept of right."[6] For "right is . . . the *existence [Dasein] of the free will*." It is "freedom as Idea" (HOPR, 46).

"The idea" of freedom and thus of right, as Hegel clarifies further, "must determine itself within itself continually, since in the beginning it is no more than an abstract concept" (Ibid., 49). This abstract and initial concept corresponds accordingly also to a merely abstract rather than a fully determined concept of right: abstract right. It is the first concept of right to appear; the as yet incomplete realization of freedom. But already, abstract right has the function of liberating the free will from the mere arbitrariness of determination and takes on a decisive function in the whole of statist community. It is helpful to reconstruct this primary level to see what it can mean to be already excluded from abstract right and the duties linked to it.[7] Abstract right is in Hegel the first objective (and therefore external) form of appearance and of the reification of the free will. "Right is in the first place the immediate existence which freedom gives itself" (HOPR, 56) and in this sense it is another embodiment of what Hegel calls "personality . . ." (Ibid., 50). Here one should pay careful attention to the following: the idea of freedom develops also in the sphere of abstract right in three different stages, which present three different embodiments of personality. Initially, objective is here to be understood as "possession which is property-ownership," then it relates to another person in the contract—the second stage—and ultimately appears as a difference not of different free wills but as a difference of the will "as related to itself" (Ibid., 56), as wrongdoing and crime. In addition it is important that these abstract legal relations and determinations for Hegel can primarily be understood when being considered as part of the logically prior state. Abstract right is part of the state and does not just delineate a historical index of his genesis.[8] But what is personality? It is "the basis (itself abstract) of the system of abstract and therefore formal right" and involves as such "the capacity for rights . . ." (HOPR, 55). It means that "as *this* person: I am completely determined on every side . . . and finite, yet nonetheless I am simply and solely self-relation, and therefore in finitude I know myself as something *infinite, universal* and *free*" (Ibid., 54).

Thus Hegel wants to claim that personality describes a pure self-relation. As fundament of right, personality is in this relation to itself purely abstract because it is still completely undetermined. Since it is derived from free will and the free will is only then truly free if it is relieved of all heteronomous determination—of needs, desires—one can claim that abstract personality[9] on this level is "a pure negativity."[10] The free person is in this passage only determined by that which it is not. For the same reason the right is also limited in this sphere to the purely negative: to "not infringe personality and what personality entails" (HOPR, 55). Due to its abstractness it contains the *capacity* for rights as a possibility. But to not only have this *capacity* for right in a merely abstract way, only as possibility, one needs an actualization of it. In this sense one can say: "legal subjectivity is, therefore, both internal and external to ourselves."[11] It is internal as possibility and external as reality and actualization of this possibility. The objectivity signifies the reality of the possible. Only the objectification makes the possibility appear as something else than a merely abstract and purely negative determination, as mere possibility.

Freedom exists only as objectifying, realized freedom; this is Hegel's fundamental insight. At the same time the cited commandment of right can be understood at another, deeper level. It is a duty *to* be a person to realize one's own freedom. It is therefore a duty not to remain in abstract interiority and draw back into one's abstract personality and mere *capacity* of right, but rather to objectify it. Therefore in the *Encyclopedia* Hegel can give a different, more content-related form to the commandment of right which is already implied in the form it receives in the *Philosophy of Right*: "[i]s a duty to possess things as property, i.e. to be a person. When it is posited in the relationship of appearance, of relation to another person, it develops into the duty of others to respect my right" (HPM, 218). Property is thus the "initial mediator"[12] which necessarily has to appear in the forming process of personality since it marks the first and decisive moment of the actualization of freedom. Or differently put: the person as free will does not appear in the world of objectivity as long as it does not become objective for itself. "So persons relate to each other through the media of things."[13] For, as explained, "the free will is not to remain abstract, it must in the first place give itself an existence . . ." (HOPR, 51). Only in the objectification has the person reached objective existence. "In property the person is joined together with itself" (HPM, 217), since only through property, only through "'this' or 'mine'" (HOPR, 62) does the person become objective, it becomes *this* (determined) person. In this way will becomes "an actual will . . ." (Ibid., 61). As Jeanne Lorraine Schroeder rightly states:

> Property is a means by which the abstract person objectifies itself. The self as abstract will claims to be essential reality, but the existence of external things, that is, objects and our dependence on external reality contradicts this. The self therefore, needs to appropriate external objects—it must own property. The self becomes particularized and concrete, rather than abstract, through ownership. Potentiality becomes actuality.[14]

Property marks in all regards that which is proper to the person because it gives it an existence which is distinguished—through property—from other persons. "Therewith the abstract, external sphere of property, posited in private right is conceived of as a condition of possibility for the realization of freedom in its entirety."[15] If the person becomes *this* person, at all *a* person which is itself objective through property, this means that mere possession is not sufficient. The transition from possession to property is performed in a way that my possession is recognized as legitimate in a form in which I recognize the other's possession as legitimate. Here in this transition,[16] the imperative of the *Philosophy of Right* repeats itself: be as possessor a property-owner and respect other possessors as (equal) property-owners. Property describes a generalized realization of freedom. It has the function of "embody[ing] one's will"[17] which is also the reason why Hegel has to "jettison the time-honored distinction in personal and law of property which Kant was able to take over without hesitation" (RHS, 107). For things are only as possessions of persons in whom their own will become an object for them. It is important to take into account that with the possession the original abstractness of the free will has entered into objectivity. The will wills something as his. But a possession of which only I know and which only I will as my possession, is a possession which can be taken from me or lost at any time, since it has not yet become property.[18] What is property?

Hegel marks three aspects which property has to contain: possession, usage, relinquishing. The fundamental element is possession, which describes an intersubjectively recognizable relation of an object with a specific person. Object signifies "any bodily thing (res corporalis) insofar as it can legally traffic" (RHS, 269). Possession for Hegel is in all respects relational and always already oriented toward intersubjective relation of recognition. It delineates the link from which one can understand what it means to be a person and respect the others as persons. For possession names for Hegel the intersubjective relation, by means of which an object is attributed to a subject and thereby excludes other subject from the possessions of this object. Possession excludes others but only to create the possibility of the recognition of others.[19] But possession needs the legal recognition of others. Although it includes "the promise of relationship,"[20] a mere promise is not the reality of this relationship.

The second element of property is its use. In it the person relates actively to the object in his belonging. But how the usage looks depends on the specificity of the object itself, and therefore it is at the same time the solipsistic moment of property and posits the person as dependent upon it. Hence as a moment of heteronomy enters into the constitution of the free will, that Hegel consequently attempts to sublate by the introduction of relinquishing. The will depends too much on the specific use value that he does not himself determine. The relinquishing again posits the nullity of the object or thing against the free will of the person. If the use was heteronomously determined by the possession, in relinquishing it the free will liberates itself from this heteronomy and posits itself as reflected in his freedom. The will again gains his dominance over the object and the freedom from it. As Hegel writes: "The reason I can alienate my property is that it is mine only insofar as I put my will into it. Hence I may abandon (*derelinquiere*) as ownerless anything that I have or yield it to the will of another and so into his possession, provided always that the thing in question is a thing external by nature" (HOPR, 77).

It is necessary to emphasize the objectification of this relinquishing to avoid relinquishing the (external) existence of the person along with it. The possibility of evading this complete form of relinquishing consists in attaining the objective confirmation (of the relinquishing) by another objective person so that the relinquishing of a thing by a subject intersubjectively gains objectivity. Hegel describes this procedure in his handwritten notes beginning with the notion of use as follows: "I myself a thing—purpose that I perish as thing, nature and become free—resurrect—this is my purpose . . ." (HGPR, 143). The resurrection of the free person as an objective relinquishing of the object enables the contract. For the contract unites two persons in the common will which at the same time conceives of both as separated from one another, each having rights and duties. Possession has become recognized property. The contractual partners are both equal and different; they actualize the identity of identity and difference. This moment of relinquishing and the moment of the exchange of property are decisive for the realization of personality because it is the moment of objectivity and makes it understandable through the intersubjective relations of multiple persons to each other.

The logic of property always already relies on a preexistent relational structure which contains the possibility of mutually recognizing persons. Property cannot be thought independently of ethicality: property is by definition social. Yet these reciprocal relations of recognition have to be constantly reinitiated, actualized and thereby reproduced in their reality. Schroeder correctly claims that "property serves a function in the creation of sociality by giving the person sufficient content to bear the weight of subjectivity."[21] The subjectivity of the proprietor is social and this sociality forms itself via the mutual intersubjective relationships which property introduces. Here one can see what it means not to be under the legal commandment and to withdraw from the imperative to be a person: it means not only to fall out of the sphere of objectivity but also to fall out of the sphere of intersubjectivity. Not to be a person means not to realize one's freedom, to be unfree, a-social and thus to have no rights and no duties. For freedom as realized is always embedded into intersubjective relations that enable this realization in the first place, but only becomes effective through property relations. To fall out of these relations signifies to fall out of freedom and therefore not to have enough content to bear the weight of subjectivity. For only property enables "a scope for action and makes possible the extending and expanding of personality. [. . .] Property remains a permanent apparatus for the individual to carry out a life-plan, to give reality to a conception of his own good, his further development."[22]

But to be able to discuss this, it is helpful to devote some thoughts to what for Hegel is the first possession, the first external way in which the person appears: the body. For "I possess my life and my body, like other things, only as my will is in them" (HOPR, 110). So here one may demonstrate something which I have already grasped by means of the notion of the *organ without a body*. The rabble has no external appearance. Can one thus claim that the rabble is without body in a sense that he himself does not *possess* a body?

For Hegel anyone is as proprietor "in natural life" insofar as "I find myself in *possession*" (HGPR, 111) of my body. But this immediate possession has to become a willed possession to constitute oneself as a person. "Insofar as the body is an immediate existent, it is not in conformity with spirit. If it is to be the willing organ and soul-endowed instrument of spirit, it must first be *taken into possession* by spirit" (HOPR, 62–3). The naturality and immediacy of this first possession has to be sublated and the body has to be truly taken into possession if it is to become a willing organ. It is only when this happens that the "human being . . . takes possession of himself and becomes his own property and no one else's" (Ibid., 69). In this sense the bodily taking possession is the "first mode of appropriation."[23] If it does not take place, the will remains in an external relationship to his immediate form of appearance. Herewith the central passage for the rabble-discussion is given. For "the possession of our body and spirit which we can achieve through education, study, habit, etc., and which exists as an *inward* property of spirit" (Ibid., 59) has to be preceded by a prior appropriation which breaks with the immediate presence of the body. For the bodies to become an inward property of spirit one has to "form a habit in them" (HGPR, 122). I have elaborated upon this process of appropriation of the body in the discussion of the logic of habit. It consists in the perpetuated re-formation of the supposed first naturality of the body in the second mediated naturality of habit which produces the unity of will and body. Only through habit does the will know the body as his existence and the volition of the body become part of his self-feeling. Hegel clarifies the matter as follows: "man stands only because and only so long as he wills it; standing is therefore the habit of the will to stand" (HPM, 57). But if one recalls Hegel's judgment to the effect that, "if man makes himself to be without rights and also keeps himself *unbound* of duties . . . then this is the rabble" (HPRV, 222), it follows as an immediate consequence of this that the rabble who unbinds itself from right and duty, also unbinds itself from the conditions of possibility for being a person, since it even suspends the possibility of property acquisition. It consequently negates the personality and presents as a result the actual and complete negation of the capacity for rights: "*capitis diminutio*" (HOPR, 57) maxima.

That Hegel's reference to the unbinding is coherent becomes intelligible when one recalls the most comprehensible definition of duties from his hand-written notes: "duties are *binding* relations, relationships to substantial ethical-ity . . ." (HGPR, 304, my emphasis). Unbinding means to lose the relationship to substantial ethicality, and thereby also one's own freedom. For Hegel, *property entails obligations* and this means that to take a position which even suspends the possibility of property acquisition is to break off from the reciprocity of the dialectic of rights and duties. *Property entails obligations; not to have the possibility of acquiring property deprives one of rights.* In this position one is unbound: from the mutuality of relations of recognition; from one's personality and thus from the duties toward other persons as well as toward one's own rights. For "I would not longer be a person and would place myself outside the realm of right," because the person "is a person only by virtue of his property."[24] But if there is only freedom within the reciprocal relations to other persons, then the rabble is unfree since it has lost the relation to the ethical and fundamentally also to right and duty. But one needs to accentuate here that an impossibility of act-ing already takes place with the poor and this impossibility does not have to do solely with one's duties. This means that already in poverty one deals with an impossibility of providing one's own subsistence through own labor—to real-ize one's freedom and in this way to fulfill one's duty and acquire property—which does not at all have its origin in a self-determination of the free will but in the movement of civil society. But two points must be noted. The first concerns the body; the second is linked to Hegel's diagnosis that the rabble despite failing to provide for itself, nevertheless claims the "right to receive subsistence" (HOPR, 221).

The rabble, although emerging from the binding and bound relations of ethical community, unbinds itself from them. This unbinding I have speci-fied with the concept of the *organ without a body.* Now the question arises of how to conceive of the bodylessness with regard to the first, immediate possession of the will: the body. The early Hegel delineates a fundamental aspect of poverty by claiming that it "becomes impossible for poverty . . . to bring something before itself . . ."[25] This clarifies that the poor remain in their mere physicality.[26] They become lazy, foul, since an external impos-sibility to bring something before themselves is imposed on them and this renders habit positive: this impossibility of bringing something before one-self signifies that for the poor it is only possible to remain in that which they are: mere bodies. The poor persist in the habit of their own body that belongs to their self-feeling, but it is impossible for them to 'realize' this in any way other than a bodily way. In poverty human being is reduced to his mere physicality as the sole realization of freedom.[27] This becoming-positive of habit produces the process of putrefaction at whose end no determination of existence remains. Does this necessarily mean that the rabble does not have a body?

Yes and no. Yes, because it is in a way bodiless in the sense that all determinations of existence have been dissolved and it no longer appears externally in a body proper to it. It cannot experience any residual form of intersubjective recognition—not even of the own body as property. Completely unbound from the binding relations of the ethical community this full unbinding leaves, according to the Hegelian logic, no determination of existence left, not even that of the body. No, because it is still present in this in-existence and does not simply disappear: it is present, has a peculiar being-there which is not a legitimate one. It itself never appears as existent, as actual, since it only appears in and as the poor. Hegel can thus never be sure if the rabble is, as was or will be really present. He sees the poor and marks in them the *possible-impossible place of the rabble*: a presence which does not follow the laws of existence. He marks with the name 'rabble' the possibility of a possibility which lies in the body of the poor—and so in anyone, latently—of whom the rabble is and remains indistinguishable. Its only appearance is therefore at the same time its disappearing (in the indistinguishability). But one cannot ground any dialectics of rights and duties on indistinguishability or apply to it. There are no resources to call that rational and represent that which cannot be distinguished.[28] At the same time it becomes clear that the rabble cannot possibly appear as existing as long as those determinations of existence are upheld which are necessary for Hegel: rational external reality as an objectification and realization of the freedom of the will which in this way posits itself in a rational relation to itself. That the rabble does not have a possession, i.e. not even of a body—because his body is the body of the poor—clarifies again that the rabble as matter of the ethical space cannot be one body among others. In and with the rabble one can foresee the conclusion that it cannot appear since already the poor is only capable of appearing in a reduced way. If the poor is still body—although this is all that is left of his (ethical-social) appearance—the rabble is bodily since it emerges where the question arises as to whether the body of the poor might be nothing more than a mere possession and is in no way intersubjectively recognized property. Hence for Hegel: "If my body did not belong to me, I could not manifest my will in the world, because the words and actions emanating from me would not be mine."[29]

What would be a property (or possession) which I am prevented from relinquishing other than a body for which the possibility to act is externally made impossible? A body of which the possibility to be a willing organ—and to realize the freedom of the will through labor—is taken. The poor are bodies that have lost the possibility of realizing their freedom through labor force. But the poor are still persons since they remain the proprietors of their body. The rabble is situated at this logical passage of the antinomy. It is at the same time the *possibility and impossibility of its appearance*. This structure is named by the notion of the *organ without body* which here takes a clearer shape. Since the organ names the possibility of appearing; the (double) bodilessness—which is expressed in the problem of indistinguishability—names its impossibility. The appearing of the rabble is its disappearing.

But what right may be claimed by the one who is in this way is unbound from right? Hegel's answer is clear: none. Because the right as first immediate existence of freedom requires at least one thing: freedom wanting to be realized. But the rabble still addresses something as its right: its own subsistence. The rabble states in here mere being-here, in its mere presence bare of all determinations a *right without right* which cannot but appear as irrational to Hegel; as arbitrary demand. But for Hegel, and this is again important to recall, always only appear the poor. If one vulgarizes his criticism of the rabble one can claim that it seems to be nothing—although this diagnosis in all regards contradicts Hegel's own deduction—but the poor who is no longer willing to work and pulls back to a position that he should be provided for. But here matters stand differently. If Hegel underlines that the lack which the rabble articulates only under civic circumstances "immediately takes the form of a wrong" because "against nature a human being can claim no right" (HOPR, 221) he unwillingly notes an insight which runs counter to his own critique of the rabble. But if the wrong, that is the lack for the poor, is addressed by the rabble in a way whose logic is the following: if society is the existence of legal relations and these produce at the same time a wrong, these legal relations are nothing but illegal relations; this is why the rabble opposes the existing circumstances and articulates a right which goes against existing right. Since the *right without right* which the rabble addresses names the position of a "*right not to need rights, not to use rights or be used and used up by them.*"[30] A right of subsistence which does not rely on criteria, accomplishments or other things, but is rather freed from all determinations of existence which should be assignable to its bearer. A *right without right* that is not calling for any determinations of existence produces an internal infinitization of the judgment because there is no possibility either of attributing it or not attributing it, due to existing determinations. The rabble-right is a right without legal comfort, without legal entitlement. It is rather the unfulfillable entitlement of an infinite judgment that does not refer to any determinable subject of this right; a right of existence which is none; a right of mere presence.

Initially one might suspect that the rabble does not articulate a positive judgment whose content and form would be the confirmation of the existing, determined facts but rather a negative judgment whose content would be its indignation against these facts. But the rabble-position is not taken up in a negative judgment. Rather the rabble-attitude only appears for Hegel as a negative judgment; negation of objectivity or as moral evil. For Hegel, due to this radical claim, the rabble always appears as mere particularity, as resentment-rabble. But the loutish *right without right* which does not correspond to the Hegelian concept of right can be read as a subjective affirmation of the mere predicateless, attributeless, i.e. fully indeterminate in-existence or presence. It is in this regard a demand for the impossible.

One can append these remarks since Hegel deals with crime in analogy with the forms of judgment. He distinguishes the nonmalicious wrong, fraud, and crime, and shows them to correspond with the forms of judgment of negative, positively-infinite and negatively-infinite judgment. The nonmalicious wrong "is the most venial of the types of wrongdoing" because it appears merely as a negation of the particular and not of "the genus." "If I say 'a rose is not red', I still recognize that it has a colour" (HOPR, 95). I negate the particular color without fundamentally negating that the rose entails the determination of color. The nonmalicious wrong comprises "the sphere of civil suits" in which the "recognition of the right as the universal and decisive factor" (Ibid., 95) is assured—only one believes the rose is blue, the other that it is red—and therefore there is no punishment for nonmalicious wrongs. It is "a straightforward negative judgment, where, in the predicate 'mine', only the particular is negated" (Ibid.). The nonmalicious wrong is like an illness which negates a particular state of health, blocks this or that life-function, but not the universal of life as such. The universal is respected, the particular negated. The fraud however respects "the particular will . . . but universal right is not" (Ibid., 96). The universal is violated in a way that in its place an abstract semblance of the universal is posited. To fraud corresponds a judgment of the form 'a woman is not a tree,' 'the table is a table' which seem to present forms of judgment and present correct sentences but do not postulate a true but only a merely abstract universality. To refer to a clear comment on this form of "infinite judgment expressed positively or as a tautology" (Ibid.) as formulated by Mark Tunick: "The corresponding judgement in our case of fraud is something like: 'the amount you should give me for this diamond is the amount you are willing to give me for this diamond.' Someone who recognizes the universal idea of right would say something else: 'the amount you should give me for this diamond is the amount it is worth'."[31]

Fraud posits the abstract semblance of a universal against the true universal, but does not negate the particular which remains respected in its demand for universality and right. The substitution of the rational universality of the right by a seeming universality represents a violation of it and is therefore punished. Crime is ultimately a "negatively-infinite judgment." For he who commits "a theft . . . does not, as in a suit about civil rights, merely deny the particular right of another person to some one definite thing. He denies the right of that person in general . . ." (HLH, 307). Crime altogether negates the universality of right's claim to legitimacy. It therefore no longer resembles the illness but rather the "death" in which "subject and predicate utterly diverge" (Ibid.). What can it mean against this background that the rabble inscribes an infinitization of the judgment? The decisive factor is that the rabble neither establishes a negatively-infinite judgment—it is not a criminal—nor a positively-infinite judgment, but rather a sort of *infinitely-infinite judgment*.

To be clear here: Hegel's criticism of the rabble is a critique which can be read either as critique of the positively-infinite judgment, since the rabble claims a universal which is merely abstract or as a critique of the negatively-infinite judgment since it negates the universality of existing legal relationships and unbinds himself from them. But it is neither a fraud nor a criminal; it rather falls out of the right by untying itself from it. It marks a wrongdoing that does not fall under the Hegelian categories of wrongdoings. Here one can see the range of the rabble's unbinding from right. For Hegel the rabble is not right without being able to offer a category which could comprise him. For the rabble falls neither under the negating categories of abstract right (nonmalicious wrong, fraud, crime) nor under those of morality. Therewith it unbinds itself even from the distinction into positively- and negatively-infinite judgment: it establishes an *infinitely-infinite judgment*. If ethicality represents the sublating mediation of morality and right in the state, the problem of categorization does not appear only on the stage of morality or right but also on the stage of their mediation—the ethical. Hence there is a further perspective if one takes seriously Werner Hamacher's link between that which I call *right without right* and the infinite—infinitely-infinite—judgment. The rabble takes the position of an *un-right*. The prefix 'un' of *un-right* then refers neither to the wrong inscribed in right nor to a positive (natural) right.

The rabble neither refers to a *right before the right* nor does it take, as Hegel tends most often to suggest, an *illegal* position, i.e. an irrational particular position. Rather it takes the position of an *un-right* which is more and less than the Hegelian concept of the wrong *[Unrecht]*. The *right without right* of the rabble is an *un-right* in such a way that it even undermines the distinction of right and wrong. Neither is it right—which would amount to a positive judgment—nor is it wrong—which would amount to a crime, i.e. a negative judgment. Rather it is a right *beyond* right and wrong; a right that only takes the merely indeterminate presence as the sole starting point from which to denounce the lack taking place within existing legal relations as a wrong. At the same time such an *un-right* is a right *beyond* good and evil, for the 'un' suspends these moral distinctions. Due to this double suspension (of morality and right) the *un-right* presents an *infinitely-infinite judgment*. Such an *un-right* which does not rely upon any determination except the mere presence of an indeterminate in-existence which is nothing but there, and necessarily generates an unbinding of the existing relationships of rights and duties.[32] The *un-right* has nothing proper to it; it does not start from any determination and therefore appears as impossible; impossible right; right of the impossible. It is not based on any externally present property, not even that of the body. And at the same time it is in its entitlement not only the negation of all determinations, not simply a negative judgment. As demonstrated, the rabble is less than a mere particularity because it has even lost the nonambiguity of its particularity and it is more than a mere particularity because it makes itself and is immediately universal. The *un-right* of the particular-universal rabble is connected to anyone. The *un-right* always contains a universal dimension. Therefore it is an *un-right to equality*. Due to this universality it is also an *un-right to justice*.

From what we have elaborated so far, the question arises as to how the rabble relates to the decisive concept which the Hegelian *Philosophy of Right* takes as its starting point: free will. Does the rabble have a free will? Can it have one?

Chapter 11

To Will Nothing or Not to Will Anymore: The Rabble as Will and Representation?

Against the idea of normal desires, we must sustain the fighting idea of a desire which always affirms as existing what is without name. Because it is the common part of our historical existence, we must affirm the existence of what is without name as the generic part of this historical existence: that is probably the revolutionary conception today, with the possibility that that sort of transformation would be a local one, and not always a general one or a total one. And, as you can see, it's not at all desire against law. The formula is generic will against normal desires.

(Alain Badiou)[1]

The psychological problem . . . is, how can he, who to an unheard of degree says No, does No to everything . . . can never theless be the opposite of a nay-saying spirit.

(Friedrich Nietzsche)[2]

The *Philosophy of Right* is a philosophy of freedom, but as freedom for Hegel can only be conceived of as freedom of the will, it is to the same degree a philosophy of the (free) will. In this first qualification one central component of Hegel's conception is already articulated: freedom is no accidental determination of the will that would be contingent or external to it. It is rather "its substance and its essence."[3] To draw nearer to the question of how the rabble-position relates to the 'atom' of the *Philosophy of Right* I will initially reconstruct the concept of free will that Hegel delineates and then determine whether or not the rabble can have a free will.

True freedom can only be as freedom of the will; true willing exists only as free. As Hegel formulates this in a nearly Kantian manner: "Will without freedom is an empty word, while freedom is actual only as will, as subject." Without subject, without will no freedom and without freedom the will is only an empty shell. This is why Hegel can come up with the infamous analogy that "freedom is just as fundamental a character of the will as weight is of bodies" (HOPR, 26). He wants to be clear here that freedom is not a contingent external quality of the will but its unique and essential quality. This analogy points to the fact that the body is just as little contingently heavy as the will is contingently free. In the realm of nature weight is the fundament, while the objective world is a "world of freedom" (HPRV, 42). But this also points to an essential difference: if a body has the property of being heavy in a way which it can neither be known to it nor willed by him, the will can and must know and will its own freedom. This means free will is only truly free will if it knows itself as free will and if it adjusts its willing to itself. This also means that man is not "on the one hand, thought and, on the other, will, and that he keeps thought in one pocket and will in another," since the will is itself "thinking translating itself into existence, thinking as the urge to give itself existence" (HOPR, 26). Because of this definition Hegel can claim that thought and will are both: immanently intertwined but at the same time different from one another—as the *unity of the difference* of practical and theoretical behavior. Between them there is a constant movement of mediation. Will and thought are aspects of the same that exist in a differential unity. The movement of this differential unity is elaborated by Hegel in three steps: initially Hegel determines the will in general (universality), then he determines the particular, the natural and reflected will (particularity), and finally he determines the will that is in and for itself free; the will that can be considered as a truly free will (singularity).

Initially will is "pure thought" (HPRV, 43) as it has the determination which it initially gives itself only as "something inward" (HOPR, 27), as idea. With this first delineation of the will Hegel has named an essential criterion with which to differentiate between man and animal: the animal, although also essentially practical, has no idea of that which it desires and wills to realize or satisfy. Imagination alone makes man human.[4] But it is necessary that this imagination is translated: from the interior to existence. Only in so doing can the will be in accordance with its own concept, because freedom is only freedom as realized freedom. But if will is initially interior then this disposition is linked to the capacity for abstraction: it can willingly set aside all particular determinations—of drives, desires, etc.—and know itself at this first stage as independent and abstractly free—as universality against these particularizations. The will can outpace all particularities and in a first step know and will his freedom completely independently of them. The will in its universal dimenson, as will tout court, appears as free due to this capacity. Freedom here means: freedom *from* all particular determination. In this way the will is a universality that has "extinguish[ed]" (HOPR, 29) all particularities. It is the "pure *thought* of oneself" (Ibid., 28). If thinking means "to generalize" (Ibid., 27) it is clear why the will is here pure thought. The will generalizes itself. He is able to engender a pure indeterminacy in itself and knows his freedom as something that can abstract from any concrete condition. But this "possibility to renounceof renouncing everything" (HVORL4, 112) is what makes human being human; a merely negative freedom—of understanding. The freedom to abstract from everything that is concrete is the possibility of being free, a freedom of (inner) imagination that is a long way from its own realization.

The will has to pass over from this absolute possibility of determination into the positing of determination; otherwise it remains in abstraction—also in abstraction from freedom. This particularization of the will makes it step into existence. This is possible only if it wills *something*. But why is this transition necessary? Because, Hegel answers, if it were to remain in abstraction from all particularities, knowing itself in pure self-relation, the will would encounter a contradiction: willing itself as universality without determinations this universality would itself become a mere particularity by becoming an (abstract) negation of determinations. A universality which is the negation of another— of determination for example—is not universality but a particularity. For as indeterminate it becomes the abstract contrary of determination and to that extent—since one can say that pure possibility is the contrary of reality—this indeterminacy is not universal but an (indeterminate) particular. In this way one gets two particularities: the determination and the indeterminacy but no universal. The universality of undeterminate freedom internally converts into the particularity of determination—of being completely abstract, of being the negation of determination, of being indeterminately determined. Abstract will only wills nothing but this nothing is itself only the negation of something. The volition of the absolute possibility that seems limitless confines the will to willing 'something' particular, i.e. the negation of something. Indeterminacy is not true freedom but limitation since it is only "one side of two" (HPRV, 45). "One tells a man—he should keep his will boundless, not will anything determinate . . . it is befitting—dissatisfaction—he should not will anything . . ." (HGPR, 53). The will willing nothing is no will anymore for Hegel. By surmounting this contradiction, the will reaches the second level at which it posits its determination. The determination of will thereby negates the first negation of all determinations and sublates it. The will arrives at the positing of a determination. The will that in the first stage only thought itself now gains a direction by willing "something—as mine" (Ibid., 53). It orients itself toward something and this leads it from its pure moving in itself to its particularization.

But this also contains a limitation. As pure negation introduced a limitation to the will, the pure affirmation of a particular determination does so, too, because the will loses itself in it. Therein the content of the determination can derive either from the nature of man, his drives, needs, preferences or "from the comcept of spirit, the right or the ethical" (HVORL4, 117). The positing is here not a heteronomous determination of will as it makes something 'his,' i.e. it freely posits a content as that which it wills. Man is for Hegel this contradiction of absolute indeterminacy and posited determination. The union of both aspects Hegel calls "particularity reflected into itself and so brought back to universality, i.e. it is *individuality*" (HOPR, 31). The will that knows itself as free in the concrete determination and nonetheless posits a determination sublates the one-sidedness of the first two stages and is the particularity as universality, the universality as particularity. Why this transition is necessary is obvious: if the will is limited in being absolute by indeterminacy and in being particular by determinacy it knows that these limitations do not correspond to his essence. If it wants to understand itself as free it enters into contradiction as long as it does not think both together but as merely coexisting.[5] It is important not to misperceive the interleaving of universality and particularity in the free will in a way that the universal dimension of freedom remains present such that the will could withdraw at any time from its particularization. Rather, Hegel enumerates different examples which clarify how the dialectical linkage of universality and particularity in the singularity of the will have to be conceived of. He calls love and friendship[6] paradigms of the individuality of the will. This marks that the will wants something other than him and is to this extent determined, at the same time it *is* in this determinate relation with itself and wills itself as free. This means that determination of the will is not only content-related but also form-related: 'something' has become an end of the will.

'End' then signifies primarily an inner determination of the will which can be conscious as easily as it can be unconscious. But this is initially a purely subjective end and it has to become objective and realized. Therefore in consequence the end leads to action but this action is subordinated to the laws of the objective world. To be a proprietor is initially a merely subjective end that should ultimately be realized. But the realization of this end and of one's own freedom as a person have to correspond with the objective possibilities of property. "We thus have a world, an object, a material in front of us in which we can perform our end . . ." (HVORL4, 123). In this way the end gains through its being performed a different, objective form. As merely internal the aim remains insufficient, and to sublate this lack the will enters into activity. In the realization of its aim the will constantly remains with itself since it is only active to realize *its* aim objectively. "When I am hungry my sensation is different from my will to be sated. Mine is now the activity, this device to sublate this lack and put my subjectivity in the form of objectivity." (HPRV, 46)

The determination of the end and its carrying out is here purely formal because this structure marks the foundational structure of the will and is in the beginning completely independent of terms of content. How does Hegel determine the contents of the will? Initially one can note that the end carried out does not lose anything in its being carried out; rather it is a necessary determination of the will which remains the same in its performance. In this way the "representationality of the will is itself determined" (HVORL4, 125). But also the content is immediately and naturally given to the will (free will in itself) and necessarily passes from the immediacy over to the mediation (free will for itself). Accordingly the free will in itself is a will which is determined by the immediacy of the natural—by "the impulses, desires, inclinations" (HOPR, 35).

On this stage the freedom of the will is always in danger of handing itself over to arbitrariness. As Hegel remarks: "Not all impulses are rational, but all rational determinations of the will also exist as impulses" (HVORL4, 128). That the will posits aims for itself, means that it posits and determines the drive—and this differentiates man from animal—as its drive. But this moment of the determination is one that necessarily surmounts the naturality of the impulse. For the determination of the drive by the will, in which its rationality and freedom lies, becomes necessary since any drive "exists alongside others which are likewise all 'mine', and each of which is at the same time something universal and indeterminate, aimed at all kinds of objects and satiable in all kinds of ways" (HOPR, 36). The will becomes resolving, deciding will by positing a content—of its satisfaction—in the undetermined universality as which the impulse appears and takes it as its aim. Therefore the contents of the will are in no way external. Although the will initially seems—as natural will—to be immediately bound to external contents—the will to be sated is immediately bound to a specific sensation—but the will gives these immediate sensations "the form of 'rationality'" and this means "giving them this form makes them finally 'mine' . . . ."[7] The resolving is a form of individuality since the will maintains itself in the decision—"the original seed of all determinate existence" (HOPR, 36)—and still determines itself. The will thereby becomes the will of a determinate individual. The 'I decide' signifies the formula of singularity: the will that decides and thereby refers to 'something' that is immanent to the decision. The will has made itself finite by moving from the mere possibility of determining itself to decision itself, but remains in mere formal freedom, since the content which it decides to take on does not come from itself but from nature.

Through this contradiction between free self-determination of the will and heteronomous natural content the will is driven into reflection: it can leave the heteronomous determination that it has taken up and take another. The will becomes by knowing about the possibility to free itself a "choosing will" (HVORL4, 130). That it can choose means that it posits not only a pre-given content as its own but furthermore is able to chose between the multiplicity of given contents of impulses. It decides itself in a twofold manner: 1. for an already given impulse and 2. for a possibility of its satisfaction which at the same time remains conditioned by the impulse itself. This is the *structure of choice*. In it the indeterminacy and determinacy of content coincide. Arbitrariness signifies "contingency as it is as will" (Ibid., 131). For, in it the will is unfree because it contains the formal freedom to abstract from any content and to chose any other, but its contents are still externally given. The will here is still dependent upon the givenness of the content—for example the food-impulse determines the content of its satisfaction. This way of givenness of the content does not correspond to the freedom of the will. It is free in its capacity to choose and it is unfree in its dependence on the contingently given content. Arbitrariness is therefore "rather the will as *contradiction*" (HVORL2, 142) since, in it, freedom and unfreedom merge. For this reason the will which can abstract from any content ultimately does not surmount the given and necessarily finite contents. "I do not surmount finitude even if I do not decide at all" (HVORL4, 132). For, as shown, the absolute abstraction from all determinations is only a one-sided determination of the freedom of the will—the internal limitation of indeterminacy. The mixture of freedom and unfreedom that is arbitrariness here mirrors in the nature of human beings, the drives. For the drives count on the one hand as positive since they lead immanently to ends, i.e. directions of the will, while on the other hand any single drive is negative, evil, since it is an exclusive unity which negates the other drives and in its unhindered effectivity finally has the negation of life as its consequence. Therewith the drives are driven out of the immanent contradiction and "the demand for the *purification* of impulses" (HOPR, 40) arises. This demand makes a whole out of the mutually exclusive drives by means of the idea of a reflected totalization[8] and produces the ideal of an all-around, harmonious satisfaction: the eudaimonic "ideal of bliss" (HVORL4, 135).

This ideal "in this external manner purifies it of its crudity and barbarity" by producing a universality in thinking which surpasses the logic of each single drive. But at the same time this thinking reflection in which lies "the absolute value in *education*" (HOPR, 41), i.e. the production of a universal, is in itself contradictory since it remains bound to the naturality of the drives—even if on a more universal level—and imagines a complete satsifaction of all of them. Beyond that there is no unifying principle of determination. In imagination the multiplicity of drives appears again in the universality that gets produced and this precisely in the idea of bliss: 1. it is conceived of as harmonic satisfaction in a way that still follows the model of the satisfaction of impulses and remains in too contingent a form, a form which depends upon external means for this satisfaction; 2. it cannot offer a universal principle of itself and remains constitutively in a merely particular form because in it 3. "there is still not present . . . any genuine unity of form and content" (Ibid.). The bliss unites two aspects: universality which shall be for me and the determination that universality is not empty or abstract. But it takes its determination solely from the drives.

Out of volatility the demand for a universality comes to light, a universality which would acquire the determination not out of something contingent but out of itself. Determination and universality shall no longer be in such a contradictory relationship but should proceed to a "*self-determining universality*" (Ibid.). In short: will and freedom and not bliss should become the end. This transition is inserted by the contradiction introduced by bliss itself. But how to answer to the demand that a universality is determined in a way that is appropriate to it? Hegel's answer is: by thought alone. "The self-consciousness which purifies its object, content, and aim, and raises them to this universality effects this as thinking *asserting* itself in the will. Here is the point at which it becomes clear that it is only as thinking intelligence that the will is genuinely a will and free." (Ibid., 42)

Hegel reaches the point at which he derives from the dialectical movement what he stated at the beginning: thought and will are the same in a number of different regards. The fact that the will now has split into two, relates back to itself and determines itself, Hegel calls the true will. It is divided from itself as the unity of the two. It is true since "concept and reality correspond." This means that the will determines itself in a way that the content of its volition is itself, "that is to say, freedom wills freedom" (Ibid.). The reality is the free will and the concept is the free will which relates itself to this reality. This "agreement" (HVORL4, 142) of reality and concept of the will is the truth of the will. The will has become its own object and also become actual.

It reaches freedom because it has entirely determined itself and has liberated the content and form of this determination from contingency. It is the unity in difference to itself. Therewith the will freely determines what it wills and this determination concerns universality itself: the free will wills itself in the form of freedom. "This idea has to be kept and the whole of science and the ethical life consist therein to realize it . . . This idea may seem vague, i.e. we do not have an image of it, no example, no possible cases, we can, as one says, not think of anything" (HPRV, 54).

The free will has become its own end which Hegel also calls the 'with itself'[9] of the will. In this reflexivity of the will having become its own object the will at the same time has its true reality, since he passed over to determination and remains neither in the mere possibility of determination nor in an external determination, in this return to itself, it does not stand against something foreign to it, to a limit that would make it finite. The will has stepped out of the limitations and has become "the *infinite in actuality* (*infinitum actu*), because . . . its objective externality is inwardness itself" (HOPR, 42). The idea which can be gained from this infinite-actual are presented by the different stages of the *Philosophy of Right*: abstract right, morality, ethicality. On all stages what is dealt with is the actual infinity of the free will which wills itself as free.

Why can Hegel say that the will is universal despite the fact that it appears as determined? He initially excludes different notions of universality which do not concern will at this stage: 1. the communality which starts from common determinations; 2. the "*all-ness*" (Ibid., 43) which presents the whole of all determinations; 3. the abstract universality "like blue which does not exist as such" (HVORL4, 142) but only as the color of an object. Beyond these three concepts of universality he aims at showing that the free will having become its own object marks a "universality concrete in character": "the concept of the free will — is the universal which embraces its object, thoroughly permeates its determination and therein remains identical with itself" (HOPR, 44).[10] Hegel defines the side of the reality of the will as the side of the subjective will and the other as the concept of the will. Therewith it is imperative to recall that both sides are in an identity of difference.

Here the will again—on the subjective and objective sides—disintegrates into the already derived determinations. The subjective will is 1. the certainty of itself as free will and that is as self-consciousness,[11] as Hegel also claims, which is expressed by the equation "I = I" (HOPR, 44); subjectivity as self-certainty; 2. the particular will as arbitrariness from which the possibility of evil also appears; subjectivity as particularity; 3. the one-sided form since the determination of an end of the will in itself has a merely internal and not an objective form; subjectivity as an end which is not carried out. Objective will, the concept of will, disintegrates into: 1. the absolutely objective will, which is the true will; 2. the objective will which is finite because it lacks the distance to its object and thereby lacks the subjective form. It is in "the will absorbed in its object or condition . . . the will of the child, the ethical will and also the will of the slave, the superstitious person" (HOPR, 44)[12]; 3. the objectivity as one-sided form as opposed to the subjectivity that signifies the immediacy of external existence. After this tour de force through the Hegelian logic of will it is now necessary to investigate the extent to which the famous but also "cryptic formula"[13] which delineates Hegel's definition of the free will in and for itself, the truly infinite will—"*the free will which wills the free will*" (HOPR, 46)—is suspended by the rabble. I have demonstrated that in the rabble-attitude a dissolving continues to write itself which makes all determinations of existence disappear. Can one here claim that the rabble wills the nothing? Is the rabble a merely abstract will? Possibly the most famous historical figure of such an abstract will which Hegel discusses is situated by him in the French Revolution. It is therefore instructive to examine Hegel's description.

Excursus: Hegel's Criticism of the French Revolution

The French Revolution marks for Hegel the historical index of the world-historical event in which "man's existence centres in his head, i.e. in Thought, inspired by which he builds up the world of reality" (HPH, 447). This event acquires world-historical relevance because in it "for the first time real existence and validity had been conferred on abstract right."[14] But this abstractness which receives historical validity in the French Revolution is the reason for its fatality. For in it a will that is directed against everything that exists expresses itself and not only proves to be capable of abandoning all concrete determinations—this makes it evental—but therein also proves to be destructive, fanatical. If the French Revolution for Hegel is a revolution of the free will, since it historically proves one of the constitutive dimensions of its own freedom, the abstraction from all concrete determinations also marks a peculiar lack that infects it and is still present in the deduction of the free will in the *Philosophy of Right*.[15] For the negation of all determinations creates an internally limited position which is not able to produce any "firm organization" (HPH, 369)—asserting abstractions in reality means to destroy reality. Any concrete determination, any concrete organization has by definition to fall short of the demand of abstract freedom and has to appear to the will as mere semblance. For "when distinctions appear, it finds them antagonistic to its own indeterminacy and annuls them" (HOPR, 30). Thereby free will remains in a "fetishistic circle of self-reifying negation"[16] which is capable of beholding a misconduct in any attempt at concrete determination. This limitation of abstract freedom can only externally recognize in any determination its own limitation. All concretion falls short of it and any conviction which attempts to give an objective face to freedom is suspicious. "It is the essence of fanaticism to bear only a desolating destructive relation to the concrete" (HPH, 358) because the only interior and pure possibility of freedom has no objective criteria of evaluation. Rather the conviction and attitude can only be judged by attitude and conviction and therefore "suspicion reigns" (Ibid., 450).

For without objective criteria with which the subject can judge subjective attitudes and since attitudes are only internal, suspicion arises that the attitude might not correspond with the purity of freedom. The capacity of the will to abstract from everything, which historically appears for the first time with the French Revolution, is not only directed against objective impurities which necessarily in any attempt to determine freedom, but also against the subjective impurities of which the abstract free will cannot know anything. It has to constantly doubt whether its purity might have been infected with seeds of impurity. For Hegel the will of the French Revolution is a pure will which, to sustain purity, has to evacuate all—objective or subjective— contaminations. This is why this will has a *destructive character*. This is why "the law of suspects . . . for Hegel [is] not a distortion or a contingent deviation from the revolution but its essential outcome and finds its perfect corollary in the mass-production of the corpse—the theoretical sniffing out of alterity here implying its practical sniffing out in the will's own cycle of tautological self-affirmation."[17]

The French Revolution offers the historical paradigm of a will that does not want to know anything but itself. The abstraction that it is defined by can therefore lead only into terror which considers any realization as betrayal. This is the definition of fanaticism, for "fanaticism is just the refusal to give scope to particular differences" (HOPR, 255). Pure freedom of the will, such a "freedom of the void" (Ibid., 29) which leads to a fanaticism of freedom is therefore the philosophical explanation of revolutionary violence. Pure freedom is always pure terror for Hegel: "a fury of destruction" (Ibid.) as a paranoid will which sustains its one purity against any concretion; a destruction of all determinations and relations with the aim of maintaining the absolute possibility of freedom; a pure ascetic will. As Badiou has remarked, Hegel's thesis is unambiguous:

> the Revolution presents the subjective figure of absolute freedom . . . In these conditions what is the only certainty? Nothingness. Only the nothing is not suspect . . . The logic of purification, as Hegel astutely remarks amounts to bringing about the nothing. Ultimately death is the sole possible name of pure freedom, and "dying well" the only thing that escapes suspicion. The maxim . . . is that . . . it is impossible to seem to die.[18]

The will which appears in the Revolution is a nihilistic will since it wills the Nothing.[19] But at the same time it is important that the historical appearance of the pure freedom of the will cannot be reduced to a mere contingency. Rather its appearance will have been historically necessary because: 1. it poses in a radical way the question of the political realization of freedom—a problem which it is not able to resolve[20]; 2. it conceives of this question in terms of the will's self-determination—which is the decisive principle for the Hegelian definition of the state; 3. history is for Hegel itself the ground on which the idea has to realize itself—the French Revolution is a *historical sign* for an essential aspect of the will and freedom. For the revolution clarifies that freedom is a universal right of all men and does not respect ancestry or class. This is its world-historical importance. So the "abstract right gains it logical force and its ontological status from the facts that it abstracts away from all that has merely come to be historical . . ."[21] The French Revolution marks the historical genesis of a principle of trans-historical validity: the radical and complete(ly) (abstract) character of the freedom of the will.

Now, can one conclude from what has been said so far that the rabble has a free will? Starting from the assumption that it has one, one can situate more precisely which type it would be: the will of the rabble cannot be a will that simply does not will anything anymore or that wills the nothing as such, since the rabble does not take the position of a complete negation of existing right, but the position that undermines this distinction, the position of *un-right*. The claim that is proper to its will is not completely abstract but rather quite concrete. The rabble demands the guarantee of subsistence while ignoring all attributes and properties: an *un-right* of equality for anyone and of justice for anyone. The loutish insistence on the assurance of its own subsistence marks a concrete demand which only abstracts all determination when it comes to the question for whom this *un-right* is valid. This means that it abstracts from everything concrete since its will refers to a right which befits anyone. The loutish insistence on the assurance of its own subsistence marks a concrete demand which only abstracts away all determination when it comes to the question for whom this *un-right* is valid. This means that it abstracts from everything concrete since its will refers to a right which befits anyone.

The will of the rabble is on one side different from the subjective will of the French Revolution since it does not consider any concretion as a failure and therefore persist in the pure possibility, but rather introduces a concrete demand. But it is on the other side similar to it, since the rabble-will is also marked by a radical ignorance of concrete determinations. But this abstraction only concerns the bearer, the subject of the *un-right* that it claims. The claim of the *un-right* is a concrete demand for subsistence for an association of indeterminately anyone. Such a demand does not end up in contradictions when realized, i.e. in the process of its universalization. Rather the demand of this *un-right* is realizable without limitations. The rabble can no longer have a free will which out of free self-determination abstracts from all concretions of the will. Rather it is initially marked by a fundamental passivity that remains inscribed in its position due to the material condition of possibility for its emergence, i.e. poverty. The will of the rabble cannot be a free will because it is always already determined by an impossibility of acting which is present in poverty. The rabble is primarily a figure of passivity.

This means that one can note a first aspect of the will of the rabble: its will is separated from the concept of freedom. It is always already determined by the necessarily present objective, material condition of his emergence. This is why it does not accord with the concept with which Hegel begins his *Philosophy of Right*. The will of the rabble resembles, due to its passivity, more a willing than a will.[22] The rabble does not will freely, not self-determinately. Rather it wills due to an objective impossibility subjectively something impossible; it wills an *un-right* of equality which expresses a completely concrete demand as well as introducing a completely indeterminate, attributeless bearer of of this *un-right*. One can say that such a willing enables us to think a concept of freedom which always and necessarily stands under the conditions of its material genesis. If one can speak of freedom at all then this freedom is a freedom to will the impossible; a freedom with conditions[23]; a freedom which is at the same time no longer the central element of the will.

But how to conceive of the combination of concrete demand and the indeterminate subject of this demand? The *un-right* which the rabble claims is first an *un-right* of the guarantee of one's own subsistence. The *un-right which* the rabble wills is directed to a subsistence without determinations and due to this indeterminacy the *un-right* is *hic et nunc* universal. It includes—without exception—anyone because the rabble is only directed toward itself in its willing of the *un-right*. But he is due to the *logic of double latency* and due to his indeterminacy no merely particular figure. By claiming its own subsistence as its right and willing such an *un-right*, this willing of its own subsistence reverses internally to become the willing of the subsistence of all. This means: 1. that the willing of the rabble is directed toward something concrete (its own subsistence) which 2. in its particularity and concretion is not merely particular but due to its indeterminacy universal. The rabble does not will the nothing as abstraction from all determinations but it wills itself and it has no determinations. One can emphasize here that the rabble wills itself as Nothing; it wills itself and in so far as it has no determinations—it is Nothing. The rabble willing itself as Nothing does not will an internally limited and abstract, empty freedom but rather it wills the perpetuation of its own willing and this willing is universal. The rabble wills itself as Nothing and relates to anyone in so doing.[24] The rabble-willing is not internally marked by any limitation resulting from abstraction and it has its foundation not in a free self-determination of the will. It is rather fundamentally determined by an impossibility from and at which it appears, which it transforms into a impossible demand, into an *un-right* of equality.

From the previous remarks there results the following *five fundamental characteristics of the willing of the rabble*: 1. the willing of the rabble does not decide anything, it does not resolve anything, it does not judge. This is why the rabble has a willing rather than a will. The *un-right* that it claims implies no judgment, no decision with regard to those for whom it is valid. 2. The willing of the rabble is and remains determined from the place where it can emerge. It is precisely in this sense not free. Rather the concept of freedom introduced by the rabble is the freedom of the impossible demand of the *un-right* of equality which always already is determined by its material, objective condition. The willing of the rabble does not correspond to the Hegelian will. 3. It wills nothing possible. Rather it is directed onto something that seems impossible and remains impossible for Hegel. But this impossibility is not an impossibility of abstraction but the rabble-willing is due its material localization and determinateness a willing of a completely concrete, determinate impossible, of a point of impossibility (of the Hegelian state). 4. The rabble-willing is directed to something concrete—onto itself—but this particular is due to its indeterminacy reversed to become a universal. The impossibility which the rabble wills by claiming his own subsistence as *un-right* is not limited to itself. Rather, due to the *logic of double latency* its indeterminacy is the reason why the rabble in its willing is directed onto an equality of anyone with anyone which does not know any limitation—not even the limitation of existence. 5. The willing of the rabble is therefore linked to what Hegel calls indignation. Willing and indignation are necessarily linked such that the rabble is indignantly willing—willing the abolition of the condition of possibility of its own emergence. Thus the willing of the rabble is not a universal capacity, rather it occurs locally—in the poor—and will only as such a local willing have been universally implied. If one can say for Hegel that the concept of free will determines the ethical community, the state and finally politics, it becomes clear that the willing of the rabble implies a different politics, a different form of equality and community.

This politics can first not be a politics which begins from a linkage of will and freedom. Rather in it, equality and not freedom is primary. This is to say secondly that this politics cannot be thought of as a politics of the realization of the possible. Its insignia is the birth in and from an impossibility. This means thirdly that this different politics has to be as much a politics of universality as is the Hegelian politics. But at the same time the question arises as to whether it can still be a politics of statist unity? Can one think a rabble-politics of equality—without the state? This question must lead into a fundamental definition of the Hegelian state: the state prevents the emergence of pure multiplicity.

Chapter 12

The Sole Aim of the State and the Rabble as Un-Organic Ensemble

The State is not founded upon the social bond, which it would express, but rather upon un-binding, which it prohibits. *Or, to be more precise, the separation of the State is less a result of the consistency of presentation than of the danger of inconsistency.*

(Alain Badiou)[1]

In the *Encyclopedia*, a passage can be found, which defines the task of the state in a way that is unique in Hegel's writings:

The aggregate of private persons is often called the *people*; but as such an aggregate it is *vulgus*, not *populus*; and in this regard it is the sole aim of the state that a people should *not* come into existence, to power and action *as such an aggregate*. Such a condition of lawlessness, ethical impoverishment, of general irrationality: in this condition the people would be only a shapeless, wild, blind force, like that of the stormy elemental sea, which does not, however, destroy itself, as the people—as spiritual element—would do. (HPM, 243)

Hegel makes one insight absolutely clear. The state founds the unity which makes a people into a people, i.e. it can bring it to appear as an organic unity. If this unity, which the state has due to its organic structuring—that refers to the organic structuring of the concept itself—and which is guaranteed through the unity of the person of the monarch, is lost, then nothing remains but a completely unbound people, a *vulgus*, that which the rabble everywhere brings to light, as possibility, as the matter of the ethical space (in and for itself). The people as *vulgus* presents a merely aggregated, unstructured connection, the unorganic, unethical and irrational mass which is necessarily driven to self-destruction. Or put differently: for Hegel *vulgus* is a multiplicity without unity which is always already violent and merely particular. Therefore the organic, which is to say, unifying structuring of the state has to prevent "the appearance of a *mass* [*Menge*] or an *aggregate* and so from acquiring an unorganized opinion and volition and from crystallizing into a powerful bloc in opposition to the organized state" (HOPR, 290).[2] The people unbound from statist unity is a mere unstructured mass whose mass-likeness gives the reason that it decays into a mere aggregate of particularities. Therefore Hegel can claim that this is a mistaken concept of people because "if one rationally speaks of the people, it is essentially at the same time a state . . . the people without state deserves no respect . . ." (HVORL4, 676).

For one can not have a unified and organic concept of something which does not know a unity and organic structuring. Thereby one would only reach the idea of a mass or an aggregate but "the concept has nothing to do with any aggregate" (HOPR, 262). The Hegelian state ensures the unity of the organized multiplicity (of the free will). Therefore in it "no one of its moments should appear as an unorganized aggregate [Menge]. The *many*, as individuals . . . are of course something connected, but they are connected only as an *aggregate*, a formless mass whose commotion and activity can therefore only be elementary, irrational, wild, and frightful" (Ibid., 291). This passage is instructive since it connects different determinations. If there is a moment that is inorganic, it is an inorganic aggregate which has mass but not form(ation). Such an unstructured, inorganic set of the many is a mere aggregate which seems to have no determination, not even that of a form. It is a formless mass which introduces a pure unsubstantial togetherness of the many who lack the unifying structuring. The commotion of this mere set of the many is wild, elementary, irrational, horrible. The investigation of the rabble as *organ without body* has led us into a discussion of the movement of the rabble which resonates here. The movement of the inorganic set of the many is wild and irrational, since it does not go in one direction but is multidirectional: in a literal sense, explosive. It is elementary and frightful, since it does not know any stopping point, appears everywhere and perpetuates itself eternally.

One can note: a multiplicity which is without unity and appears as an inorganic set of the many is for Hegel chaotic, elementary, unorganized, and ultimately irrational.[3] But as has become clear the rabble is 1. unbound from the organic structures of the state and 2. even from its own proper appearing. The rabble would in this sense be a formless mass, a mere agglomeration, an unorganized set of the many, the *vulgus*. The rabble would as such a *vulgus* be as much included in the state as excluded from it. But here one can, albeit in a way that is perhaps forced, ask the question: Which elements does this set of the formless mass contain? Hegel here uses the notion of the "Menge" synonymously with the notion of "mass" but an interesting perspective results if one takes one connotation of it—namely the mathematical connotation of "set"—and uses it as a starting point. If the rabble is on one side the matter of the ethical space, the matter in and for itself, can this matter without form, without determination, be understood as a set, as multiplicity without unity? Can such a pure multiplicity without unity be thought at all? It is instructive to undertake here a short excursus through the mathematical theory of sets[4] in order to achieve a different perspective on how to understand the inorganic set of the many. The question I shall thus attempt to answer is: Which elements does the rabble-set have? A reply to this question promises to let us conceive more precisely just why the rabble is a problem in the Hegelian state.[5]

Excursus: Intensional and Extensional Concepts of Sets

Around 60 years after the publication of Hegel's *Philosophy of Right*, the *Contributions to the Foundation of the Theory of Transfinite Numbers* were published by Georg Cantor. In them one finds a first definition—founding naïve set theory—of what a set is: "By set what is understood is the grouping into a totality [S] of quite distinct objects [s] of our intuition or our thought [which are called the *elements* of S]."[6] The remarkable thing in this definition is that Cantor leaves open the question of whether the grouping of objects works due to a common property, a concept encompassing all objects, or if the grouping is a result which does not assign a common attribute. This means that Cantor does not respond to the question of whether the grouping is a grouping of states, citizen, all natural numbers etc. or if it is conceived in the same way as the grouping of all the things that right now lie on a random desk or are trawled by a fishing net.[7] The distinction between these two types of grouping is articulated in Bertrand Russell as the difference between intensional and extensional concepts of the set.[8] While the intensional conception of what a set is—whose representatives were initially Frege and Russell—presuppose the primacy of the concept with regard to its application to given objects, the extensional understanding proceeds in the reverse order: "a set is simply a result, the result of collecting together a certain bundle of elements."[9] Against this background it is not difficult to conceive of Hegel's critique of the set as a mere agglomeration of the many as a criticism of the *extensional* conception of sets. A set which one calls a people as a merely aggregative grouping is for Hegel irrational, inorganic, vulgar—*vulgus* and not *populus*. The *populus* by contrast represents for Hegel a uniform grouping due to a property assignable to all. Thereby for the people in the state it is at least valid to think of it as constituting a unity if one presupposes one common property belonging to all of the elements of the contained multiplicity—the free will. The Hegelian people are an intensional and not an extensional set. The extensional set names rather the threat of disintegration of the state in the inorganic and merely mass-like togetherness of the many.

But the debate around the—intensional or extensional—definition of the concept of sets is not only a mathematical game. Rather as a consequence of it, an influential problem occurred for the intensional definition of sets, which became known as the 'Russellian antinomy.' Frege is the first to define unambiguously a set as unity of all object to which a specific property can be assigned[10]—formalizable as, for example, $\lambda(\alpha)$, whereby λ would name the property and α the multiplicity or objects which share the same property. With this it is possible to 1. comprehend the notion of property in an absolutely formal way and 2. conceive of it with regard to a free variable which is determined from it as the sole constant.[11] This means that any object, any term which has a certain property—for which the proposition that the term α has the property λ is true—belongs as an element to the set of terms which have this property. But—and here the problem begins—this assumption presupposes that 1. there are objects, terms which can be grouped due to a property they have in common and 2. that properties have to be unambiguously assignable so that it is never a question whether they befit the terms or not. As innocent as these two presuppositions might seem, they produce the starting point of a fundamental mathematical problematization of the intensional concept of sets.

In 1901 Russell formulates a paradox which begins from these two premises and remains insoluble for the representatives of the intensional determination of sets. If one assumes that a set is constituted intensionally, then one can distinguish between sets that belong to themselves and those that do not. This distinction does not contradict either of the two premises. But in consequence this means that some sets are self-belonging—the set of all collections of books is itself a collection of books—and some are not—the set of all women is itself not a woman. Russell's paradox now poses the question as to whether the set of all sets belongs to itself.[12] What follows from this construction is that no direct answer can be given, since both answers seem to be equally valid and—worse—one answer necessarily implies the other. The paradox leads to the equivalence of a proposition and its negation: the set of all sets belongs to itself and does not belong to itself.[13] Cantor describes the consequence of the paradox as follows: "[O]n the one hand a multiplicity can be such that the assumption that *all* of its elements 'are together' leads to a contradiction, so that it is impossible to conceive of the multiplicity as a unity, as 'one finished thing'. Such multiplicities I call *absolutely infinite* or *inconsistent multiplicities*."[14]

With the definition of an inconsistent multiplicity Cantor implies not a possible unity of opposites in the way that the inconsistent multiplicity could be unified by its irregularity. He rather insists, as one can claim with Badiou, "that the multiple . . . be delivered *without concept*" (BBE, 43). A set in the extensional understanding does not know any predetermined conditions of belonging. With this definition Cantor already implies some characteristics which the historical development of set theory will realize theoretically: 1. that it is possible to think a concept of multiplicity which cannot be grouped under any property and which even suspends the fundamental form of qualitative predetermined unity; 2. that 'something' is no longer collected into a unity, but rather that there is no way to distinguish between what is an already existing unity and what is not. So Cantor implies that a multiplicity can be thought as a pure multiplicity, i.e. as a multiplicity of multiplicities; 3. this to-be-collected-into-a-unity does not mean that the multiplicity, that is an element of the unity, i.e. of the set, itself has any essential attribute. Rather the collection into a set works solely according to the mere relation of belonging to this set, i.e. following an operation of collection which 'externally' happens to the elements—for example to the fishes in a fishing net. What is important here for our purposes is that this threefold implication means that set theory—in its consequences— can no longer distinguish between objects, groups of objects, or even between elements and sets.[15] For the extensional conception of sets leads to the fact that one has to think the supposed unity which becomes an element of the set itself as an extensional set.

Thus any multiplicity collected in the form of a unity is itself nothing but a multiplicity. The determination 'to be an element of something' is not a quality, not a determination of being anymore, but rather founds itself on the contingent operation which collects the elements together to form a set. This determination names a relation through which 'something' (the element) is collected by 'something else' (the set whose element it is) and presented as its element. This means that that which is presented as an element of a set does not distinguish itself by any immanent determination, any intrinsic predi- cate from something else. The differentiation is an effect created by the col- lection alone—for example the books which lie on a desk are different from those that are not lying on it *only due to the fact that* they are lying on the desk. Ultimately this means that the extensional conception of sets does not presup- pose the existence of qualitatively determined objects. Rather an existence is exclusively implied in a way that one can deduce from the already existing elements that which will have existed contingently before the collection of ele- ments into a set—the fish in the fishing net are part of the set of the fish in the sea whose existence one can only deduce from the fish caught in the net, since it is necessarily implied but not presupposed.

The intensional conception of sets presumes *that* something, objects exist, and some of them have a certain property such that they can become the ele- ment of a set; the extensional conception abandons this assumption of exist- ence. It rather begins with a (existentially) undetermined assumption: *if* there is something, i.e. *if* objects (fish in the sea) exist, then there also exists a set of object to which a certain property can be assigned (caught by fishermen) and that therefore can become an element of a set (the set of fish in the net). With this indeterminacy, existence is no longer presupposed. Rather it is implied that if the existence of something is given, then at the same time the existence of something else is implied, the existence of a part, which can be assigned a particular determination.[16] One does not take the assumed existence of the fish in the sea to be indicative of the fish in the net, that all have the qualitative determination of being caught, but the fish in the net are indicative of the implied existence of the set of fish in the sea. This is also to say that one can only retroactively say something about that which lies before the collection into a set. Only when there is a part for which a determination is correctly applied and which is therefore collected into a set, can one say something about what logically lies 'before' this collection. Otherwise one cannot say anything about this 'before'—not even that it exists. This also means that there is and has to be always 'something' which does not fully coincide with the collection into a set, i.e. whose existence one can only retroactively conclude, as it is implied. Otherwise there would only be intensionally constituted sets.

As a consequence, there has to be 'something' that marks the collection of elements into a set as an operation. If the collection collects certain things together as elements of a set, then this 'something' that became an element implies the existence of 'something' which can only be thought retroactively as that which lies 'before' this collection. This does not describe a "logic of a lacuna," i.e. something which would have been "forgotten" (BBE, 54) by the collecting operation. Rather there are only collections in the form of sets. But nevertheless, something is collected which will have been 'before' the collection and at the same time can only be made accessible by and from it. But if, as set theory shows, all internal qualities which the intensional conception presupposes are subtracted, the sole determination that is left is that of the multiplicity. If set theory thus presents pure multiplicities, multiples of multiples, then the question necessarily arises as to *what* set theory collects into such a multiplicity; *what* will have lain 'before' the collection into a pure multiplicity. This leads to the fact that even this last determination has to be subtracted since that which lies before multiplicity cannot *be* a multiplicity: one needs to think a multiplicity which is not a multiplicity (as there are only multiplicities). Set theory solves this problem with the introduction of an axiom: that of the empty set.

This axiom is the only axiom of set theory that claims an existence: the existence of the void. That which will have lain 'before' the pure multiplicity and which is only presentable *within* it in the form of a name. For the void of the empty set is inserted as a name which claims the existence of that which is not presentable, even after the subtraction of all possible determination, even of multiplicity. To clarify, one can reconstruct the path from the intensional to the extensional conception as follows: if intensional sets collect their elements due to shared properties, the extensional conception subtracts these properties and claims the existence of neither properties nor given objects. It only presupposes that everything which appears in a set in the form of an element is itself a set and therefore consists of something else, i.e. the set is a multiplicity of multiplicities. In this sense a clear definition of what a set is is impossible since a set does not have any distinctive criteria. If for example one can decompose the set of the books on the desk into its elements, which makes each of them into a book and one can continue with this infinitely, then it becomes clear that any element of a set is again composed of elements and the same will go for any element. But what is the multiplicity of multiplicities which results from this infinite decomposition ultimately composed of? What is the pure multiplicity which results from this process of decomposition made out of?

Here the axiom of the empty set enters. It states that there is a set which does not have any elements. The decisive import of this axiom was formulated by Badiou: "there exists that to which no existence can be said to belong" (BBE, 67). Set theory thus prescribes the existence of something that does not have any criterion of existence, since nothing belongs to it as an element. This makes it clear that the concept of existence which the extensional conception implies depends on the concept of belonging. A set to which elements belong exists, since it is determined by the elements that belong to it. Sets are only specified by the elements which belong to them. Therefore one can conclude that the empty set does not have any determination of existence, since it has no elements. This is why the existence of the empty set 1. is introduced axiomatically, for its existence cannot be otherwise assigned and 2. its existence is postulated by a pure act of naming. If the empty set cannot be determined by its elements, that which it collects is nothing but a pure name (the void, existence without existence). The axiom does not say anything about the empty set; it only posits its name as the name of an existence without existence.[17] This is important: because the multiplicity in its pure form is composed of something which logically will have lain 'before' it and this 'before,' due to the axiomatic positing of set theory, is delineated as an empty set, the empty set is a part of any set.[18] This does not mean that the void appears as an element in any set. Rather the void is that with which one necessarily ends up with if one continues the decomposition of multiplicities. The void is therefore that which in the last instance the elements of the elements of a set are composed of. It is in this sense omnipresent, not having a fixed position, included in all sets as a part. One can also say: since any set α is composed of 'something' that it collects (β) and this element is also composed of something (γ) then there is a limit to what can be presented as an element in α, but which nonetheless is a part of it by being an element of β. Something can be an element of β and not an element of α. The empty set is part of any set because the multiplicity of multiplicities is composed only of it. It is universally included.[19]

What role do these remarks play for the question discussed here? A result of this historical excursus offers a different perspective on Hegel's critique of the inorganic and irrational aggregate of the many as a mere mass or set. One can read Hegel criticism of such a *vulgus* as criticism of the people as an extensional set. The people as extensional set is no longer structured as a unity derived from a common quality or property. Rather such a vulgar determination of the concept of the people for Hegel cannot display any substantial bond, consistency or stability between its members. If one does read the

Hegelian critique in this way one can see precisely which threat Hegel wishes to confront:

1. Due to the *logic of double latency*—anyone is latently rabble. The rabble refers to the fact that the state itself is composed out of the rabble which is implicitly everywhere, which logically will have been 'before' the organic unity, although this 'before'—as the peculiar 'place' of the matter of ethical space—can be thought only retroactively after the formation of the state. The rabble therefore marks the irruption of the ethical matter in and for itself which is without common or given qualities. The rabble—as the *un-right* of equality clarified—marks the consistent primacy of equality over freedom.

2. The determination of the rabble as *organ without body*—separation from the organic unity within this unity; subtraction of all determinations—refers to the fact that the rabble does not exist. It names a set which in an irrational and inorganic way presents a merely abstract ensemble of the many, which, negating the organic unity, stands against the state. It is a set which has no determination of existence, i.e. no element. The rabble is a set without element and therefore universally implied. This is why one can claim that the rabble takes a similar position in Hegel's *Philosophy of Right* as the empty set in the post-Cantorian set theory. The rabble also has no determinations of existence as it emerges after the process of putrefaction of the poor and at the same time, as complete in-existence, it refers to anyone in the state. The rabble is a set without elements which therefore is a part of all elements. Hegel's critique of the *vulgus* can be read as critique of the rabble that at the same time does not capture its true nature. For Hegel an understanding of the people as a mere mass-like togetherness of the many is internally reversed so as to become a regime of violence and opinion, since in it any particular individual would posit itself as universal. Any such particularity would stand as universal and such a state of nature comprised of particularities would necessarily end in a cataclysm of violence. But Hegel's critique of the *vulgus* can at the same time not be a critique of the rabble.

For the rabble as in-existence, which lack all determinations, rather marks the emergence of something that generates the insight into the matter of the ethical space. The emergence of the rabble as *organ without body* is the irruption of the void, of something which has no determination, into the intensionally conceived unity of the organically structured state. On one hand one can only confirm Hegel's critique of the rabble as *vulgus*. For such an extensionally constituted set is incapable of reaching a substantial, organic unity. Rather it is only constituted by a contingent operation. However, Hegel's criticism also misses something since he draws from this the conclusion that such a collection is necessarily irrational since it would conceive of the state as a mere aggregate of ultimately qualityless multiplicities.[20] The Hegelian rabble-critique is a critique of the effect which is linked to the insight of the matter of the ethical space, decomposing the state. Even the Hegelian state perpetuates itself through a prohibition of unbinding the organically structured unity into the equality of anyone. The rabble emerges as *organ without body* in the organic structuring of the state and appears within it—and for Hegel—only as the negation of all determinations, as insisting inexistence, as void. But can one claim here that the rabble is in a certain sense nothing more than a mere name, just like the void, the empty set such that Hegel cannot do more with regard to the rabble than just posit his existence, his name? I have already shown that Hegel cannot know if the rabble is present or not, if it ever will be present. For it has no external determination of existence. Is the rabble the void of the Hegelian *Philosophy of Right* which is nothing but a name? To answer these questions a short detour through the *Encyclopedia* and Hegel's theory of names is essential.

Frank Schalow has indicated that in Hegel "[l]anguage ceases to be a system of signs to be employed by thinking as a mere tool. [. . .] Rather, language emerges as having vitality and power of its own right."[21] I will limit myself here to a short reconstruction of Hegel's theory.[22] One also should recall that the name also serves an important function in the *Philosophy of Right*. It is the name of the monarch, the absolutely arbitrary connection of the contingent proper name of an individual with the multiplicity of the free wills and the ethical institutions which creates and maintains the organic unity of the state. The name functions in this determination in ethicality as the symbolic unity of the state which allows for the potential infinity of the different free wills to conceive of themselves as being unified because in any act of the monarch—in the empty 'I will'—the totality of the specified and different acts of the will of all are both, concretely—in an individual, i.e. a will—and universal—the 'I will' being the universal form of the resolving will which can be assigned to all of them—is present.[23] The name of the monarch is a pure name which however can create and maintain the statist unity only due a common determination— the free will. Against this background it is possible to reconstruct Hegel's definition of the name:

In the *Encyclopedia* one can find the Hegelian theory of the name as an element of the theory of signs, in the second part of the psychology, in the chapter on representation.[24] The chapter marks the transition from intuition to thinking; it marks the process of becoming-subject which begins from an externally found and in this way abstractly, sensually inflicted content and proceeds to internalize and universalize it. In this process, as Derrida remarked, "the sign is understood according to the structure and movement of the *Aufhebung* by means of which the spirit . . . accomplishing itself as internal freedom, and thereby presenting itself to itself for itself, *as such*."[25] Hegel proceeds in three steps. Initially, recollection, with which he begins here, lifts an intuition "out of the *particularity* of space and time" (HPM, 186) into the universality of space and time, i.e. in the inner time and the inner space of the subject. In this way the intuition as an initially contingent moment can at any time be recalled by the subject and is subordinated to his free access. Thereby it becomes the "product of intelligence,"[26] because the content of this intuition is "posited as *mine*" (HPM, 185). To use a word of the early Hegel: in this way "the spirit steps out of himself and looks at *his* intuition, i.e. the object as *his . . . the image.*"[27] The intelligence has the free disposal of intuition and can arbitrarily recall it, decompose it into its components and subsequently re-compose it in new ways.

All of these processes are operations of the imagination and lead step by step to the genesis of what Hegel calls a symbol. The intuition is in the beginning internalized by the subject and can then be recalled. Imagination is not only able to reproduce but also to edit it. Initially there is still a similarity between the produced intuition and the employed material of this intuition. It already gives testimony to a creative editing of the material of intuition but it still remains determined by this material. This is the contradiction of the symbol. For it is for Hegel still afflicted with sensual intuition so that it can only produce a universal as a *"particular* aspect of the object raised to the *form* of *universality"*—from the red rose is derived the color red—or as *"concrete universal"* (HPM, 191), for example as genus—from the red rose is derived the plant. The symbol is nothing but the particularity that is only a formal universality because it constantly lacks the universal content. The intuition is particular because it is constantly limited to the particular spatial and temporal conditions of *this* intuition. The symbol is a universal form with particular content. True universality comes into relation with intuition only when imagination becomes *"intuition*-producing . . . *sign making fantasy"* (Ibid., 192). This means that only when any similarity between the universal and the intuition which it presents is abolished, can one speak with Hegel of a true universality:

> Now the universal representation, liberated from the content of the image, makes itself into something intuitable in an external material *willfully* chosen by itself, and thus produces what has to be called, a *sign*. The sign must be proclaimed a great accomplishment . . . The willfulness emerging here . . . must first be learned. (HPM, 193–4)

To learn the meaning of signs and the possibility of reproducing this meaning affords memory. For the sign introduces a completely arbitrary relation between itself and its meaning: "the absence of any natural relation of resemblance, participation or analogy between the signified and the signifier . . ."[28] Only at the moment in which the sign appears as completely arbitrary and externally posited can it gain a truly universal meaning. "The process of the sign is an *Aufhebung,"*[29] because it is a process of purification in whose movement the particularity of the initial sensual intuition is negated. The determination of the sign reached here—as an intuition which does not stand in any relation of similarity to the intuition is signifies—offers the fundamental determination of the name. One can see that "names properly are, viz. *external-ities* which of themselves have no sense, and only get signification as *signs* . . ." (HPM, 196). Names are signs which due to the arbitrariness of the relation—between themselves and the intuition they signify—have no signification as long as they are not understood as bearers of signification independent of intuition. Žižek rightly encapsulates this as follows:

> The result at which we thus arrived is a "representational language" com-posed of signs which are the unity of two ingredients: on the one hand, the universalized name, mental sound, a type recognized as the same in differ-ent utterances; on the other hand, its meaning, some universal representa-tion. Names in "representational language" possess a fixed universal content determined not by their relation to other names but by their relationship to represented reality.[30]

This remark is important as Hegel introduces in this context a threefold dis-tinction into what he calls memory. The first is the *"name-retaining* memory" (HPM, 199) which represents the subjective presupposition to be adjusted to the fundamental needs of language: naming. Here the partition into three repeats itself on a more universal level. To recall names means to be able to abstract from the specific context of its signification and to remember the connection between two different intuitions as the unity of the name. As with imagination, the abstraction from the particular spatial and temporal context of its uttering means that it can be reproduced autonomously and in different contexts. This is something that *"reproductive* memory" (HPM, 199) can do. But here this form of memory is still too much infected with the external content of the sign. There needs to be not only a reproduction of a connection between different intuitions in the form of an intuition but also a habit of the same. That something is mechanically remembered is the condition to be able to freely deal with language. There needs to be a learning of signification which leads to an automatization of its usage, to finally be able to speak and write freely. The mechanical memory—the quoting by heart of a series of words without consciousness of their signification—indicates the transition to thinking. For the sign remains within the realm of signification and sense and only when the meaninglessness of the name appears as a constitutive moment of the sign of any word, Hegel can claim that "it is in names that we *think*" (HPM, 199). This means that only due to a mechanical repetition which can only occur when there appears an intuition which is no longer linked to an utterance with an inscribed meaning that thinking for Hegel becomes thinkable. The sole stabil-ity which is inscribed into the mechanical reproduction of meaningless signs is the 'I' which presents the empty bond between them. Thereby the meaning of a name is longer constituted due to an intuition which would—however arbitrarily—represent it, but through a different form of relation.

Here one should start to look at Hegel's early lectures in which he delineates a helpful definition of the name. There he writes that we answer to the
question: "What *is* this? *It is* a lion, donkey, etc. *it is*, i.e. it is something yellow,
having feet—etc.—an autonomous being, but a *name*, a tone of my voice—
something completely different to the way it is in intuition and this is its true
being."[31] This passage clarifies that names are not related to an external reality
which would be secondarily named by them. Rather a lion is initially nothing
but a "tone of my voice," "words in my mouth."[32] As soon as one claims: 'this is
a lion' the relationship between antecedent reality and secondary signification
changes. 'Lion' refers not to a preceding reality, to the intuition of a huge animal with four paws, from which one could articulate that one is dealing with a
'lion.' Rather the relation of 'objectively' present properties and their denomi-
nation changes. "The paradox of symbolization resides in the fact that the
object is constituted as one through a feature that is radically external to the
object itself."[33] The name puts something into a symbolic unity which in itself
does not have the objective aspects but only relates to the series in which they
are placed by the name.[34] This means that 'lion' here is not the end of a series
of objective determinations—animal, eating flesh, having a mane, etc., i.e. this
is a 'lion'—so that its name would be an abbreviation for a multiple, objective
content of a row of determinations. At the same time this also does not mean
that the name 'lion' is the beginning of a series of determinations and would
make *one* series of determinations appear such that one could understand it as
a series of explanations: the 'lion' having a mane, is an animal, etc. Neither can
one conclude from the series of determinations to the unity of the name which
abbreviates the determinations and follows a *logic of the 'i.e.'*—x has a series of
determination, *i.e.* it is a 'lion'—nor from the unity of the name to the multiplicity of concrete determinations which would explain it and introduce a *logic
of the 'because'*—x is a 'lion' *because* it has the following determinations.[35] Both
logics—of abbreviation and explicitation—stand in a inverse relationship to
one another: the logic of explicitation inverts the logic of abbreviation.

If the explanation—the name at the beginning of a series of determinations
that explicitate it—inverts the abbreviation—the name at the end of a series of
determinations—for Hegel the name unites *both* functions at the same time.
This means that the name explicitates the series of determinations which it
immediately abbreviates. To make this clear with reference to the example,
this means that the name 'lion' operates according to this logic: x is a lion,
because it is an animal, eats flesh, has four paws, etc. *i.e.* x is a lion. Because the
name appears twice—at the beginning and the end—what the signification
of the name will have been is constantly retroactively re-determined; a kind of
self-determining and self-differentiating tautology. The name as the foundation of the series of determinations which explicitates and abbreviates it can
only be in a relation to itself if this series of determinations exists. An example
of this logic found in Žižek may help to clarify things:

first socialism is posited as the simple abbreviation of a series of markers that designate effective qualities ("When we have enough food, electricity, flats, books, freedom . . ., we have socialism"); one then inverts the relationship and refers to the series of markers in order to "explicate" socialism ("socialism means enough food, electricity, flats, books, freedom . . ."); when we perform another inversion, however we are not thrown back to our starting point, since "socialism" now changes into "Socialism", the Master-Signifier—that is no longer a simple abbreviation of this series of markers but the name of the hidden ground of this series of markers that act as so many expressions-effects of this ground.[36]

The name sutures a series of determinations which only appears as a series because of this suturing. Any further determination determines in consequence what the determination of the name—'lion' for example—will have been, so that the name is both the unity and the multiplicity of determinations. The name is in itself completely empty, a meaningless utterance as long as it is not conceived as a sign, i.e. as a series of determinations which gives a signification to it but which at the same time is constituted by it as *a* series. Thereby the name contains a constant procedure of self-determination—mediating the series of determinations which it generates and abbreviates. The question 'what is this?' refers to the necessity of a symbolic unity for the multiplicity of determinations which retroactively makes them into a series of determinations. This for example is also what the name of the monarch does for Hegel, which answers the question: 'what is this?' with a 'this is a state.' Only due to the name of the monarch one can say that x is a state, *because* x has a series of determinations, *i.e.* x will have been a state.

How does this relate to Hegel's diagnosis: "if man makes himself to be without rights and also keeps himself *unbound* of duties . . . then this is the rabble" (HPRV, 222). Initially one can see to what extent the rabble can also be understood as a name. But Hegel seems to proceed here in a way different to that which is indicated by the logic of the name. He begins from a series of determination—better: with negations of determinations—from which the rabble results. The being that is without rights and unbound from duties, *i.e* is the rabble. Thus Hegel employs 'rabble' as an abbreviation. 'Then this is the rabble' means: x has a series of determinations, i.e. x is rabble. But already a few lines before Hegel talks about the rabble and therefore follows the logic of the name that we have just exhibited: "He who is paltry does not yet belong to the rabble. What is characteristic for the rabble is the attitude . . . and the production of the rabble presupposes a state of society"[37] (Ibid.). In this passage Hegel proceeds in the opposite manner: x is rabble *because* it has a certain attitude and this attitude presupposes a state of society. One can see here to what extent the rabble follows the logic of the name. For 'rabble' or "what one usually calls rabble" (Ibid.) is the name for an x, because x has a series of determinations. But two things need to be remarked: 1. that the logic of name is valid here means that x is 'rabble,' *because* x has a series of determinations, *i.e.* is rabble; 2. the remarkable thing with the series of determinations which the name 'rabble' abbreviates is that this series—which explicitates the name—for Hegel is a endless series of negations of determinations. But what does this mean?

One can come up with an answer if one again recalls: x is 'rabble,' *because* x negates everything that is present, or a series of determination, *i.e.* it is 'rabble.' This logic shows that the name 'rabble' abbreviates a series of negations of determinations, i.e. that it can only be explained by this series. But for Hegel the name 'rabble' as the negation of a series of determinations is itself determined: a determined name. 'Rabble' names for Hegel the complete, absolute negation of all determinations and as such a negation it is determined. 'rabble' seems to be the name of nothing which persists in the complete void of determinations. But one should not overhastily understand the rabble as an abstract entity, as a negation which leads to a merely abstract nothing. If the name 'rabble' is the abbreviation of a series of negative determinations which negate all positive attributes it is because it can only be explained by such a series of negations. The name 'rabble' is determined by a series of—determinate—negations and it therefore appears as the peculiar foundation of this series of negations. Because these negations are understood as determinate negations, the name 'rabble' abbreviates such a series and this series explicitates it.

What is interesting is that the logic of the name is inverted for a second time here: not only is the name 'rabble' the abbreviation of a series of (negative) determinations which explicitate it, but what explicitates it is that which it is not. But it *is*. The name 'rabble' marks an indeterminacy which is explicitated by a series of (negative) determinations and this is why it can abbreviate this series. If the name is the linkage of the *logic of the i.e. and of the because* then Hegel proceeds by claiming that the name as abbreviation presents the universality of a series of determinations. But this universality is merely abstract, an abstract name which just names the formal unity of the series of concrete determinations which it at the same time has to ignore. This abstract unity is automatically internally reversed to become the necessity to resolve this abstraction and to explictate the names as abbreviation through a series of determinations—otherwise the name would be nothing but a further determination, or as Hegel has it, a senseless exteriority. If the name is the dialectical linkage of abbreviation and explanation—the abbreviation as negation of determination is again negated in the series of determination which the name has founded—this means that the rabble is the abbreviation of a series of negations which can only be explained by this very series. To force this argument one can claim that the rabble as name is an abbreviation of nothing and cannot by explained by anything. But this nothing is not abstract, it is rather a *concrete nothing* because it can be explicitated through a series of negations of determinations. One can claim that the 'rabble' as the name of the matter of ethical space can be explained as the unity of the series of negated determinations which the 'rabble' as name of the *organ without body* abbreviates. The organ without body refers to a negated series of determination which will always already have been founded by the matter of the ethical space. The rabble is the absolute negation of all determination and to this extent the name 'rabble' is a name of the absolute negation, a name of nothing. More precisely this means that the name 'rabble' is the concrete product of a series of (negative) determinations. The concrete nothing then means an indeterminacy which does not result from the abstract negation of the totality of determinations. Otherwise the name 'rabble' would be the name of a particularity, a particular name, and therefore not a true name in Hegel's sense. Rather, the concrete nothing, which is named by the word 'rabble,' is an indeterminacy which results from the series of (negative) determinations that can be (potentially) infinitely continued. Therewith Hegel prescribes in the name 'rabble' an existence which has no determination of existence: 'rabble' is the name of a nothing, a concrete nothing that result from an endless series of negations. 'Rabble' names an indeterminacy which emerges in the Hegelian philosophy of the state.[38]

This can clarify: 1. that the rabble takes an analogous position to the empty set in set theory. For the rabble can similarly only be determined by a series of negations and is an abbreviation of (the) nothing (in politics) because it can only be explicitated through this series of negated determinations. At the same time this nothing is not the abstraction of all determinations, but results as a concretion in the negation of determinations, from a series of negated determinations. The peculiar matter of the ethical space that the rabble is, is nothing but a name, a name of nothing. Therefore it can emerge from the movement of civil society—of the "*world of appearance* of the ethical" (HOPR, 180) as Hegel writes in a telling way—and at the same time not have its own appearance. The rabble as the matter of the ethical space, as that which will have been 'before' the ethical, can only be grasped by the fact that its name, as an abbreviation of a series of negated determinations, as the name of nothing, appears in the ethical. 'Rabble' is the name of the peculiar matter of the ethical which does not have any determinations and which can only be grasped with the appearance of the name 'rabble' in the ethical as that which will always already have been prior to the ethical. 2. This clarifies to what extent the rabble, although it can only 'appear' in this world of appearance, its appearance is its disappearance. For what appears behind the name 'rabble' is nothing, a series of negations of determinations which does not know any determinations; not even existence or appearance are left un-negated. At the same time the appearance of this name is not a mere fantasy, no abstraction but a concrete—local—appearance of the name, because it results from a series of negated determinations. 'Rabble' is the name of a local emergence, of a concrete irruption of the matter of ethical space into the space of the ethical. But this irruption of the matter—as matter—is an irruption of an inconsistency into the organically structured order of the state; an irruption of a disappearing which has no appearance of its own. Thereby a void irrupts which provides an insight into the pure multiplicity, the extensional set of the *vulgus*. 'Rabble' is the Hegelian name for the emergence of an indeterminacy which decomposes the state.

Conclusion: Hegel's Rabble—Hegel's Impossibility

Spirit that does not appear, is not.

(G. W. F. Hegel)[1]

This is where Hegel vacillates, namely, in the vicinity of this rock that we Marxists call the "primacy of practice". . . .

(Alain Badiou)[2]

In the rabble Hegel encounters an impossibility. This impossibility confronts his *Philosophy of Right,* which is a philosophy of freedom, with a demand for equality that it cannot put up with. The investigations have shown that the rabble names a complex problem which is not an arbitrary occurence in Hegel's philosophy of the objective spirit, in that which is traditionally called his 'political philosophy.'[3] But what confronts Hegel in and with the rabble? Summarizing the previous results one can claim that Hegel's answer is clear: the rabble names the absolute negation of all determinations. Its attitude is equated with the negative understanding, it is morally deprived, shameless, evil, shy of work and as such a negation of all the necessary rational determinations of the free, active and rational subject in the ethicality of the state. It is as abstract negation, a mere particularity.

But I have demonstrated, the Hegelian answer is insufficient even according to its own logic. Hegel misperceives that the possibility of the emergence of the rabble is necessarily inscribed into his conception of the state, since the world of appearance of the ethical, civil society, itself unavoidably and indispensably produces poverty from a certain historical moment of its development. At the same time poverty can no longer be counterbalanced by any additional dimension of the economy of salvation because, as Hegel clarifies with regard to the Reformation, modern society is marked by the fact that poverty can no longer be considered to be an honoring but only a lack. Here a first impossibility is present: it is impossible that poverty, the condition of possibility for the emergence of the rabble is not produced. This impossibility is the impossibility of civil society, its inability to uphold its own principle. What results from this presents itself as a further impossibility. For the poor it becomes impossible to do what Hegel wanted to demonstrate: that it is only possible to realize one's freedom within the state. Hegel encounters in poverty a first fundamental problem, a problem of categorization as he can no longer describe poverty being artificially produced by civic economy as a natural lack. But at the same time he cannot recognize this violation of its own principle as a wrong. Otherwise the world of appearance of the ethical would be a concatenation of illegality. But this problem of categorization only arises with the emergence of the rabble. For it emerges due to a genuinely subjective operation which Hegel calls attitude, then there appears with it the demand for a right, which enables us to classify the impossibility linked to poverty as a wrong, and posits a right valid for anyone against the existing right. Hegel encounters an impossibility of categorization because he cannot dismiss the *un-right* of equality and justice which the rabble claims as a merely particular demand. Hegel thus marks a place at which an impossible demand for the equality of everyone arises which is no longer bound to the laws of the movement of the state and civil society. The rabble confronts him with the impossibility of categorizing this demand.

Although the rabble makes itself by way of a radically contingent and purely subjective operation, it is not what Hegel constantly wants it to be: a mere particularity. the necessarily produced condition of possibility of the rabble gives us an insight into what I have called the *logic of double latency*. Anyone in the state is latently poor and therefore latently rabble. The rabble is thus not a mere particularity but as a particularity it latently contains a universal dimension. Through the *logic of double latency* a primacy of equality over freedom becomes clear: that anyone is latently rabble is the formula of this impossible equality. This is at the same time an insight into that which lies logically 'before' the organic structuring of the state and what I have called the matter (in and for itself) of the ethical space. What does this insight into the equality 'before' the state mean? Hegel initially marks with the necessary production of poverty a place at which, as soon as the rabble emerges—as *organ without body*—another concept of equality, differing from Hegel's, becomes thinkable. At the same time, it is in this structural place, necessarily present in the state, that Hegel's failure appears most clearly. For if Hegel attempts to develop the state in a way that in it any subject should realize its own freedom actively and this realization is guaranteed by the universalized right and the statist institutions, then in the impossibility of realizing one's own freedom on the part of the poor, it becomes manifest that the appearance of the state—in civil society—necessarily produces suspensions of equality and justice. That the rabble cannot emerge from anywhere else but the poor means that Hegel has indicated in his *Philosophy of Right* the place from which a call for a different, more fundamental equality than that of the statist equality (of attitude) can arise, for a different conception of justice than that with which the state fails, even more: a call for a sublation of the Hegelian state.

Such a call can only emerge from the objective impossibility (of realizing one's freedom), but it is a subjective, subjectivized call and it is not the poor that call but the rabble, who indignantly accuse the state by presenting the necessary production of the condition of the rabble's emergence marks the place in which one might establish a thinking of transformation that does not correspond to the model of change on which the Hegelian conception of the state relies. That Hegel's *Philosophy of Right* as a philosophy of freedom is at the same time a 'political philosophy,' a philosophy of objective spirit, in this context means that the rabble is a limit, a limitation of this 'political philosophy' of the state. If for Hegel the free will is the atom from which the political universe of the state is composed, then the will of the rabble presents the atom of a different politics; a politics which necessarily cannot be the politics of the Hegelian state.

The 'rabble' marks in Hegel the impossibility of a (different) politics which is not founded upon the free will. Rather it begins with the insight—necessarily linked to the rabble—into the equality of anyone with anyone. If the rabble names a fundamental problem of categorization and localization in Hegel's political thought, for which it does not know answer and in which it fails, then the question arises as to whether it can still be encompassed in its founding category: the free will. That the Hegelian legal philosophy is a philosophy of the *free* will and of its realization is clear from the fact that the will corresponding to the rabble—a will lacking freedom—can only take the place of an unfree will. For the rabble has no free will but a will which wills the impossible, an *un-right* of equality and it can only do so, because it is always already determined by the material, external condition of its own possibility (poverty). The will of the rabble is furthermore directed only onto itself; by its indeterminacy it is as a particularity latently universal. The will of the rabble is separated from freedom which only occurs as that which refers to its own conditioning. Conditioned wills are not free wills for Hegel and therefore they contradict their own concept. The will of the rabble is for Hegel an unfree and therefore impossible will because it does not will freedom, but rather equality. The will of the rabble is an impossible will which wills the impossible.

What is revealed by this Hegelian failure? Two things are important: 1. the rabble marks within the Hegelian Philosophy a problem of categorization which can neither be resolved by the means of Hegelian logic nor find a clear place within it; 2. this means that in the Hegelian philosophy of objective spirit a problem of indistinguishability arises which refers to a different concept of indeterminacy, and one that is no longer subordinated to the Hegelian indeterminacy. One can draw nearer to this point by taking account of the fact that two aspects coincide in the rabble: universality and latency, and by viewing these in light of our prior investigations. The rabble as particularity is universal, where universal means latently to include anyone in the state, but universality is only understood as a latent, a potential one. The rabble marks a latent, potential universality which includes anyone since it names that which can only be grasped through the structures of the state but which at the same time lies 'prior' to it. It marks the structural place in Hegel's 'political philosophy' in which his philosophy is confronted with politics in a way that no longer fits the philosophical categories of politics. The logic of politics, which becomes thinkable here, begins from the primacy of equality and not freedom. But such a politics necessarily has to appear impossible to Hegel. What Hegel marks as the absolute negation of all determinations under the name 'rabble' is the place in which an equality becomes conceivable which transcends the Hegelian concept of the state and makes it possible to think of transformation in a way that cannot be grasped in Hegel's concept of transformation. For the change which Hegel marks with the rabble neither begins with an inscribed possibility nor with a possibility being realized; it rather starts from impossibility. One can claim that under the name of the 'rabble' the Hegelian philosophy is confronted with a logic of (a different) politics which bursts through the philosophical frame of its description. For it necessitates a new thinking of equality, an equality which cannot be conceived of in legal or statist terms, and it necessitates a new thinking of transformation that suspends the category of the possible, by putting the impossible first. The logic of such a politics is irreducible to the logic of philosophy which sutures politics and philosophy. Although 'the rabble' appears to Hegel only as a particularity which he attempts to think as the abstract negation of all determinations, Hegel's greatness is to have named here the place from which we might conceive of a different politics, a politics of equality and impossibility. It will not respect rights or the state in any of its organizational forms or forms of action. At the same time this necessitates a transformation of philosophy. This is why Marx will use the rabble to grasp the singular logic of politics in a way that will lead him to the proletariat. What in Hegel is marked as indeterminacy, as the absolute negation of all determinations, is the irruption of a different thinkability of politics *into* philosophy. This happens at a point where Hegel was not Hegelian enough.

Coda: Preliminary Notes concerning the Angelo-Humanism and the Conception of the Proletariat in Early Marx

Moreover, it goes without saying that all forms of the state have democracy for their truth . . .

(Karl Marx)[1]

One can also say that democracy, as a philosophical category, is that which presents equality. Or again, democracy is what prevents any predicates whatsoever from circulating as political articulations, or as categories of politics which formally contradict the idea of equality.

(Alain Badiou)[2]

Early Marx knows the rabble.[3] Not only does he know of the indignation constituting it,[4] he also knows that the economic movement in its historical development always already produces the condition of his emergence. But the early Marx is not a thinker of the rabble but of the proletariat. How to get from the rabble to the proletariat? Initially one can take up one element that already has proven to be essential for the discussion of the will and attitude of the rabble. The Hegelian rabble emerges at a point of impossibility of the realization of one's freedom, from poverty. For "it becomes impossible for poverty to bring something before itself."5[4] Its emergence at this impossibility means that the rabble recognizes this objectively existing, external impossibility as such and starts from it to claim an *un-right* of equality which due to the *logic of double latency* includes anyone. Marx, as I want to claim, begins precisely from the same point with his delineation of the proletariat. For it "confronts . . . society with its own impossibility."[6] The path leads from the rabble to the proletariat because one can demonstrate that the proletariat contains all characteristics which I presented above. Marx reacts thus to the irruption of politics in philosophy and to the possibility of thinking transformation in a way which does not correspond to the existing (dialectical) categories. To specify this thesis two things are needed: 1. a proof that the proletariat in the early Marx is conceived of in a way that it can be consistently related to Hegel's rabble and 2. an answer to the question if in Marx the irruption of the matter of ethical space into the structured ethical-statist space is understood as suspension of the structures of ethicality and organization, or if Marx understands this irruption of inconsistency as an initial moment which in its consequence leads to a conversion of the impossibility into a previously unknown possibility and allows for a multiplicity of this conversions.

The question is therefore how to verify the mentioned formula of the transition 'from the rabble to the proletariat (and back)' in the early Marxian texts. In this way it will be possible to show how the difference between Hegel and Marx is the difference between the rabble and the proletariat. How does the early Marx define the proletariat? The possibly most famous definition can be found in his introduction to the critique of the Hegelian philosophy of right from 1843/44. It is the

> the formulation of a class with *radical chains*, a class of civil society which is not a class of civil society, an estate which is the dissolution of all estates, a sphere which has a universal character by its universal suffering and claims no *particular right* because no *particular wrong*, but *wrong generally*, is perpetuated against it; which can invoke no *historical*, but only *human*, title; which does not stand in any one-sided antithesis to the consequences, but in allround antithesis to the premises of German statehood; a sphere, finally, which cannot emancipate itself without emancipating itself from all other spheres of society and thereby emancipating all other spheres of society, which, in a word, is the *complete loss* of man, and hence can win itself only through the *complete re-winning* of man. This dissolution of society as a particular estate is the *proletariat*. . . . By heralding the *dissolution of the hereto existing world order*, the proletariat merely proclaims the *secret of its own existence*, for it is the factual dissolution of that world order. (MCHR, 256)

One can recognize the historical specificity of the rabble-problem—in the artificially produced poverty. On can recognize the *un-right* of equality and justice that the rabble claims—in the wrong in general. One can recognize the dissolution of all determinations which breaks into the structure of community—as factual dissolution of world order—and finally, one can recognize the constitutive indeterminacy of the rabble—in the complete loss of man.[7] Marx also diagnoses that civil society from a certain historical point of its development constantly produces the conditions which make an emergence of the proletariat thinkable. Therein the proletariat, as the Hegelian rabble, is determined by a complete "impoverishment [*Entwesung*] . . ." (MEPM, 288). The proletariat is also a particularity which is immediately universal since its emergence produces the insight into the *logic of double latency* and indicates that anyone in civil society and the state is latently proletarian. Marx describes not only the necessarily present condition for the emergence of the matter of the ethical space, he also—like Hegel—distinguishes between this condition (poverty, working class) and an emergence (rabble, proletariat). This is why the proletariat is a class which is no class and therefore constitutively distinguished from the working class.[8] For the working class still falls—like Hegelian poverty—under the socioeconomic determinants of society and does not as such pose a problem of categorization. Marx clarifies thereby that the proletariat can be conceived of neither in terms of a *creatio ex* nihilo,[9] since it always remains bound to the conditions of its emergence, nor as a necessary result of historical development. As Marx explicitly remarks, the idea of a stable historical development which would produce emancipatory change is simply nonsensical: "The category of *gradual* transition is first historically false and, secondly, it explains nothing" (MCH, 119). The emergence of the proletariat is not derivable from historical categories—of gradual transition.[10]

Rather one has to think the difference between the historical genesis of the condition of emergence—"revolutions need a *passive* element, a *material* basis" (MCHR, 255)—and the emergence of the proletariat—the emergence of the "*truth of this world*" (Ibid., 244). As Michael Löwy has rightly stated: "The conditions for the self-emancipation to emerge can be either conjunctural . . . or structural . . . . It is the historical coincidence of these two orders that transform it into an idea-force of the broad masses of people."[11] With this a further insight is possible if one recalls the Hegelian distinction of luxury- and poverty-rabble. If Marx in his conception of the proletariat takes up determinations of the rabble, it is obvious that he refers to the poor rabble. But what does then happen to the luxury-rabble? As soon as the 'proletariat' appears in the place of the Hegelian rabble it becomes apparent that the luxury-rabble is the only true rabble. One can again see here that only the poor rabble and not the rich one poses a problem of categorization. The poor rabble becoming-proletariat in Marx produces the insight that in civil society and the state there will always have been only one true rabble: the rich one, the luxury-rabble, the capitalist. For it the Hegelian judgments prove to be absolutely accurate: it is morally evil, i.e. corrupt, a mere negative understanding, which considers the ethical community only from the perspective of private interest. With Marx one can answer the question of the true rabble for which the Hegelian analysis is consistent: it is the luxury-rabble.

But to return to the distinction of condition of emergence and emergence itself, it is necessary to ask how to conceive of the 'absolute loss of man' which marks the proletariat. Therefore I will shortly refer to the theoretical apparatus which Marx presents to think the genesis of this complete loss: the theory of alienation. I want to read a few selected passages and address only the question how to generally situate the theory of alienation or more precisely: if alienation is a historically contingent or necessary context. One can find an instructive answer in the early Rancière:

Well, the problem of the origin of the alienation of labor poses itself: either alienation is an accident and we are now referred back to a problematic of the origin of the bad history, which is assimilable to that of the philosophy of the Enlightenment, or alienation is a necessary process which is inherent to the development of humanity. It is the second solution which will be chosen by Marx in the third manuscript [of the economic and philosophical manuscripts] in which the alienation of the human essence will appear as the condition of the realization of a human world.[12]

Alienation is a historical necessary condition. The impoverishment [*Entwesung*][13] of the human being is necessary for the constitution of a truly human world. So, why is there a necessity of alienation? Man has to externalize his own essence in the development of the economic and historical process; he has to become the impossible human being to be able to become truly human. This means that all determinations of the essence of the human being have to be externalized for a true determination of the essence of the human being to become thinkable. For the early Marx, it is necessary that the essence of man has no determination, no attribute, no property, because any determination *proper* to man would prevent him from producing universally[14]—which is what makes him human. The historical process that empties the essence of man of all determinations is necessary to not constantly fall back into a particularization of the universal. This is to say, it is necessary in order not to constantly reduce and limit the universal of human production to that which is *proper* to and particular for man. A universality which depends on determinate properties that are able to totalize the essence of man is no true universality. This is how one may render the intuition that stands behind the necessity of alienation. It should therefore be read as an intervention against any particularization of universality, but also as an attempt to develop a new, truly universal universalism. To think human essence as an essence with determinations *proper* to it would imply to understand this essence as a *proprietor* (of its properties). To avoid any logic of (private) property linked to the determination of the essence of man—which even in its most universality, Hegelian variant cannot avoid that it is possible to be excluded from the system of rights—and to develop a universal perspective of the equality of anyone with anyone as a starting point, the essence has to be thought of as being indeterminate. The theory of alienation finds its systematic place in the Marxian attempt to think a true (political) universalism—a different humanism.[15]

From the claim that universality, a notion of universal equality, can be thought *in actu*—not reducing "equality as the *basis* of communism" (MEPM, 364), to any particular attribute—one can derive the necessity to think absolute alienation, to think the *complete* loss of man. At first man has to become "non-being [*Unwesen*]" (Ibid., 343).[16] Being the negation of the essence, man neither must have an essence nor does he not have one. He is a non-being [*Unwesen*] and this is what designates his constitutive indeterminacy. One can here recall the helpful distinction between three forms of judgment in Kant's

Critique of Pure Reason:[17] The positive judgment assigns an attribute to a subject ("X is dead"); the negative judgment negates this attribution ("X is not dead"), and this is what makes it possible to translate this judgment into a positive one ("X is not dead, which is to say, X lives"). Finally, the infinite judgment assigns a nonattribute to a subject ("X is undead, which is to say, neither X lives nor X is dead"). Thus, the infinite judgment undermines the given possibilities of distinction. But the insight into the constitutive indeterminacy of man, into the human non-being [*Unwesen*], into the void of his essence, is what is only offered with the emergence of the proletariat. With it becomes clear, following the *logic of double latency*, that man will always have been a non-being.

If one attempts to ground equality in a (constructible) determination of human essence, the universality of man is always already lost[18] and the talk about true equality can only degenerate into "a mere phrase" (MEPM, 124). This is to say, Marx does not hope for de-alienation, for *Ent-Entfremdung*, for a return to an "original state of paradise" (Ibid., 122) preceding alienation. This is precisely what Marx vehemently criticizes in the theorists of national and political economy. It is rather the "impoverishment [*Entwesung*]" (Ibid., 134) of man that builds the condition for the fact that the proletariat as soon as it emerges at its evental site[19] implies an immediate dimension of universality which is addressed to anyone, because it is *for* anyone.[20]

If man is characterized by a universal dimension, then this universality can only be truly universal if it passes over into a process of universal production. Starting from the emergence of the proletariat and the insight linked to it one cannot simply persist in the rupture with civil society and the state; the rupture rather needs to lead into the process of a reorganization of the existing circumstances in accordance with the universality of mankind. The evental appearing of the proletariat has to be read as the inauguration of a process in which a subject that (principally) includes anyone comes to universal production (of an equality of anyone with anyone). But if in Hegel the rabble makes itself, how does Marx think the evental emergence of the proletariat and of universal production? Marx's answer is clear: an "*actual* [*wirkliche*] communistaction" (MEPM, 123) is needed. The actual communist action names an event; an evental irruption into the structures of historical societal dynamics which lets the specific "universality of man" (Ibid., 75), the matter of the ethical space, following the *logic of double latency*, appear as something that logically lies "before" (although it is always only accessible "after") the structures of the state and of civil society. In this way an equality without any limiting determination becomes thinkable which encompasses anyone. Through the event of an actual communist action, the impossibility of universal production under given capitalist modes of production and under the dictatorship of private property becomes an "impossible possibility"[21] which brings about the appearance of a new subject: the proletariat, which prior to its emergence had no determinations of existence.[22] The actuality, or better the effectivity—"*Wirk-lichkeit*" in German literal sense—of the communist action consists in the fact that it transforms the previous history and its laws into a history of "preparation" (MEPM, 110)[23] by even changing the seemingly stable laws of change.

What should become clear is that actual communist action is determined by the historically necessarily produced site of the event at which the proletariat emerges—the working class, poverty. It is therefore singular—localized—and universal because the proletariat concerns anyone, since anyone will have been latently poor and latently proletarian. If there is an evental irruption of a truly communist action and if this action brings the proletariat into existence, then here the question arises of how the young Marx develops the process of universal production which structurally follows the event. How does Marx elucidate what he himself calls universal production which is only thinkable 1.under the condition of a radical alienation of all essential determinations of man and 2. if and only if a true communist action eventually breaks the existing historical situation into two, and even changes the laws of change, and which finally, 3. depends on the subject-proletariat, that is the agent of the true communist action and thus the subject of universal production? How does Marx therefore meet the claim to think a universality which introduces an equality of anyone which is at the same time essentially bound to the *production* of this equality?

What is introduced by the true communist action is the procedural deployment of a subject which Marx describes as man's active "*species life*" (MEPM, 162)[24] One direct result of this is that to conceive of a process in which a universally producing life of the species emerges, one has to avoid any reference to anthropological categories and determinations. It is rather in this process that "truly *ontological* affirmations of essential being" (Ibid., 135) take place. Only in this process, "the brotherhood of man is no mere phrase . . . but a truth . . ." (Ibid., 124).[25] In its process universal production leads to ontological affirmations of the (fully indeterminate) nature of man which deploys the equality of anyone—the brotherhood of man—as a truth.[26]

But how can one understand this opaque formula? To start one can note that the process of universal production is immanently linked to what Marx calls "a truth" and that this truth is immanently related to ontological affirmations of an essence. Universal production is first a production of truth, which has an ontological dimension. If one now tries to bring together this first and still abstract definition of the process of universal production and the necessarily indeterminate essence of man which emerges as an effect of the actual communist action, it becomes manifest: the universal production which affirms the essence of man has to preserve the indeterminacy of this essence in the process of production. If it does not do so, it will not have been a true affirmation of human essence. But, how to imagine such a production? Or to begin slightly different: If Marx implies that these ontological affirmations of essence in the active species-life are related to man as "species-being" (Ibid., 102), how can one understand this species-being that is affirmed only in universal production? An example that Marx offers is helpful: "just as music alone awakens in man the sense of music, and just as the most beautiful music has *no* sense for the unmusical ear—is no object for it because my object can only be the confirmation of one of my essential powers . . . for the same reasons, the senses of social man are other senses than those of the nonsocial man. Only through the objectively unfolded richness of man's essential being is the *human* sensibility (a musical ear, an eye for beauty of form, in short, sense capable of human gratifications, senses confirming themselves as essential powers of man) either cultivated or brought into being." (Ibid., 109)

If one reads Marx's considerations as an analysis of the structure of universal production, things become clearer. What happens in the process of universal production—in this process that logically begins after the actual communist action—is that a constitutively indeterminate human (collective) subject cultivates "*social* organs" (Ibid., 107) that retroactively determine the essence of the human being. The invention of music signifies a retroactively occurring determination of man who will have had a musical ear. Universal production is therefore on the one hand a production of determinations of the human being which become objective and actual. These determinations are objective because they change the constitution of the essence of man in a way that they will forever have changed this essence. For man will after the invention of music forever always have had a musical ear. But this process can, on the other hand, be only fully grasped if it is considered in its proper temporality. For the determination of that which will have been human, cannot refer back to any given determinations of the human essence. It only results *retroactively and in the process* of its determination. For this reason, the temporality of universal production is the *future anterior.* The determination of the "unessential [*Unwesen*]" (Ibid., 134) that is man is therefore no longer bound to a predetermined possibility of humanity which would realize itself in this process of production. This process itself continually retroactively creates the conditions of its own possibility.[27] This is why Marx can claim that "communism . . . as such is not the goal of human development" (Ibid., 114), because the process of universal production as emerging after the communist action cannot, due to its inherent logic, know any goal. If one begins with the assumption that there is no essence of man which could be realized in the process of production; if one begins with the claim that the human being is constitutively indeterminate, one is lead to the consequence that this process of determination—whose name is "universal production"—cannot have any immanent boundaries, or inherent limitations. It rather has to be understood as—at least potentially—infinite.

The process of universal production proceeds via a constant conversion into "impossible possibilities" of that which seems to be impossible for man to do or to think. Things seem to be impossible for the human being: 1. because it bears no determinations of what is possible for it and 2. because it is always inscribed into concrete social historical and political situations that present something as an impossibility, as historically impossible. If it seems impossible prior to the invention of music that man has or can have a musical ear, what happens with the invention of music is that a new organ is generated. This specific impossibility is converted into a possibility that has to be thought in the temporality of the future anterior.[28] One can therefore also claim that the proletariat as a subject of universal production continually determines itself retroactively as that which it will have been.[29] It is a constant "beingby-itself" (Ibid., 112)[30] in the steady production of the retroactive determinations of new social organs of its own universal essence. Marx thinks, starting from the emergence of an *organ without a body*, of the proletariat, through an actual communist action, the perpetuated process of formation of a collective body which is able to add constantly and potentially infinite many organs to this body.[31] The proletariat is the subject of this process of universal production, and what is produced by it is the universality that Marx calls species-being.

This also means that there can be no condition of belonging which would regulate who can and who cannot participate in the process of universal production. Rather it is in this process that there is "a moment in which it fraternizes . . . with society in general . . ." (MCHR, 105). It addresses anyone as there are no limiting conditions of belonging. In a different context Marx offers an image that is helpful for the logic of this operation. The movement of universal production whose subject is the proletariat is similar to a constant "*somersault*, not only over its own limitations, but at the same time over the limitations of the modern nations . . ." (Ibid., 104). The somersault movement makes it possible that the process of universal production knows no boundaries or limitations: *as universal production itself, it is at the same time a retroactive production of universality.* Step by step, or better: somersault by somersault, without any law of production, without any regulation of how it proceeds and without any prior determination, in always singular historical situations, one determination after another is produced that retroactively deploys the universal dimension of the human species-being. The species-being is constitutively indeterminate and it is precisely due to the potential infinity of its connected determinations—this somersault after somersault retroactively change the essence itself—that it remains indeterminate. For the process neither allows a law of operation, a defined condition of belonging to it, nor a point at which the realization of the humanly possible would be reached. This sort of production is rather marked by what I call an immanent Bestimm*bar*keit.[32] On the one hand, the essence of man is without any determination, because it is stripped of all determinations by the existing forms of alienation. On the other hand, what universal production designates is a process of production that—in always singular historical situations—generates step by step certain determinations which retroactively always determine the ever new species-being. This means that the essence of man is and will always be a non-being [*Unwesen*].

Due to the internal infinity of the process there can be no substantialisation, no essentialisation of any determination. This is the reason why the universal production (of the proletariat) and the production of the universal (of the human species-being) is and remains bestimm*bar*.[33] Man for Marx truly lives if and only if this excess is engendered by an actual communist action that leads to the process of affirmation of the ontological determinations of its indeterminate essence. Only in the deployment of his universal species-being does man begin his true "*life of the species*" (MEPM, 76). When Marx thereby defines universal production as the life of the species, it is because this production implies a conception of life which is a "*productive life*" (Ibid.). What universal production produces is thus the universal dimension of the human species-being. In the process of deploying the truth of this species-being the true species-life of man appears, which includes everyone. Consequently, man lives if and only if he participates in the deployment of his own universality, if he works for the ontological affirmation of his own essence. It is because this production constantly creates retroactive determinations of its own essence that one can claim that this *universally* producing life is as well constantly relating itself to itself, i.e. in the process of living truly, life produces determinations of itself. For Marx, to truly think human species-life signifies to think a collective universal production that itself generates life. "[W]hat is life other than activity" (Ibid., 75)— other than universal production? If to truly live means to produce universally, to produce the universality of owns one essence, then life = practice = activity. This is why true activity, i.e. universal production, is true life, i.e. the permanent creation of one's own universality. If true life is constitutively universal active life and if therefore life can be said to be creative life, one can conclude that productive life defines a life which in its activity constantly refers back to itself. For Marx, true life is universal activity and universal activity is true life. One can now easily inscribe these interdependent definitions into Marx's formula of "productive life": Marx's conception of human species-life, the life of generic humanity, can be understood as a conception of a *life living life*.[34]

What can be seen in the development of this logic of universal production and of the production of universality in Marx for the question of the transition from rabble to proletariat? First it is clear that Marx takes up essential determinations of the Hegelian rabble. But he makes out of the determination of the content of the rabble-attitude (indignation) the actual communist action. Its evental outbreak consequently generates the process of universal production. The marking of a fundamental indeterminacy which emerges at a necessary produced condition Hegel shares with Marx. What Hegel does not share with Marx is the judgment that from the emergence of indeterminacy alone a fundamental transformation can be thought which cannot be described in given categories of change as it even changes the laws of change. If in Hegel's *Philosophy of Right* the name 'rabble' stands for an indeterminacy about which philosophy does not have to say anything except that it presents the negation of all determinations and if the emergence of the indeterminacy insists as problem within philosophy, then one can claim that it is the irruption of politics into philosophy. For this indeterminacy appearing within philosophy is the indeterminacy of an emergence, of an event of which philosophy previously cannot say anything. Philosophy is only able to mark the place from which even the laws of change might be changed. To describe the relationship of Marx and Hegel one can borrow a remark by Theunissen and turn an inscribed implication against him. Theunissen marks with a critical intention toward Marx that Marx in his critique of the *Philosophy of Right* proceeds in a way that "he turns the logic denied in it against itself."[35] If Hegel's *Philosophy of Right* is a philosophical treatise on politics in its modern and statist forming, then in the remark above is implied that politics can have a different logic than philosophy.

When Marx notes that "Hegel is not to be blamed for depicting the nature of the modern state as it is, but rather for presenting what *is* as the *essence* of the state" (MCH, 64), this comment has to be taken seriously. Hegel depicts the essence of the modern as it is and he depicts what happens in the state if there is an emergence of the rabble accurately. But Hegel presents what is as invariant structure of politics, of the state. Therewith he suspends his own insight. Taking up the implication of Theunissen's remark one can claim: Marx reads the logic of the Hegelian *Philosophy of Right* against the logic of Hegelian *Logics*. Thus Hegel depicts what is, what emerges and rightly marks the place of the rabble. For Hegel it is valid that "philosophy can give a name to it, but philosophy cannot solve it."[36] Marx, however, is not content with this marking of an indeterminacy but transforms philosophical thinking from "the standpoint of the proletariat,"[37] from the impossibility of philosophy. What happens against the background with the image of the early humanist Marx?[38] What sort of humanism is one dealing with here? If one thinks together the structure of universal production by the proletariat and the production of the universal, of human species-being, starting from the indeterminacy of human being, the non-being, an image results which differs from the traditional one. For how to think a humanism of human non-being, an in-humanism, or more precise: a humanism of impossibility? Here again Hegel can help. He writes in the register in Tübingen: "S'il y avait un gouvernement des anges, il se gouvernoient démocratiquement"[39] and thereby offers an important hint. A truly democratic organization or government would be one of non-human beings, so Hegel: A democracy of angels.

If one starts from the Marxian determination of man as non-being [*Un-wesen*], one can develop a further point. For if the Marxian conception of universal production can be read as a constant conversion of impossibility into impossible possibility, then the early Marxian humanism cannot be understood from a preset substantial determination of human being. Rather one should inscribe the Hegelian note into the conception of Marxian humanism to do justice to his description of the universal dimension of the human species-being. Taking up a remark by Badiou one can say for Marx it is valid: "Given their ability to create eternal truths in various worlds, men have within them the angel that religions saw as their double."[40] If one takes all this remarks together one can outline a *materialist definition of the angel* which helps to understand Marx's humanism. If the process of universal production is marked by the fact that it suspends any substantial determination of human being, then one can say in a first step that Marx's humanism starts from man as non-being which has no thing specifically human. If now the universality of the human species-being consist in self-determining retroactively itself in the process of universal production and is this production therefore the unfolding of a truth, in the form of an ontological affirmation of human essence, one can say that the Marx's humanism relates an *Un-Wesen* and a form of eternal truth. At the same time one can conceive of the universality of this production and production of universality in a way that it addresses anyone and describes a process which makes an equality thinkable which is constituted without condition of belonging. The universality of the active process, which marks the human species-being, immanently generates thereby a conception of democracy, more precise: of communism which is without limitation and an equality of anyone with anyone. If hence the early Marx is a thinker of the proletariat as subject of a process of universal production in which the universality of human species-being is understood starting from its non-being as equality of anyone in the form of unfolding eternal truths, one can claim that the humanism of early Marx is an *angelo-humanism*, a humanism of impossibility. Its principle is: Man only truly lives when man is an angel to man.

Marx's angelo-humanism turns politics, happening to Hegel's philosophy in the 'rabble,' against Hegel, i.e. he puts the logic of politics through the name 'proletariat' forth against the logic of philosophy and (re-)introduces the condition of politics into philosophy. Philosophy is, at least, *after* Marx conditioned by the singularity of politics. There is no political philosophy which could escape the Marxian rupture without again returning, in one way or another, to the Hegelian problem of the rabble. Marx introduces the true primacy of practice into philosophy, the primacy of the autonomy of political practice. There is no political thinking which could still refer with a sovereign gesture to the invariance of the political and suspend the conditioning of philosophy by (the singularity) of politics.[41] Hegel's greatness consists in having marked this conditioning in the name 'rabble.'

Notes

Introduction

[1] Alain Badiou, *Entretien avec Christine Goémé*, France Culture 10.02.95.

[2] ATS, p. 145.

[3] Theodor W. Adorno, *Kant's Critique of Pure Reason (1959)*, Stanford: Stanford University Press 2001, p. 9.

[4] The series of authors who commented on this transition reaches from Althusser to Žižek.

[5] One of the most famous critics of the obstructing of the thought of Marx is obviously Lenin. I have undertaken a commentary of his criticism in: Frank Ruda, *Was istein Marxist? Lenins Wiederherstellung der Wahrheit des Namens*, in *Namen. Benennung, Verehrung, Wirkung. Positionen der europäischen Moderne*, Tatjana Petzer, Sylvia Sasse, Franziska Thun-Hohenstein, Sandro Zanetti (ed.), Berlin: Kadmos 2009, pp. 225–42.

[6] Solange Mercier-Josa, *Übergänge von Hegel zu Marx. Philosophie, Ideologie und Kritik*, Köln: Pahl-Rugenstein 1989, p. 151. My translation. All subsequent translations from books or articles yet untranslated into English are provided by the author. Where an existing translation has been modified for the purposes of accuracy, this has been indicated.

[7] Alain Badiou, *Metapolitics*, London/New York: Verso 2005, p. 10. A convincing critique of 'political philosophy' can also be found in: Alain Badiou, *Peut-on penser la politique?*, Paris: Seuil 1985.

[8] Étienne Balibar, *Für Althusser*, Mainz: Decaton 1994, p. 143. "Displacement" translates the French "déplacement." All emphases, unless otherwise indicated can be found in the cited texts. At the same time I do not follow Balibar's thesis that a Machiavellian moment in Marxian thought should be played off against a Hegelian moment. I rather insist in the following on the decisive relevance of the Hegelian moment for the early Marx. See Étienne Balibar, 'Marx, the Joker in the Pack,' in: *Economy and Society*, Volume 14, Number 1, February 1985.

[9] Karl Marx/Friedrich Engels, *The German Ideology*, New York: Prometheus Books 1998, p. 29.

[10] I here borrow this formula from Werner Conze. See: Werner Conze, "Vom Pöbel zum Proletariat. Sozialgeschichtliche Voraussetzungen für den Sozialismus in Deutschland [1941]," in *Gesellschaft – Staat – Nation. Gesammelte Aufsätze*, Stuttgart: Klett-Cotta 1992, pp. 232–46.

Chapter 1

[1] MCH, p.138.
[2] Bronislaw Geremek, *Poverty. A History*, Cambridge: Blackwell Publishers 1991, p. 47.
[3] Ibid., p. 67.
[4] That this ambiguity leads to a general mistrust of the "mere appearances" and to a whole literature of simulation and dissimulation is already noted by Luhmann. See: Niklas Luhmann, *Die Gesellschaft der Gesellschaft*, Frankfurt a. M.: Suhrkamp 1998, p. 623.
[5] Bronislaw Geremek, *Poverty*, p. 50.
[6] One could easily think of the logic of suspicion that Hegel delineates paradigmatically with regards to the French Revolution.
[7] The fidelity to Luther can be found in Hegel inter alia in the following formulation: "We Lutherans – I am one and I want to remain one – only have this original belief." *Briefe von und an Hegel*, ed. V. J. Hoffmeister and F. Nicolin, Hamburg: Meiner 1969–81, Bd. 4, S. 60.
[8] See: HOPR, p. 127. There it reads: "the will is only what it posits itself to be; it is not good by nature but can become what it is only by its own labour."
[9] Joachim Ritter, *Hegel und die Reformation*, in *Metaphysik und Politik. Studien zu Aristoteles und Hegel*, Frankfurt a. M.: Suhrkamp 2003, p. 313.

Chapter 2

[1] HPM, p. 139.
[2] Paul Tillich, *Vorlesung über Hegel (Frankfurt 1931/32)*, Berlin/New York: De Gruyter 1995, Bd. 8, p. 319.
[3] Manfred Riedel, *Tradition und Revolution in Hegels "Philosophie des Rechts,"* in *Studien zu Hegels Rechtsphilosophie*, Frankfurt a. M.: Suhrkamp 1969, p. 100.
[4] Eduard Gans, *Vorrede zu G.W.F. Hegels Werke*, Berlin 1833, Bd. 8, p. XVII
[5] Hegel names the following advantages: "the opportunity of acquiring skill and education of any kind, as well as of the administration of justice, health-care, and often even of the consolations of religion." HOPR, p. 220.
[6] Family " in civic community . . . is subordinate and merely forms a basis." Ibid., p. 264.
[7] Hegel enumerates 1. the ethical (legal age of the child and the ability to acquire property and create a family) and 2. the natural movement of dissolving the family (death of the parents). See HOPR, pp. 175ff. He additionally refers to the arbitrary dissolution through divorce which does not perform the transition to civil society. See: Ibid., 174.
[8] The stage of difference should be understood as immanent, and also following a logic of development: beginning with the difference of concrete persons (immanent), and the difference between civil society, family and the state (following a logic of development).
[9] Joachim Ritter, *Hegel und die Reformation*, p. 314.

[10] Hegel calls marriage and honor the subjective bases of the state; family and estate its objective bases; family and corporation its roots.

[11] Mark Neocleous, *Administering Civil Society. Towards a Theory of State Power,* London/New York: Palgrave 1996, p. 8.

Chapter 3

[1] HVORL 3, p. 702.

[2] One has to add here: Hegel knows of this failure.

[3] It is imprecise to only indicate one proposed solution as for example Dallmayr does. See: Fred R. Dallmayr, *G.W.F. Hegel. Modernity and Politics*, New York/Oxford: Sage Publications 2002, p. 130. Avineri also sees only three options in Hegel. See: AHT, pp. 151–4.

[4] With this Hegel clearly attempts to avoid a rigid formalism of rights that he paradigmatically criticizes in Roman law (in the example of the slave relationship of Roman children). See: HOPR, pp. 174, 177–8.

[5] That this is necessarily the case can be derived from Hegel's critical discussion of the position that judges an action by only taking into consideration the conviction and intention behind it. Such a standpoint belongs to the "most abstruse form of evil" (HOPR, 138) that ultimately leads to the erasure of any notion of a good or evil action. See: Ibid., pp. 144–7.

[6] HOPR, pp. 187–8.

[7] For the pardon as a sphere of reasons for mitigation, see: HOPR, p. 129. That the pardon can only be granted by the monarch does not affect the consistency of the above argument. Also, the monarch is bound to the legal procedure which has just been carried out; he may grant an act of gracious pardon but leaves the pardoned one with the status of a criminal. See: HGPR, pp. 275ff.

[8] One can claim that desire leads man back to "mere natural needs" of which Hegel writes that they are an expression of "savagery and unfreedom." See HOPR, p. 190.

[9] For Hegel, the reference to the strength of sensual impulse in judging the motivation of an illegal action is an idea that starts from a simple stimulus-reaction model. See: HOPR, p. 100.

[10] For this see also: Giorgio Agamben, *Homo Sacer. Sovereign Power and Bare Life,* Stanford: Stanford University Press 1998.

[11] Ibid., p. 269.

[12] See: HPRV, p. 224; HOPR, p. 221 and HVORL 4, pp. 611–13.

[13] That this is consistent with Hegel is due to 1. the fact that he understands the notion of civil society both socioeconomically and also politically and here gives the primacy to the first meaning. (See: Manfred Riedel, *"Der Begriff der »bürgerlichen Gesellschaft« und das Problem seines geschichtlichen Ursprungs"*, in: *Studien,,* pp. 135–67) and 2. the fact that the immediate estate, as a result of its tendency to be submissive (See HOPR, 195) falls behind the formal estate and also because the general estate refers only to the political notion of civil society.

[14] Ibid., p. 225. One central element of capability that Hegel names skill seems to refer to Kant's definition of the citizen as *sui iuris*, master of his own deeds against the *operari*. See Ibid., p. 191.

[15] Joel Anderson, "Hegel's Implicit View on How to Solve the Problem of Poverty: The Responsible Consumer and the Return of the Ethical to Civil Society," in: *Beyond Liberalism and Communitarianism. Studies in Hegel's Philosophy of Right*, ed. by Robert R. Williams, New York: State University of New York Press 2001, p. 196.

[16] Ibid.

[17] Ibid. What this means concretely reads in Anderson like this: "For example, if I am aware that a favorite restaurant is having trouble attracting business, I may frequent it more often to help keep it afloat. If a craze for this Christmas season's 'hot toy' is leading to wild retail and production fluctuation, I may choose a different gift for a child. Or I may purchase goods that are produced by laborers earning a living wage, so as to resist the downward pressures on wages that come from uncertainty and fierce competition. In small ways, these choices help to support rational and stable growth in consumer demand, and insofar as this occurs, the general resources are increased." Ibid., p. 196.

[18] MCH, p. 46. As David C. Durst rightly remarked, any attempt to reduce the reciprocal relations of Hegel's state model to purely economical ones that would be—whether ethically or not—regulating it, transforms Hegel's state in what Plato once called a state of pigs. See: David C. Durst, "The End(s) of the State in Hegel's Philosophy of Right," in: *Beyond Liberalism and Communitarianism*, p. 236.

[19] Domenico Losurdo, *Zwischen Hegel und Bismarck. Die achtundvierziger Revolution und die Krise der deutschen Kultur*, Berlin: Akademie Verlag 1993, pp. 157–234.

[20] Ibid., p. 159.

[21] Rectitude is alongside the honor of the estate (after love within the family and confidence in the first estate) the appearance of the ethical attitude. See HOPR, p. 196.

[22] That this examination has a police character is clear: "The corporation has in its circles within its remit the dealings of the police . . ." (HVORL 3, 710)

[23] This formulation I owe to Lorenzo Chiesa.

[24] In this way Luhmann will later call day laboring a limit-case of the distinction between inclusion and exclusion. See Niklas Luhmann, "Inklusion und Exklusion," in: *Soziologische Aufklärung 6. Die Soziologie und der Mensch*, Opladen: Westdeutscher Verlag 1995, p. 263.

[25] In this sense the Hegelian corporation is not fully freed from its medieval heritage. For the medieval guild, as Luhmann rightly claims, "does not address the lowest strata [*Schichten*] . . ." Niklas Luhmann, "Jenseits der Barbarei," in: *Gesellschaftsstruktur und Semantik. Studien zur Wissenssoziologie der modernen Gesellschaft*, Bd. 4, Frankfurt a. M.: Suhrkamp 1999, p. 141.

[26] Hegel distinguishes between inner and exterior provisions. If the corporation deals with the inner, the police deal with the exterior. See: HPRV, p. 216.

[27] Hegel enumerates, in order to determine this limit, the morals, the momentary danger, the spirit of the constitution and the specific state of society. The police is, as he calls it later, determined by the "political situation." See: HVORL 4, p. 593.

[28] HPRV, p. 217.

[29] It again becomes clear here what the notion of possibility on the level of contingencies means. As Hegel had already noted in a handwritten remark to paragraph 17: "A being determined as merely possible is contingent—it can be or it cannot be." (HGPR, 67)

[30] It is of no relevance if the cited passage from the Griesheim postscript stems from Hegel or not because it only has to support the consistency of the following remarks. It is in any case indisputable that the handwritten note to paragraph 116 of the *Philosophy of Right* refers to the same notion in a quotation from Johann Michaels Heineccius. Hegel writes: "*Heinecc [ccius, Elementa Juris Civilis]* § 1235. *Pauperiesest damnum sine inuiria facientis, datum nonnisi quadrupes pauperem facere dicitur.*" HGPR, p. 216.

[31] Any person within civil society is subject to the dialectics of rights and duties; the same goes for the family.

[32] Hegel talks about eradicating [*ausreuten*] "what is merely sensuous and natural" in children. The German "ausreuten" refers to exterminating something and to cutting something off at its roots. See HOPR, p. 173.

[33] HVORL 4, p. 593.

[34] See: HVORL 4, p. 607.

[35] 1824/25 Griesheim calls this the "failure of religion."

[36] Christoph Menke, *Tragödie im Sittlichen. Gerechtigkeit und Freiheit nach Hegel,* Frankfurt a.M.: Suhrkamp 1996, p. 257.

[37] As Hegel notes: "Also the monasteries feed poverty by feeding laziness, because they care for the satisfaction of needs independent of work." (HVORL, 611)

[38] One can see here that, by rejecting the right to strike, Hegel wants to solve a problem that was also instructing his discussion of the right of distress: the right to an exception of right.

[39] Manfred Riedel, *Das Problem der bürgerlichen Gesellschaft*, p. 161.

[40] Ibid., p. 162.

Chapter 4

[1] Friedrich Nietzsche, *Beyond Good and Evil. Prelude to A Philosophy of the Future,* Cambridge: Cambridge University Press 2002, p. 162. The addition in brackets, referring to the German version of the passage, was included by the author.

[2] BBE, pp. 93–102

[3] To what extent Hegel therewith provides an insight that has been forgotten in political theory, I have tried to show paradigmatically in dealing with Foucault in "Back to the Factory. A Plea for a Renewal of Concrete Analysis of Concrete Situations," in: *Beyond Potentialities? Politics between the Possible and the Impossible,* hg. von Ruda, Frank/Potocnik, Mark/Völker, Jan, Berlin: Diaphanes 2011.

[4] Manfred Riedel, "Die Rezeption der Nationalökonomie," in: *Studien,* p. 89.

[5] Ibid., p. 95.

Chapter 5

[1] HOPR, p. 266.

[2] See the entry in: Friedrich Kluge, *Etymologisches Lexikon der deutschen Sprache*, Berlin: De Gruyter 1989.

[3] The German "Notdurft" is rendered as 'penury' in English. HOPR, p. 220.

[4] Karl Marx/Friedrich Engels, *The Holy Family or Critique of Critical Criticism. Against Bruno Bauer and Company*, at: http://www.marxists.org/archive/marx/works/download/Marx_The_Holy_Family.pdf, p. 28.

[5] Also see: HVORL 4, p. 608.

[6] See: HVORL 2, p. 682; HVORL 3, p. 703, HVORL 4, pp. 608ff.

[7] I want to anyhow address the philological objection that this passage could also not stem from Hegel and therefore the following remarks stand on shaky ground. If these remarks are not of Hegelian origin, they nonetheless show a deep understanding of the Hegelian *Philosophy of Right*. Because they explain a structural analogy that otherwise explicitly cannot be found explicitly in Hegel. One could say that here the Hegelian saying on reality and theory is valid in a different guise: If these passages do not stem from Hegel, even worse for Hegel.

[8] That he is quite correct in this can be seen from Hegel's remark that the sphere of particularities, i.e. civil society, preserves "the rest of the state of nature in itself." HVORL 2, p. 647.

[9] The rich rabble thereby adopts a position which is comparable to an anti-Hobbesian Hobbes according to the reading of Hobbes supplied by Macpherson. It declares a state of nature, which is understood in purely possessive individualist terms, and which is not regulated by contracts but by the dynamics of economy, i.e. of the state of nature itself—a sort of *visible* hand that befits the (economically) fittest. The struggle for recognition, following this logic, is a struggle for capital. See also: C. B. Macpherson, *The Political Theory of Possessive Individualism. Hobbes to Locke*, Oxford: Oxford University Press 2011.

[10] In Hegel this reads as follows: "In this case he finds himself being a gambler." HPRV, p. 230. Hegel implies that there can be a sort of natural starting capital of the gambler, when he speaks of inheritance as "acquisition . . . without labor . . . due to the contingencies of mere exterior relations." HGPR, p. 331.

[11] More precisely one would have to say that this partition into three which follows the separation of the free will into free will in itself, for itself, and in and for it itself, is again repeated on each of the individual levels. A contemporary reading that attempts to describe the repetition of any step in each of the others ad infinitum and that presents in this way a reconstruction of Hegel's system as a thought of pure infinite relations, may be found in: Jean-Luc Nancy, *Hegel. The Restlessness of the Negative*, Minneapolis: University of Minneapolis Press 2002.

[12] Josef Derbolav, *Hegels Theorie der Handlung*, in: *Materialien zu Hegels Rechtsphilosophie*, vol. 2, ed .by Manfred Riedel, Frankfurt a. M.: Suhrkamp 1975, p. 204.

[13] In Hegel's formulations: "If this estate has livelihood, it has secured its honor, does not need to give himself luxury." Or: "To show luxury, this is not necessary if he is a master." Or: "He who only has his patent has no ethical obligations. And finally he has no honor. The recognition by others he can only generate

by showing luxury." HPRV, 230. That these descriptions do not contradict those Hegel gives in his lectures on the *History of Philosophy* should be clear. "Philosophy may thus be called a kind of luxury, in so far as luxury designates enjoyments and occupations which are unconnected with external necessity as such." HLHP 1, 192. Philosophy, rather, due to its inner freedom from ends allows us to gain a true conception of 'inner luxury,' of 'inner wealth' whereas the rich rabble always already refers to a concept of luxury that is bound to ends and to pure externality. Inner and outer luxury then relate to one another in a way similar to how good infinity relates to bad infinity.

¹⁴ It is characteristic that Hegel's example of the gambler is the owner of a patent (see: HPRV, p. 230). Here the problem is already anticipated which will be named "capitalist" in later lectures. (HVORL 4, p. 609) The problem is that the split of the individual into producer and consumer, that delineates the general frame of reference, is reduced in the owner of a patent to a purely consumptive attitude. He consumes the products of other without being active himself. Obviously one can here think of the structures of the master-slave dialectics that in this case would be freed from the threat of death.

¹⁵ In the double sense of: "legal claim to x" and "claim to right as such."

¹⁶ Hegel speaks of the "power" of wealth. HPRV, p. 222.

¹⁷ The idea that this can even mean the linkage of possibility and impossibility of a (shared) universal 'structure,' may be found in: Alexander Garcia Düttmann, *Between Cultures: Tensions in the Struggle for Recognition,* London/New York: Verso 2000.

¹⁸ See the explanation of the Lacanian notion of communication as successful misunderstanding, in: Slavoj Žižek, *Looking Awry. An Introduction to Jacques Lacan through Popular Culture,* Massachusetts: MIT Press 1992, pp. 30–1.

¹⁹ Slavoj Žižek, *For they know not what they do. Enjoyment as a Political Factor,* London/New York: Verso 2002, p. 161 and pp. 164ff.; Slavoj Žižek, *Le plus sublime des Hysteriques. Hegel passe,* Paris: Erès 1999.

Chapter 6

¹ Friedrich Nietzsche, *Thus spoke Zarathustra. A Book for All and None,* Cambridge: Cambridge University Press 2006, p. 219.

² One needs to indicate here that Hegel does not speak of privation in his *Philosophy of Right.* I use the term here in a double sense: 1. as deprivation, revocation of a predicate and 2. as negation wherein the negating predicate denies the subject not only the attribute but also its essence.

³ Rolf Konrad Hocevar, *Stand und Repräsentation beim jungen Hegel. Ein Beitrag zu seiner Staats- und Gesellschaftslehre sowie zur Theorie der Repräsentation,* München: Beck 1968, p. 31.

⁴ HPRV, p. 223: "One can call this depravity [*Verdorbenheit*] that the rich assumes himself to be at liberty to do anything." Interesting in this context is also Hegel's remark in the *Encyclopedia* that "everything in the world that has become corrupt has had a good reason for its corruption." HLH, p. 229.

5   The way in which a prohibition of unbinding is inscribed into any conception of the 'state' is described at BBE, pp. 104–11.
6   See HOPR, p. 172.
7   The formal style of writing is here and in the following solely employed as an abbreviation of the logical chains.
8   I write small "i" as an abbreviation of internal (i.e. subjective operation) and "e" for external.
9   One could also claim that here the opposition of a thought of particularization of the universal and a thinking of the universalizability of the particularity opens up. The first claims that particularity has always and at all to remain stable *as* and *in the form* of the particularity. The second by contrast claims that particularity can in itself have a universal character, which as an effect of universalization suspends the stability of all particularities. See Alain Badiou, *Saint Paul. The Foundation of Universalism*, Stanford: Stanford University Press 2003.
10 Theodor W. Adorno, *Negative Dialectics*, London: Routledge 1990, p. 312.
11 Hegel seems to have recognized this peculiar position of the rich rabble and its specific danger for the ethical community clearly when he speaks about the harmful effect of the concentration of large fortunes in the hands of the few. See: HVORL 4, p. 611.
12 In this way he is, even against his will and in a manner that also Hegel cannot enjoy, included in the formal general context of mediation in the ethical community.
13 One can rather claim the poor rabble relates to the poor in a similar way to that in which the white square relates to the white ground on Malevich's painting from 1918 "White on White." See: Alain Badiou, *The Century*, Cambridge/Malden: Polity Press 2007, pp. 55ff., here: p. 56.

Chapter 7

1   HPM, 178.
2   Friedrich Nietzsche, *Thus spoke Zarathustra*, p. 159.
3   The reconstructed course here follows the maxim of early Badiou: "*Contradiction has no other mode of existence but scission.*" Alain Badiou, *Theory of the Subject*, London/New York: Continuum 2009, p. 14.
4   I employ this notion here while deliberately not discussing its determinations in Nietzsche's works.
5   Joachim Ritter, "Moralität und Sittlichkeit. Zu Hegels Auseinandersetzung mit der kantischen Ethik (1966)," in: *Metaphysik und Politik. Studien zu Aristoteles und Hegel*, Erweiterte Neuausgabe. Mit einem Nachwort von Odo Marquard, Frankfurt a. M.: Suhrkamp 2003, p. 284.
6   Already in the lectures of 1819/20 Hegel claims that the consciousness of the corruptibility of right that the rich have is the counterpart to the loss of loyalty to the right in the poor.
7   I owe this point to discussions with Christoph Menke.
8   Peter Landau, "Hegels Begründung des Vertragsrechts," in: *Materialien zu Hegels Rechtsphilosophie*, vol. 2, ed. by Manfred Riedel, Frankfurt a. M.: Suhrkamp 1975, p. 179.

[9] Joachim Ritter, "Moralität und Sittlichkeit," in: *Metaphysik und Politik*, p. 282.

[10] Honneth employs Wittgenstein's phrase with regard to the picture that holds us captive in order to delineate the structure of conceptual confusion. But could one not ask: Isn't it Hegel's inconsistency which holds us captive? Does not the conceptual confusion lie rather in Hegel (and even more in Honneth) than in the rabble?

[11] Obviously herein consists once again the rabble's proximity to the *homo sacer*. See Agamben, *Homo Sacer*.

[12] To understand this totalization not only as pathological but as evil, Honneth would need an elaborated conception of truth that also can be found in Hegel's philosophy. A conception of evil as totalization which is not described as 'pathological' can be found in Alain Badiou, *Ethics. An Essay in the Understanding of Evil*, London/New York: Verso 2001.

[13] Theodor W. Adorno, *Negative Dialectics*, p. 324

[14] I use here the phrase *absolute rabble* to differentiate him more clearly from the rich rabble. Due to reasons that will become clearer in the following, I will use the notions 'rabble,' 'absolute poverty' and 'absolute rabble' synonymously.

[15] See Sylvain Lazarus, *Anthropologie du nom*, Paris 1996.

[16] One can from this perspective only agree with Žižek when he remarks: "When a thing becomes 'for itself,' nothing actually changes in it; it just repeatedly asserts ('re-marks') what it already was in itself." Therefore the void in the for itself of the rabble is nothing but the repetition of the in itself of the void within poverty itself. See Slavoj Žižek, *The Ticklish Subject. The Absent Centre of Political Ontology*, London/New York: Verso 2000, p.74.

Chapter 8

[1] G. W. F. Hegel, *Vorrede zu Hinrichs Religionsphilosophie*, in: *Werke*, Frankfurt a.M.: Suhrkamp 1970, vol. 11, p. 49.

[2] The most systematic reconstruction of the Hegelian notion of habit can be found in Catherine Malabou, *The Future of Hegel. Plasticity, Temporality and Dialectic*, Oxford/New York: Routledge 2004.

[3] For a presentation of the history of the notion see Gerhard Funke, *Gewohnheit*, Archiv für Begriffsgeschichte, Bd. 3, Bonn 1961.

[4] Here Hegel can be read as precursor of Nietzsche's critique if asceticism. See Paul Tillich, *Vorlesung über Hegel*, pp. 120ff.

[5] HPM, 136. A helpful discussion of habit may be found in Slavoj Žižek, "Disciplines between two Freedoms – Madness and Habit in German Idealism," in Markus Gabriel, Slavoj Žižek, *Mythology, Madness, and Laughter. Subjectivity in German Idealism*, London/New York: Continuum 2009, pp. 95–121.

[6] Émile Chartier Alain, *Idées. Introduction à la philosophie. Platon – Descartes – Hegel – Comte (1939)*, Paris: Flammarion 1983, p. 200.

[7] Jun-Ho Won, *Hegels Begriff der politischen Gesinnung. Zutrauen, Patriotismus und Vertrauen*, Würzburg: Königshausen & Neumann 2002, S. 94. My emphasis.

[8] Cf. HOPR, pp. 188ff.

9   The notion of habit is synonymous with second nature. Cf. Malabou, *The Future of Hegel*, p. 77; Hegel himself articulated this in HOPR, p. 159.

10 For this reason, as Žižek claims, in the anthropology, the section on habit follows the one on madness. If habit, in its perpetuated process of universalization, constantly transforms the nature of individuals retroactively, this process does not know any stability. Habit as mechanical repetition would be a form of stabilized madness, i.e. the only thinkable and consistent form of a constitutively unstable process. Cf., Slavoj Žižek, "Disciplines between two Freedoms."

11 Malabou, *The Future of Hegel*, p. 24.

12 Manfred Riedel, "Tradition und Revolution in Hegels 'Philosophie des Rechts'," in Riedel, *Studien zu Hegels Rechtsphilosophie*, p. 114.

13 The discourse of the rebirth in the second nature stems from Hegel (HOPR, 159). Malabou rightly remarks that for Hegel "nature is always *second nature*," although she wrongly assumes that Hegel would deviate from this insight in the Philosophy of Right. Malabou, *The Future of Hegel*, p. 108. It should be clear that it is only against this background that the reference to natural right which Hegel indicates in the subtitle can be grasped.

14 Precisely this point is missed by Theunissen who claims that Hegel would in the development of the *Philosophy of Right* pervert "any relationship of persons to each other into a relationship of the substance to these persons" and would thereby interpret "the supposed basal relationship as a relationship of the substance to itself." That therewith the autonomy of persons would disappear and that they would be mere accidents of the ethical substance, is a claim that may be sustained only if one disregards the twofold determination of habit in the realm of the ethical and only considers the purely mechanical side of it. Michael Theunissen, "Die verdrängte Intersubjektivität in Hegels Philosophie des Rechts," in *Hegels Philosophie des Rechts*, ed. by Dieter Henrich/Rolf-Peter Horstmann, Stuttgart: Klett/Cota 1982, p. 328

15 Jun-Ho Won, *Hegels Begriff der politischen Gesinnung*, p. 99.

16 Bean spoke in relation to Hegel (and Bismarck) of a "subversive influence created by the idleness of the labouring classes." Cf. Philip Bean, "Law, Order and Welfare," in *In Defence of Welfare*, ed. by Philip Bean/John Ferris/David K. Whynes, London New York: Routledge 1985, p. 213. Foucault points in a similar direction when he claims that "idleness was an act of rebellion." Cf. Michel Foucault, *History of Madness*, Oxford: Routledge 2006, p. 70.

17 Karl Marx, *Debates on the Law on Thefts of Wood*, on: http://www.marxists.org/archive/marx/works/1842/10/25.htm.

18 This motto from Ferdinand Kürnberger is placed at the beginning of Theodor Adorno, *Minima Moralia. Reflections on Damaged Life*, London/New York: Verso 2005, p. 16.

19 G. W. F. Hegel, *On Natural Right and Political Science. The First Philosophy of Right. Heidelberg 1817–1818 with Additions from the Lectures of 1818–1819*, Berkeley/Los Angeles/London: University of California Press 1995, p. 210.

20 I borrow the neologism 'to inexist' from Badiou who uses it to name a mode of the being-there of a multiplicity in a world structured by a non-subjective transcendental. The transcendental, in its fundamental operation, regulates the appearance of multiplicities by ascribing them properties that lead

to differentially understood degrees of intensity of appearance. To inexist for Badiou means that according to the transcendental of a certain region of appearance which he calls 'world,' the inexistent—in relation to the other appearing multiplicities—has the lowest degree of appearance. Here I take 'to inexist' only as a name for the structure of the rabble—to be present without any determination of existence. Cf. Alain Badiou, *Logics of Worlds. Being and Event 2*, London / New York: Continuum 2009, pp. 303–24.

21 Jean Hyppolite, *Genesis and Structure of Hegel's Phenomenology of Spirit*, Evanston: Northwestern University Press 1974, p. 266.

22 Heinz Kimmerle, "On Derrida's Hegel Interpretation," in *Hegel after Derrida*, ed. by Stuart Barnett, London/New York: Routledge 1998, p. 234. To my knowledge there is no detailed reconstruction of the Hegelian theory of the hand which I myself can only very briefly touch upon.

23 The German word for action 'Handlung' refers literally to the hand. From this point of view one can foresee a different interpretation of Hegel's definition of the subject as the "*series of his actions [Handlungen]*" HOPR, p. 122.

24 Etymology shows that in German, 'Verfaulen' is synonymous with 'Verwesen.' See the entry 'faul' in Friedrich Kluge, *Etymologisches Lexikon der deutschen Sprache*, quoted from the CD Rom version.

25 I owe this formulation to Jan Völker.

26 This pun does not translate into English. The German 'Wesen' names both a being, and the nature or essence of it. 'Ver-Wesen' therefore plays on this reference inscribed into the German word for to rot, to decompose: 'verwesen.'

27 This formulation of Hegel's refers to the state. A few lines above it he talks about the severed hand that is incapable of so doing. Cf. HOPR, p. 253.

28 As Steffen Schmidt has made clear—thus underlining my reading—Hegel speaks in his early 'system of ethicality' (1802) of a distinction between the organic and inorganic nature of the ethical. The organic side names the domain of ethicality which unifies the "multiplicity and makes it into the indifferent"; while the inorganic names "this multiplicity of different subjective drives and needs" along with the objective activities which "cannot be unified completely." Cf. Steffen Schmidt, *Hegels System der Sittlichkeit*, Berlin: Akademie Verlag 2006, pp. 135f.

29 Against this background one can only agree with Slavoj Žižek's remark that Hegel therefore "insists on the necessity of war which, from time to time must allow the subject to regain the taste for abstract negativity and shake off his full immersion into the concrete totality of the social Substance *qua* his 'second nature' . . ." Slavoj Žižek, *The Ticklish Subject*, p. 82. The question of the glorification of war belongs to the category of "Hegel Myths and Legends." Cf. a constellation of texts in *The Hegel Myths and Legends*, ed. by Jon Stewart, Evanston: Northwestern University Press 1996.

30 Arseni Gulyga, *Georg Wilhelm Friedrich Hegel*, Leipzig: Reclam 1980, p. 31.

31 Hegel describes this as follows: "by the complete cultivation of his activity, the vitality of the activity expires . . ." (HPM, 61). Due to his use of the word 'complete' a peculiar Aristotelian remainder appears in Hegel's remark.

32 Already the early Hegel writes: "Life which is close to decay can be reorganized only by the most drastic means." G. W. F. Hegel, *The German Constitution (1798–1802)*, in: Hegel. Political Writings, Cambridge: Cambridge University Press 2004, p. 80.

33 Eduard Gans, *Naturrecht und Universalgeschichte. Vorlesungen nach G.W.F. Hegel*, Tübingen: Mohr Siebeck 2005, p. 204.

34 Due to this mutual relation of determination Hegel also talks about (the state as) "inward organism." HOPR, 234, trans. mod.

35 G. W. F. Hegel, *On the Scientific Ways of Treating Natural Law, on its Place in Practical Philosophy, and its Relation to the Positive Sciences of Right (1802–1803)*, in Hegel. Political Writings, pp. 102–80, 149 also cf. HVORL 3, p. 726.

36 Therefore this notion refers to the Kantian distinction of the three different forms of judgment (positive, negative, infinite) as elaborated by Žižek. If the positive judgment asserts a positive predicate of a subject (X is dead), the negative judgment deprives it of a predicate and can logically be rewritten as a positive judgment (X is not dead; X lives). The infinite judgment asserts a non-predicate of the subject (X is undead) and thereby opens up a domain that undermines the underlying distinction. Cf. Slavoj Žižek, *Die politische Suspension des Ethischen*, Frankfurt a. M.: Suhrkamp 2005, p. 49. See Also the brilliant investigation in Jan Völker, *Ästhetik der Lebendigkeit. Kants dritte Kritik*, München: Fink 2011.

37 That the rabble is lazy and evil at the same time due to the standpoint which he takes on the negative as such refers particularly to Kant. Adorno once remarked of Kant that he has "taken the work ethic of bourgeois society . . . as his own supreme philosophical standard" and therefore for him "radical evil is nothing other then laziness . . ." Theodor W. Adorno, *Problems of Moral Philosophy*, Stanford: Stanford University Press 2001, p. 131.

38 Hegel attempts in this passage to disavow the defenders of the physical theory of latent warmth. I have presented an initial commentary on this passage in Frank Ruda, "Namenlosigkeit. Von nichts zu Nichts oder vom Pöbel zum Proletariat," in: *Latenz. 40 Annäherungen an einen Begriff*, ed. by Stefanie Dieckmann/Thomas Khurana, Berlin: Kadmos 2007.

39 One can claim that in this passage something appears that drives the structure of Hegel's dialectic or Hegel's 'structural dialectic' to its limit. The term 'structural dialectic' names a dialectical thinking which knows only one form of contradiction, determinate negation. See Alain Badiou, *Theory of the Subject*, pp. 53–64.

40 See HSL, p. 87.

41 Herbert Schnädelbach, *Hegels praktische Philosophie. Ein Kommentar der Texte in der Reihenfolge ihrer Entstehung*, Frankfurt a.M.: Suhrkamp 2000, pp. 228ff.

42 My reading bears certain similarities to a thesis of Georges Bataille. As Agamben has elaborated, Bataille also proposed the notion of "unemployed negativity." "If action ("doing") is—as Hegel says—negativity, the question arises as to whether the negativity of one who has "nothing more to do" disappears or remains in a state of "negativity with no use" . . . (I would not be able to define myself more precisely). I recognize that Hegel has foreseen such a possibility; at any rate he didn't situate it at the *end* of the process he described." Quoted in: Giorgio Agamben, *The Open: Man and Animal*, Stanford: Stanford University Press, 2004, p. 7.

43 This corresponds to Hegel's claim that one needs to step out of "the night of possibility into the daylight of the present . . ." HPS, p. 242.

44 Eric Weil, *Hegel et l'Etat. Cinq conférences suivies de Marx et la philosophie du droit*, Paris: Vrin 2000, p. 96.

[45] This analogy is itself suggested by the early Hegel when he talks about the fact that "matter . . . in this way . . . does not exist in and for itself, but rather to come to this indifference it must itself have become a predicate, a sublated moment. Thus, in itself, to be matter means: it is only taken in its abstraction." G. W. F. Hegel, *Jenaer Realphilosophie. Vorlesungsmanuskripte zur Philosophie der Natur und des Geistes von 1805–1806*, Berlin: Meiner 1969, p. 22.

[46] Although this might seem a bit forced, it is not at all arbitrary. Hegel himself speaks of the ethical human being in terms of "free matter." Cf. HPN, p. 49.

[47] The rabble is therefore in a double sense unique. He is on one side the only thing that is indifferent to difference and which stands in *in-difference to (the) difference* (of determination) and on the other side one can derive from this the claim that the rabble is unique in Hegel's philosophy, which is in no other place confronted with such a problem. A definition of 'unicity' can be found in BBE, pp. 68ff.

[48] As Hegel writes: "Matter fills space . . ." HPN, p. 47.

[49] Helmut Reichelt has rightly pointed out that Marx does not measure the *Philosophy of Right* according to the Hegelian *Logic* but rather opposes the logic of the *Philosophy of Right* to the logic of the *Logic*. Helmut Reichelt, *Die Marxsche Kritik der Hegelschen Rechtsphilosophie*, on: www.marxforschung.de/docs/0703_reichelt.pdf. The reading supports the thesis by Theunissen, intended as a criticism of Marx, that the latter proceeds in his criticism of the Philosophy of Right in such a way that "he turns the logic that is denied in it against itself." Michael Theunissen, *Sein und Schein. Zur kritischen Funktion der Hegelschen Logik*, Frankfurt a. M.: Suhrkamp 1980, p. 477. This remark implies that the logic of the *Philosophy of Right* may/could be different from the logic of the *Logic*.

[50] One could also say that it repeats itself as an immediate result in the fourth stage of the dialectical process.

[51] This notion which obviously presents a counter-concept to the Deleuzian, Guattarian notion of a 'body without organs' I borrow from Žižek. Cf. Slavoj Žižek, *Organs without Bodies. Deleuze and Consequences*, New York/London: Routledge 2004. I will delineate it more precisely in what follows. Kant, who comes close to a similar insight, substantializes the rabble in the anthropological categories of a pre-social state of nature: "(B)y nature all men are rabble, and those who are not, are refined by the social order and discipline. If they would cease to exist, also the refinement would cease and all men would be such rabble." Cf. Immanuel Kant/Friedländer, Ms. germ quart. 400 p. 678 / XXV 678f.) Order and discipline take a structurally analogous position as do habit and madness in Hegel.

[52] The relation of repulsion and attraction implied here obviously refers to Newtonian mechanics.

[53] Dieter Wandschneider, *Raum, Zeit, Relativität: Grundbestimmungen der Physik in der Perspektive der Hegelschen Naturphilosophie*, Frankfurt a. M.: Klostermann 1982, p. 123.

[54] The sense in which Hegel is here repeating an Aristotelian problem becomes clear when one takes into consideration the problem of localizing the 'void' in Aristotle as developed by Badiou. The void would have to be an absolutely empty

place in Aristotle which due to this emptiness would contradict the definition of place itself because it would be everywhere at the same time. It is telling that, as a result of this contradiction, Aristotle leaves open the possibility of thinking the void as the determination of matter. See BBE, 70–80. But the rabble is thus not something like an unmoved mover because he can only be generated in relation to the (historically situated) economic movement of civil society.

55 Already the early Hegel had referred to—in his criticism of the mechanism of industrial labor—a "negative liveliness." Cf. G. W. F. Hegel, *Jenaer Realphilosophie I: Die Vorlesungen von 1803/04*, Leipzig: Meiner 1932, pp. 232, 237. He also indicates there that money has the "moving life of t he dead." Ibid., pp. 239ff.

Chapter 9

1 G. W. F. Hegel, *The Positivity of Christian Religion*, in *Early Theological Writings*, Chicago: University of Chicago Press 1975, p. 152.

2 That patriotism is (structurally) synonymous with political attitude is rightly state in Claudio Cesa, "Liberté et liberté politique de Fichte à Hegel," in *Autour de Hegel. Hommage à Bernard Bourgeois*, ed. by François Dagognet/Pierre Osmo, Paris: Vrin 2000, p. 56.

3 Cf. HOPR, p. 134. Trans. mod.

4 Endre Kiss, "Die Begriffsvariationen der Gesinnung in Hegels Denken," in: *Phänomenologie des Geistes. Hegel-Jahrbuch 2002. Zweiter Teil*, ed. by Andreas Arndt/Karol Bar/Henning Ottmann, Berlin: Akademie 2002, p. 100.

5 Robert P. Pippin, "Hegels Praktischer Realismus. Rationales Handeln als Sittlichkeit," in *Hegels Erbe*, ed. by Christoph Halbig/Michael Quante/Ludwig Siep, Frankfurt a. M.: Suhrkamp 2004, p. 297.

6 Jean-Luc Nancy, *Hegel*, p. 56.

7 Hegel clearly states that the ethical laws "are not something alien to the subject. On the contrary, his spirit bears witness to them as to *its own essence . . .*" HOPR, p. 155. This is the reason why Ernst Tugendhat is simply wrong in claiming—and thus repeating the old liberal-bourgeois topos of Haym—that Hegel's philosophy would lead to the mere justification of the existing order. Cf. Ernst Tugendhat, *Self-Conscious and Self-Determination*, Cambridge/London: The MIT Press 1989. For example, the law not to kill is fundamentally different according to whether it is read as an external norm or as a norm which one subjectively holds as necessary. Hegel's position is, contrary to Tugendhat's reading, the latter.

8 Cf. HGPR, p. 296.

9 The attitude is not a mere emotion, because it remains bound to moments of arbitrariness. But the dimension of emotion cannot be completely erased from attitude as is suggested by the etymology of the German 'Gesinnung' which already refers to sense (sensus) from which 'Gefühl' also stems. Cf. WilhelmTraugott Krug, "Gefühl," in *Allgemeines Handwörterbuch der philosophischen Wissenschaften nebst ihrer Literatur und Geschichte*, Leipizg: Brockhaus 1833, vol. 2, pp. 139–43.

[10] In this way the child has the right to be educated as a realization of its freedom to become a member of civil society (which is initially merely present in itself) and at the same time it has a duty to its parents to subordinate itself to this education. Cf. HOPR, pp. 172–9.

[11] Leo Rauch, "Hegel, Spirit and Politics," in *Routledge History of Philosophy, Volume IV, The Age of German Idealism*, London/New York: Routledge 2003, p. 278.

[12] Theodor W. Adorno, *Sexual Taboos and Law Today*, in *Critical Models: Interventions and Catchwords*, New York: Columbia University Press 2005, p. 75.

[13] The formulation of "a right to have rights" can be found in the handwritten notes to § 94. Cf. HGPR, p. 181. Hegel is therefore the inventor of this phrase, and not Arendt.

[14] Cf. HOPR, pp. 176ff.

[15] In Pippin's reading one would need to claim that the fact that in modernity the principle of subjectivity becomes important supplies proof of "the historically effective character of practical reasons" and shows that those should never be valid as "instances of an a-historical type." However, this interpretation misses the fact that with the historical moment in which the principle of subjectivity becomes the guide for the constitution of the state, this principle becomes irreversible, and this means that it must enjoy an a-historic validity. This means that, in a historical setting, as soon as the subject has entered into a free and rational self-determination, any revision of this principle is a violation of its rationality. Therefore in Hegel something takes place within the specificity of history which exceeds the historical place of its appearance. Cf. Robert P. Pippin, "Hegels Praktischer Realismus," pp. 302–3.

[16] Cf. in contrast Karl-Heinz Ilting, "Rechtphilosophie als Phänomenologie des Bewusstseins der Freiheit," in *Aufsätze über Hegel*, pp. 135–65.

[17] Ludwig Heyde, "Sittlichkeit und Ironie. Hegels Kritik der modernen Subjektivität in den *Grundlinien der Philosophie des Rechts*," in *Die Folgen des Hegelianismus. Philosophie, Religion und Politik im Abschied von der Moderne*, ed. by Peter Koslowski, München: Fink 1998, p. 316.

[18] This implies that in the supposed finitude of every determination of will the true infinity of the will's freedom appears.

[19] What goes for the child goes for the ethical human being: "he stands only in so far as he wills to stand; as soon as we no longer will to stand, we collapse; standing is, therefore, the habit of the will to stand." HPM, p. 57. The standing [*Stehen*] and the estate [*Stand*] share one structure. Both are expressions of the will relating to the objective reality and want to be stable within it.

[20] For the notion of political constitution which I largely leave undiscussed, cf. RHS, pp. 134–57.

[21] Hegel clearly points to this when he comments concerning the attitude: "The Truth is freedom having itself as end in its realization; to be active, to realize oneself, this is the true in and for itself." HVORL 4, p. 641.

[22] One can notice a general rationalization of the affective dimension if ethicality. One can thus conceive of the emotion, understanding and reason in a structural analogy to the community of sentiment (family), of understanding (civil society) and of the state (reason).

[23] David James, *Hegel's Philosophy of Right. Subjectivity and Ethical Life*, London/ NewYork: Continuum 2007, p. 111. James is right—*to state the obvious*—that in civil society the bourgeois is initially bourgeois. It is precisely in relation to this passage that the early Marx will begin to criticize Hegel, for while elaborating his concept of the state, he still depends on the determination of the corporation and thereby remains infected by the logic of civil society and its atom—interest.

[24] This is the reason why Hegel is not in danger of becoming 'totalitarian,' as Berlin claims. Berlin—whose views are inherited by Popper—develops/proposes the thesis that Hegel's 'political philosophy' develops the universal out of the isolated interest. If that were the case he would not be able to avoid a situation in which any possible content could come into the sphere of the state. Therein Berlin sees the threat that one interest can assert itself against all others and could be claimed to be universal. That in this reading the important distinction between morality and ethicality is structurally lost—which Hegel precisely introduces to avoid this consequence—is what Berlin misses completely. Cf. Isaiah Berlin, *Two Concepts of Liberty*, Oxford: Clarendon Press 1958, pp. 18ff. Cf. also Slavoj Žižek, *Did Somebody say Totalitarianism? Five Interventions into the (Mis) Use of a Notion*, London/New York: Verso 2002.

[25] Jun-Ho Won, *Hegels Begriff der politischen Gesinnung*, p. 79.

[26] One can resume Hegel very briefly if one reads the following sentence only in relation to attitude: "The state in its constitution penetrates all relationships." HVORL 3, p. 752.

[27] From this passage one could derive a modified understanding of what Balibar calls—with Spinozist undertones—the transindividual. Transindividual would then name the attitude in Hegel's state Cf. Étienne Balibar, *The Philosophy of Marx*, London/New York 2007, pp. 30–3. Already Avineri—although only in relation to labor—employs the notion of the transindividual with regard to Hegel. Cf. AHT, p. 91.

[28] For this reason Hösle's thesis that Hegel wants to "diminish" the subjective dimension in the state is correct and incorrect at the same time. it is Correct if one understands the subjective dimension exclusively as a moral dimension; incorrect if one considers Hegel's idea that the state is nothing but a collective subject, as this substance. Cf. Vittorio Hösle, "Der Staat," in *Anspruch und Leistung von Hegels Rechtsphilosophie*, ed. by Christoph Jermann, Stuttgart/Bad-Cannstatt: Frommann-Holzboog 1987, p. 190. The subject is regarded as substanceless as long as it does not relate itself to the ethical substance in the ethical attitude. At the same time one needs to add that this substance is never some stable entity but is rather a constant renewal of multiplicities of relations.

[29] One can remark here that due to the constitution of Hegel's notion of attitude it does not seem surprising that Rosenzweig who wrote an early book on Hegel's state—if one follows the convincing reading of Eric Santner—attempted to develop an ethics of responsibility. Cf. Eric Santner, *On the Psychotheology of Everyday Life. Reflections on Freud and Rosenzweig*, Chicago: University of Chicago Press 2001, pp. 86–129. The cited phrase can be found on p. 9. My interpretation here opposes the comment by Pippin that "it is not clear, I will

suggest, how the citizens are to 'understand' the state [. . .]." I want to claim that this 'understanding' is a knowledge about the unconscious. If one can interpret this relation which attitude names still in terms of a hermeneutical understanding is however certainly questionable. Cf.. Robert B. Pippin, *Hegel's Political Argument and the Problem of* Verwirklichung, in: *Political Theory*, vol. 9, no. 4 (Nov. 1981), p. 531.

30 Dolar made this point with regards to Lacan's reading of the cogito: *"the subject emerges only at the point of a nonrecognition*: [. . .] a "this is not me," "I was not there,"""" although they are produced by the subject him/herself. Mladen Dolar, *Cogito as Subject of the Unconscious*, in: *Cogito and the Unconscious*, ed. by Slavoj Žižek, Durham/London: Duke University Press 1998, p. 14.

31 Eric Santner, *On the Psychotheology*, p. 26.

32 Christoph Menke, *Tragödie im Sittlichen*, p. 49.

33 Ibid., p. 55. Jean-Luc Nancy has rightly claimed that Hegel's standpoint is one in which "it is no longer just a matter of changing form, of replacing one vision and one order by some other and some other order, but in which the one and only point—of view and of order—is that of transformation itself." Jean-Luc Nancy, *Hegel,* pp. 6ff.

34 Giorgio Agamben, *The Open*, p. 7.

35 Karl Marx/Friedrich Engels, *The Holy Family*, p. 28.

36 Early Hegel defines inner indignation as the "highest inner conflict of the will, inner indignation and hatred" produced by the "inequality of wealth and poverty." Therewith inner indignation signifies not only the mere conviction of the poor against the rich. But rather the scission of poverty and wealth itself. Indignation as the name for the tearing up of the ethical bond is the highest inner conflict. I will in the following claim, against Hegel, that this inner indignation produces clear external effects and does not remain in mere interiority. Cf. G. W. F. Hegel, *Jenaer Realphilosophie. Vorlesungsmanuskripte zur Philosophie der Natur*, pp. 232ff.

37 For the notion of contradiction, see Alain Badiou, *Théorie de la contradiction*, Paris: F. Maspero 1975.

38 Here Marx's word—directed against Stirner—fits: "The belief that consciousness is to blame for everything is his dogma which makes him a rabble and the rabble a sinner." Karl Marx/Friedrich Engels, *The German Ideology*, 1998, p. 408, trans. mod. Hegel would be in this sense a rebel against the rebellion of the rabble which he understands merely as a morally evil attitude remaining for itself. He misjudges therewith the range of his own description. At the same time one can see in the rabble-problem what the early Badiou remarked: "We must understand what Lenin repeated all over the place: the retrospective good news that Hegel is a materialist!" Alain Badiou, *Theory of the Subject*, p. 3.

39 Also Hegel wants to say that appearance is not a mere semblance but in it there is always an essence expressing itself which exists only as appearance although it does not coincide with it.

40 Hegel here takes up a distinction from Kant. For him the rabble and the *vulgus* therefore coincide: "By the word *people* (*populus*) is meant the *number* of human

beings united in a region, insofar as they constitute a *whole*. This number, or even a part of it that recognizes itself as united into a civil whole through common ancestry, is called a *nation* (*gens*); the part that exempts itself from these laws, the unruly crowd within this people) is called a *rabble* (*vulgus*) whose illegal association is the *mob* (*agere per turbas*); this conduct that excludes them from the quality of a citizen." Immanuel Kant, *Anthropology from a pragmatic point of view (1788)*, in Kant, *Anthropology, History, and Education*, Cambridge: Cambridge University Press 2007, p. 407. What Kant names *agere per turbas* is what I reconstruct as dissolving in Hegel.

41 G. W. F. Hegel, *Politische Schriften*, Frankfurt a. M.: Suhrkamp 1966, p. 160.

42 Werner Conze, *Vom Pöbel zum Proletariat. Sozialgeschichtliche Voraussetzungen für den Sozialismus in Deutschland [1941]*, in: *Gesellschaft – Staat – Nation. Gesammelte Aufsätze*, Stuttgart: Klett-Cotta 1992, p. 222.

43 One can find a commentary on the historical signification of the word in Werner Conze, *Proletariat – Pöbel, Pauperismus*, in: *Geschichtliche Grundbegriffe. Historisches Lexikon zur politisch-sozialen Sprache in Deutschland*, Stuttgart: Klett-Cotta 1984, vol. 5.

44 Niccolo Machiavelli, *The Prince*, London: Penguin 2003, p. 58, trans. mod.

45 Agemir Bavaresco has aligned the *vulgus* with "multitudo" and "turba." Cf. Agemir Bavaresco, *La théorie hégélienne de l'opinion publique*, Paris: L'Harmattan 2000.

46 G. W. F. Hegel, *Politische Schriften*, p. 161.

47 Friedrich Nietzsche, *Thus spoke Zarathustra*, p. 350.

48 On the logic of 'transcendental illusion' see Slavoj Žižek, *Tarrying with the Negative. Kant, Hegel, and the Critique of Ideology*, Durham/London: Duke University Press 2003, pp. 89–91.

49 If one reads the affirmation of the impossibility as the logic of the rabble-attitude and his will, there are two ways one can take from there. On one side it is conceivable for one to insist on the interruption of the structure of the ethical and on the suspension of any action and organization. On the other it is thinkable to understand the interruption of the ethical structure as a first moment which in what ensues, through actions, leads to the conversion of an impossibility into a possibility that had previously not existed and to repeat such a conversion a potentially infinite number of times. One can say that the first way is Agamben's, the second Badiou's.

50 This phrase I borrow, out of context, from Peter Hallward. Cf. Peter Hallward, *Depending on Inconsistency: Alain Badiou's Answer to the "Guiding Question of All Contemporary Philosophy,"* in: *Polygraph. An International Journal of Culture and Politics, 17 (2005), The Philosophy of Alain Badiou*, p. 9.

51 Here it is interesting to refer to Badiou's remark that the time of classical revolutionary politics was the future, but the time of post-classical politics is the future anterior. Here as well the actuality of the rabble-problem becomes clear. Cf. Alain Badiou, *Peut-on penser la politique?*, p. 107.

52 It is important to note is that to think stasis—the basic idea of any Platonic ontology—precisely does not mean to think ontological inertia in a pure form but one necessarily needs the movement of dialectics and also the retroaction

to gain a consistent concept of stasis. Stasis therefore always already presupposes the movement which it produces so that it can be retroactively grasped as that which lies 'prior' to movement. Stasis is always already *production of stasis*. In political terms, Badiou has recently named such a production with the old word 'communism' Cf. Alain Badiou, *The Communist Hypothesis*, London/New York: Verso 2010. For Hegel one can note: in the rabble, idealism—the name 'rabble' marks a pure ideal place without its own appearance—and materialism—with him the insight into the matter of the ethical space is generated—coincide.

53 Herbert Marcuse, *Reason and Revolution. Hegel and the Rise of Social Theory*, London: Routledge 1955, p. 150. One can also say that for the rabble the Hegelian dictum is not valid to the effect that "When all conditions of a fact are at hand, the fact steps into concrete existence" (HSL, 416). For 1. the rabble does not step into existence and cannot 2. be grasped by the presence of the conditions peculiar to him. The whole question is if one thinks the relationship of dialectics and non-dialectics dialectically or non-dialectically. The author is preparing an elaboration of this question under the title of a *dialectics of dialectics and non-dialectics*.

54 *Briefe von und an Hegel*, ed. by. V. J. Hoffmeister/F. Nicolin, Hamburg: Meiner 1969–81, vol. 2, pp. 85ff. This passage from one letter to Niethammer which I cite here in full—not only because of the obviousness of its prose but also in order to be precise: "I stick to the fact that the world spirit has given the time the order to advance. Such a command will be obeyed; this entity strides irresistibly forward like an armored, firmly united phalanx and with such an imperceptible movement through thick and thin as the sun strides. Uncountable light infantry against and for the same flank all around it, they mostly do not know what is happening and all get struck on the head like being struck by an invisible hand. All the tarrying story-telling and the make-believe stroking the air is of no help against it. There can be something which reaches the shoe laces of this colossus and spreads a bit of shoe polish or excrement on it but it is not able to loosen them . . . The most secure (namely inner and outer) option is to keep sight of this advancing giant." The rabble would in Hegel's image be no more than the bit of excrement on the shoe of the world spirit, which surprisingly can bring him down.

55 G. W. F. Hegel, *Jenaer Realphilosophie. Vorlesungsmanuskripte zur Philosophie der Natur*, p. 232.

Chapter 10

1 Alain Badiou, *Metapolitics*, S. 96.
2 Quoted by Manfred Riedel, "Einleitung," in *Materialen zur Hegelschen Rechtsphilosophie*, Vol. 1, ed, by Manfred Riedel, Frankfurt a. M.: Suhrkamp 1975, p. 23.
3 Why Hegel considers the concept of right in the *Philosophy of Right* as "presupposed" (HOPR, 18) is explained in Christoph Menke, *Tragödie im Sittlichen*, pp. 202–32.
4 Robert Pippin, "Hegel, Freedom, The Will," in *Grundlinien der Philosophie des Rechts*, ed. by Ludwig Siep, Berlin: Akademie 1997, p. 37.

5 Cf. Manfred Riedel, "Dialektik in Institutionen," in *Zwischen Tradition und Revolution,* pp. 43ff.

6 Ibid., p. 44.

7 My reading attempts to show that the sphere of abstract right which is the first part of the *Philosophy of Right* is not an arbitrary idea of Hegel but has a systematic relevance. contrast, for example, Knowles' claim: "How can we make sense of all this? It must be admitted that here Hegel seems to be pulling one rabbit after another out of a hat, each fantastical, each magical, each mystifyingly unintelligible." Dudley Knowles, *Hegel and the Philosophy of Right,* London: Routledge 2002, p. 48.

8 By deriving abstract right from the free will Hegel does not adopt the liberal position which begins from the free individual as the starting point for the community.

9 One can remark here that the abstractness refers to the fact that personality as fundament of right is gained by abstracting from all determinations which define an individual living in the state.

10 Jeanne L. Schroeder, *The Vestal and the Fasces. Hegel, Lacan, Property and the Feminine,* Berkeley/Los Angeles: University of California Press 1998, p. 30.

11 Jeanne L. Schroeder, *The Vestal,* p. 11.

12 Jeanne L. Schroeder, *The Vestal,* p. 19.

13 Peter G. Stillman, "Property, Contract and Ethical Life Property, Contract, and Ethical Life in Hegel's *Philosophy of Right,"* in *Hegel and Legal Theory,* ed. By Drucilla Cornell/Michel Rosenfeld / David Gray Carlson, London / New York: Routledge 1991, p. 206.

14 Jeanne L. Schroeder, *The Vestal,* p. 34.

15 Joachim Ritter, "Person und Eigentum ," p. 267.

16 This conclusion deepens when one considers the fact that Hegel is the inventor of the notion "private property". Cf. the entry on 'Eigentum' in Johannes Hoffmeister, *Wörterbuch der philosophischen Grundbegriffe,* Hamburg: Meiner 1955.

17 Tom Rockmore, *Marx after Marxism. The philosophy of Karl Marx,* Oxford: Wiley-Blackwell 2002, p. 28.

18 Here one can conclude that the luxury-rabble always retains the status of a mere possessor. At the same time Hegel never goes as far as denying legal security to his wealth.

19 One has to insist here against the widespread misreading, which attempts to align Hegel with Locke, that Hegel does not justify the possession of a particular property in a normative way. Rather he takes it as the logical starting point of the abstract person. This is to say, that Hegel is no theorist of primordial accumulation.

20 Jeanne L. Schroeder, *The Vestal,* p. 43.

21 Jeanne L. Schroeder, *The Vestal,* p.24.

22 Peter G. Stillman, Property, Contract, and Ethical Life, pp. 207ff.

23 Angelica Nuzzo, "Freedom in the body," in *Beyond Liberalism,* p. 121.

24 Herbert Marcuse, *Reason and Revolution,* pp. 194–5.

25 G. W. F. Hegel, *Jenaer Realphilosophie. Vorlesungsmanuskripte zur Philosophie der Natur,* p. 232.

[26] This reduction of the poor (worker) to his mere bodily functions is what the early Marx will start to criticize.

[27] Here one could draw a parallel to Luhmann who notes that in modernity only 'bodies' are left in the domain of exclusion. See Niklas Luhmann, *Inklusion und Exklusion*, p. 262. The possibility of reading Hegel and Luhmann together on this question I have presented in, "Alles verpöbelt sich zusehends! Namenlosigkeit und generische Inklusion," in: *Soziale Systeme. Zeitschrift für soziologische Theorie*, Jg. 14, (2008),ed. by Sina Farzin/Sven Opitz/Urs Stäheli, pp. 210–28.

[28] Here a remark of Badiou concerning Leibniz gains another meaning. He states that: "The state is programmed to solely recognize as apart, whose count it ensures, what the situation's resources themselves allow to be *distinguished*." (BBE, 283) For Leibniz it follows that the indistinguishable which cannot be separated by a name are necessarily identical. Hegel here obviously goes further than Leibniz by distinguishing between poor and rabble although without resolving the problem of indistinguishability.

[29] Peter G. Stillman, "Property, Contract, and Ethical Life," p. 211.

[30] Werner Hamacher, *The Right Not to Use Rights. Human Rights and the Stucture of Judgments*, in *Political Theologies. Public Religions in a Post-Secular World*, ed. by Hent de Vries/Lawrence E. Sullivan, New York: Fordham University Press 2006, p. 681. That for the rabble it cannot be a question of using the dimension implied in the right not to use rights, should be clear.

[31] Mark Tunick, *Hegel's Political Philosophy*, p. 27.

[32] It should be clear that this *un-right* is close to the Arendtian 'right to have rights.' Since I cannot pursue this linkage here I refer to the far-sighted investigations of Werner Hamacher, in *'The Right to Have Rights (Four-and-a-Half Remarks),'* in *South Atlantic Quarterly* 103:2/3, Spring/Summer, Durham NC 2004. At the same time I see a problem in Hamacher's conception of a right to have rights which is bound to the notion of existence that for him has to be the decisive notion of this right. His reference to the right of "bare human existence," the notion of existence—even stripped of all determinations—refers to a transcendental—obviously that of language—which makes this existence thinkable in the first place. I however claim that the rabble here even suspends this form of transcendental since he 1. In-exists and 2. Does impossibly appear. Badiou expounded a similar criticism with regard to Agamben. Cf. Alain Badiou, Intervention dans le cadre du Collège international de philosophie sur le livre de Giorgio Agamben: la Communauté qui vient, théorie de la singularité quelconque, on: http://www.entretemps.asso.fr/Badiou/Agamben.htm.

Chapter 11

[1] Alain Badiou, *Politics: A non-expressive Dialectics*, in *Beyond Potentialities? Politics between the Possible and the Impossible* ed. by Mark Potocnik/Frank Ruda/Jan Völker, Zurich: diaphanes 2011, p. 20.

[2] Friedrich Nietzsche, *Ecce Homo. How to become what one is*, p. 109

[3] Herbert Marcuse, *Reason and Revolution*, p. 185.

[4] This is why Hegel can write in the *Aesthetics*: "In this way man breaks the barrier of his implicit and immediate character, so that precisely because he *knows* that he is an animal, he ceases to be an animal and attains knowledge of himself as spirit." HA1, p. 80.

[5] Hegel makes it clear that this does not take place when one considers the will as indeterminate and "also determined . . ." Cf. HOPR, p. 32.

[6] Cf. HOPR, 33.

[7] Robert Pippin, "Hegel, Freedom, The Will," p. 51.

[8] Hegel calls this a "whole of happiness." Cf. HOPR, p. 41.

[9] Cf. HVORL 4, p. 141 and HOPR, p. 43.

[10] For the notion of concrete universality see AlenkaZupančič, *The 'Concrete Universal' and what Comedy can tell us about it*, in *Lacan: The Silent Partners*, ed. Slavoj Žižek, London/New York: Verso 2006.

[11] Cf. HVORL 4, p. 142.

[12] This enumeration becomes clear when one also understands the ethical will as the absorption of the will into its object so that the will is ethical but its— subjective—content is unethical. The ethical will presents the most universal objective will in the enumeration.

[13] Herbert Marcuse, *Reason and Revolution*, p. 188.

[14] Jürgen Habermas, Hegel's Critique of the French Revolution, in *Theory and Practice*, Beacon Press 1973, p. 82.

[15] One can here cite Ritter's right insight that Hegel's philosophy "*is up to its most inner incentives a philosophy of revolution* . . ." Joachim Ritter, "Hegel und die französische Revolution," p. 192.

[16] Rebecca Comay, *Dead Right*, p. 379.

[17] Rebecca Comay, *Dead Right*, p. 385.

[18] One can claim that such a will is always contaminated by what Badiou calls a destructive "passion for the real." Alain Badiou, *The Century*, pp. 53–54.

[19] In this critique, Hegel anticipates Nietzsche.

[20] Cf.. Joachim Ritter, "Hegel und die französische Revolution," pp. 196ff.

[21] Jürgen Habermas, "Hegels Kritik der Französischen Revolution," p. 133.

[22] A discussion of this distinction can be found in Alain Badiou, *La volonté. Cours d'agrégation (2002–2003)*, on: http://www.entretemps.asso.fr/Badiou/02-03.2.htm.

[23] Cf. Alain Badiou, *Conditions*, London/New York 2009.

[24] In a certain sense in the willing of the rabble there is a proximity to the 'International': "We are nothing, now let's be all."

Chapter 12

[1] BBE, p. 109.

[2] The following comments will in a certain sense present an idea which relies on the connotation of the German word '*Menge*' which can mean 'a lot,' 'mass,' or 'set' in the mathematical sense of the term.

³ To what extent Hegel perpetuates a problem that already instructed the Platonic dialogue, Parmenides, becomes clear if one recalls Badiou's precise investigation: BBE, pp. 31–7.

⁴ A good short overview of the history of set theory may be found in Peter Hallward, *Badiou. A Subject to Truth*, Minneapolis: University of Minnesota Press 2003, pp. 323–48. A more detailed account is given by Shaughan Lavine, *Understanding the Infinite*, Cambridge: Harvard University Press 1998.

⁵ The excursus establishes a connection that Hegel himself criticizes: the linkage of philosophy and mathematics. Hegel's well-known criticism first of the indeterminacy of the number and secondly of the mathematical concept of infinity which is in concurrence with the philosophical one. I want to leave this consciously aside because I only want to point to a consequence which results if one takes up the connotation of the concept of the "Menge" which is not deployed in the Hegelian text. On Hegel's relation to mathematics, see Alain Badiou, "Philosophy and Mathematics," in *Conditions*, pp. 93–113.

⁶ Georg Cantor, "Beiträge zur transfiniten Mengenlehre," in: *Mathematische Annalen* 46, 1895, p. 481. That the development of set theory—even with Cantor—dissolves all of the concepts involved in this definition can be read in BBE, pp. 23–52.

⁷ The subsequent examples function only as clarification—although they necessarily introduce inaccuracies. I accept them for the purpose of greater clarity.

⁸ Cf. Bertrand Russell, *Introduction to Mathematical Philosophy*, London: Simon & Schuster/Touchstone 1920, pp. 12ff.

⁹ Peter Hallward, *Badiou*, p. 323.

¹⁰ That this assignation is far more complex can be seen from the reconstruction in Alain Badiou, *Number and Numbers*, Cambridge/Malden: Polity Press 2008, pp. 16–23.

¹¹ Cf. GottlobFrege, *The Foundations of Arithmetic: A Logico-Mathematical Enquiry into the Concept of Number*, Evanston: Northwestern University Press 1980.

¹² An illustrative version of this paradox became famous: If a barber only cuts the hair of those who not do cut their own hair, does he cut his own hair? If yes, then he does not only do the hair of those which do not themselves do it. If no, then he does the hair of those whose hair he does, which is to say who do not do their hair themselves and therefore he does his own hair. See also: Howard Eves, *An Introduction to the History of Mathematics*, New York: Brooks Cole 1975, p. 476.

¹³ To what extent this had a "downright catastrophic effect" for the intensional conception of set theory cf. Constance Reid, *Hilbert*, London: Springer 1970, p. 98.

¹⁴ Letter to Dedekind, July 28, 1899, quoted from the translation of Michael Hallett, *Cantorian Set Theory and the Limitation of Size*, Oxford: Oxford University Press 1996 p. 166.

¹⁵ My remarks are in a certain sense historically imprecise because one can find this threefold determination only after the axiomatization by Zermelo and Fraenkel. Cantor still distinguishes between objects and groups of objects. However, as the axiomatization seems to me to be a necessarily implied effect of the Cantorian theory, I believe my argument accords with the logic of the matter in hand. Also see Ernst Zermelo, *Untersuchungen über die Grundlagen der Mengenlehre*, in: *Mathematische Annalen* 65, 1908.

[16] One can formulate here alongside the set theoretical axiom of separation which can easily be presented in a formal way. I therefore refer to Badiou (Cf. BBE, 60–6) The assumption of the intensional conception can be written as follows: $(\exists\beta)(\forall\alpha)[\lambda(\alpha)\rightarrow(\alpha \in \beta)]$. This reads: there exists a beta and for all alpha it is the case that if alpha has a property (lambda), then alpha is an element of beta. Already in the typeface—and I will be dealing exclusively with this—it is clearly the presupposed existence (written $\exists$) of beta which names a multiplicity in which a certain domain can be singled out (alpha) which contains elements which share a certain property. The assumption of the extensional conception leads to a different formalization: $(\forall\alpha)(\exists\beta)(\forall\gamma)[[(\gamma \in \alpha) \, \& \, \lambda(\gamma)]\rightarrow(\gamma \in \beta)]$. This reads—and I shall deal only with the first part: for any alpha there exists a beta, etc. That this formalization does not begin with an existential presupposition but only with an implication—of 'something' (β) if it is correct that alpha exists. This transforms the whole thinking of the constitution of sets. $\exists$ and $\forall$ are called (existential / universal) quantifiers. The difference between intensional and extensional conception is therefore a difference in the order of quantifiers

[17] I have shown to what extent the distinction between two forms of existence (a determinable existence and one which has no other determination than that of existence) is necessary for any political analysis of concrete situations in "Back to the Factory. A Plea for a Renewal of Concrete Analysis of Concrete Situations," in *Beyond Potentialities? Politics between the Possible and the Impossible*, ed. by Mark Potocnik, Frank Ruda, Jan Völker, Berlin: Diaphanes 2011.

[18] For the set theoretical notion of the part cf. Abraham Adolf Fraenkel, *Einleitung in die Mengenlehre. Eine gemeinverständliche Hinführung in das Reich der unendlichen Grössen*, Berlin / Heidelberg/New York: Kessinger Pub. 1972, pp. 15ff.

[19] One can also claim that this is the set theoretical formulation of the *logic of a double latency*. Important consequences of this will become clearer in the following. Also see Alain Badiou, *Number and Numbers*; also the important remarks concerning the excess of inclusion over belonging in BBE, pp. 84–6.

[20] One needs to indicate that herein consists a fundamental ambivalence of Hegel's critique: on one side it can be read as a critique of an unorganized form of being together of the kind dear to anarchism. This can only be supported. On the other side it is a critique of a contingent emergence of an in and for itself indeterminate particularity whose universality Hegel does not recognize. This critique cannot be sustained, since the contingent emergence of something which is indeterminate in no way excludes that in consequence there can be (the invention of) a strict and disciplined organization.

[21] Frank Schalow, *The Question of Being and the Recovery of Language within Hegel's Thought*, in *The Owl of Minerva* 24, 2 (Spring 1993), p. 179.

[22] Cf. Also Karl Löwith, "Hegel und die Sprache," in *Sämtliche Schriften I. Mensch und Menschenwelt*, ed. by Klaus Stichweh, Stuttgart: Metzler 1981 and Jacques Derrida, "The Pit and the Pyramide: Introduction into Hegel's Semiology," in *Margins of Philosophy*, Sussex: University of Chicago Press 1982.

[23] Cf. My article oriented at the works of Žižek and Nancy: "The Name of the Monarch: Hegel's Communist Conception of the State" (in preparation).

[24] HPM, pp. 184–201.

[25] Jacques Derrida, *The Pit*, p. 76.
[26] Ibid., p. 90.
[27] G.W.F. Hegel, *Jenaer Realphilosophie. Vorlesungsmanuskripte zur Philosophie der Natur*, p. 180.
[28] Jacques Derrida, *The Pit*, p. 84.
[29] Ibid., p. 88.
[30] Slavoj Žižek, *The Metastases of Enjoyment. On Women and Causality*, London/New York: Verso 2005, p. 44.
[31] G.W.F. Hegel, *Jenaer Realphilosophie. Vorlesungsmanuskripte zur Philosophie der Natur*, p. 183.
[32] I here follow the commentary of Žižek. Cf. Slavoj Žižek, *The Metastases of Enjoyment*, pp. 46–50.
[33] Ibid., p. 48.
[34] Cf. John McCumber, *The Company of Words: Hegel, Language, and Systematic Philosophy*, Evanston 1993, pp. 130–43.
[35] McCumber clarifies the explanation with the formula: "$M_{n+1} \Leftarrow (M_{n=x} \ldots\ldots M_n)$", where $n > x$ ('explication')" and the abbreviation by the formula: "$(M_{n-x} \ldots\ldots M_n) \Rightarrow M_{n+1}$, where $n > x$ ('abbreviation')." Ibid., p. 132. M stands here—as a token for a marker—both inside the brackets as that which I have marked as the series of concrete determinations and outside of them as a name. The explanation leads from a name to the unity of a series of determinations, the abbreviation leads from a series of determinations to a name.
[36] Slavoj Žižek, *The Metastases of Enjoyment*, p. 49.
[37] This is the first passage in the manuscript of 1821/22 in which Hegel talks about the rabble.
[38] To what extent Hegel is wrong to think the rabble following the logic of negation, I have noted several times by showing that he is here presented with a problem of categorization which cannot be conceived merely in terms of negation.

Conclusion

[1] HPR1, 120.
[2] Alain Badiou, *Théorie du sujet*, p. 19.
[3] Cf. Eugène Fleischmann, *La philosophie politique de Hegel: sous la forme d'un commentaire des Fondements de la philosophie du droit*, Paris: Gallimard 1964. A problematization of this notion, not relating to Hegel, but relevant for the question discussed above may be found in Alain Badiou, *Metapolitics*, pp. 10–26.

Coda

[1] *MCHR, 89.*
[2] Alain Badiou, *Metapolitics*, p. 93.
[3] I will develop my reading with reference to the texts up to 1844. My concluding remarks stand in a twofold relation to Althusser: On one side they share the idea

concerning the Marxian economic-philosophical manuscripts that "One day we shall have to study this text in detail and give a word-by-word explanation of it . . ." Cf. Louis Althusser, *For Marx*, London/New York: Verso 2005, p. 158. On the other side they do not share the thesis that the criticism of the Hegelian state philosophy can only be grasped in the context of Feuerbachian philosophy (Cf. Ibid., p. 37). Rather I want to claim that the texts of early Marx can be properly understood against the background of the rabble-problem.

4   Karl Marx/Friedrich Engels, *The Holy Family*, p. 28.

5   G. W. F. Hegel, *Jenaer Realphilosophie. Vorlesungsmanuskripte zur Philosophie der Natur*, p. 232.

6   Stathis Kouvelakis, *Philosophy and Revolution. From Kant to Marx*, London/New York: Verso 2003, p. 331.

7   Marx also speaks of "absolute poverty" (MEPM, 290). In the *Holy Family* one can even find the determination of inexistence that marked the rabble. Marx writes: "But not having is not a mere category, it is a most dismal reality; today the man who has nothing is nothing, for he is cut off from existence in general, and still more from a human existence, for the condition of not having is the condition of the complete separation of man from his objectivity. Therefore, not having seems quite justified in being the highest object of thought for Proudhon . . ." See: Karl Marx/Friedrich Engels, *The Holy Family*, p. 32.

8   This distinction has often not been acknowledged in the contemporary discourse (also within the Marxist tradition). Badiou rightly remarked concerning this form of "vulgar Marxism" that "it thought the working class as the class of workers . . . Yet this did not prevent knowledge (and paradoxically Marxist knowledge itself) from being forever able to consider 'the workers' as falling under an encyclopedic determinant (sociological, economical, etc.) . . ." BBE, p. 334. That this distinction remains a provocation for some thinkers is explicit in Laclau's debate with Slavoj Žižek in which Laclau, first quoting and then commenting on Žižek, claims: "'Marx distinguishes between working class and proletariat: the working class effectively is a particular social group, while the proletariat designates a subjective position [. . .].' Now, to start with, Marx never made such a distinction." Ernesto Laclau, "Why Constructing a People is the Main Task of Radical Politics," in: *Critical Inquiry* 32 (Summer 2006), p. 659 sq. The quote from Žižek is from the following text: Slavoj Žižek, "Against the Populist Temptation," in: *Critical Inquiry* 32 (Summer 2006).

9   This indicates why Marx refuses any form of anarchic politics. The agent, the subject of emancipatory transformation cannot be conceived of an-archistically.

10 Marx criticizes in this passage a wrong depiction of the historical development. That my reading remains consistent, I will demonstrate by showing that the proletariat can only break into the bourgeois order when a contingent, subjective operation supplements the necessarily produced condition.

11 Michael Löwy, *The Theory of Revolution in the Young Marx*, Chicago 2005, p. 16.

12 Jacques Rancière, *Le concept de critique et la critique de l'économie politique des 'Manuscrits de 1844' au 'Capital'*, in Louis Althusser/Etienne Balibar/Roger Establet/Pierre Macherey/Jacques Rancière, *Lire le capital*, Paris: Quadrige, 1996, pp. 103, et sq.

[13] The German notion of "*Entwesung*" is here more precise than the English "impoverishment," because it implies two semantic components: 1) a loss of essence/being (Wesen)and it renders 2) this loss as a process.

[14] Cf. MEPM, p. 327.

[15] Cf. for this also Frank Ruda, *Humanism Reconsidered, or: Live living Life*, in: *Filozofski vestnik, What is it to live?*, vol. XX, no. 2, 2009 And Lorenzo Chiesas comradely and critical remarks in Lorenzo Chiesa, *The Body of the Structural Dialectic, or, the Partisan and the 'Human Animal'*, unpublished typescript.

[16] I here add the German "*Unwesen*," because it is important to note that the German term "*Unwesen*" implies that the essence [*Wesen*] of man is a negation of that essence itself [*Un-wesen*] which should not be conceived of only in terms of negation, but also as an indicator of an existence.

[17] I adopt this argument from Žižek. See: Slavoj Žižek, *In Defense of Lost Causes*, London/New York: Continuum 2010, p. 286.

[18] One would have to develop further how and why any reactionary politics grounds its thought in the principle of constructability. See also BBE, pp. 265–326.

[19] I refer here to the relation of eventual site, event, and subject in Badiou. The working class can be considered as the eventual site of the proletariat. See also: BBE, pp. 104–11 and pp. 173–90.

[20] That universalism in this regard can be understood as a universal address within a potentially infinite process becomes intelligible if one also considers Badiou's theory of fidelity and investigation. See: BBE, pp. 201–64.

[21] Alain Badiou, *Peut-on penser la politique?*, p. 101.

[22] That any event leads to the appearance of something previously in existing Badiou claims in *Logics of Worlds*, pp. 355–80.

[23] One could claim that the actual communist action changes the transcendental of change of the existing bourgeois world.

[24] This expression in German is "*werktätiges Gattungsleben*," which implies an activity and the creation of a material work. It shall become clear that my reading differs from Agamben's, as he is starting from the Aristotelian notion of genus. Giorgio Agamben, *The Man without Content*, Stanford: Stanford University Press 1999.

[25] The English translation does not render the German "*Wahrheit*" as "truth" but as "fact of life," I therefore modified the translation.

[26] As also Alain Badiou claims: "Truths are eternal because they have been created, not because they have forever been there." See: Alain Badiou, Séminaire sur: *S'orienter dans la pensée, s'orienter dans l'existence (2)*. Session of October 19, 2005.

[27] This is why it is false to read the early Marx simply as an Aristotelian.

[28] Universal production here comes close to the Hegelian logic of habit which constantly transforms retroactively the constitution of human nature.

[29] Habermas misses precisely this point. He indicates that Marx understands identity as "forming of . . . identity" but does not take the temporality of the forming into account and thus misses to link it to the necessity of alienation (and thereby to the indeterminacy of human being). Jürgen Habermas, *Knowledge and Human Interest*, Boston: Beacon Press 1972, p. 40.

30 I modified the translation because the sense of the German expression "*Durchsichselbstsein*" which Marx employs here, literally means to be the cause of one's own being. This precise sense gets lost if one translates it as "self-mediated being."

31 Here again a counter-notion to the Deleuzian notion of the body without organs appears. Marx rather develops the concept of a body with (potentially) infinite organs. Marx is no Deleuzian.

32 This term is not translatable into English and its precise sense would be lost if rendered as "determinability." This is because "Bestimm*bar*keit" should be read in two ways: something can constantly be determined because it is stripped of all determinations (it is "bar aller Bestimmungen," as one could put it in German) and also produces this double condition constantly as any retroactive determination changes the basis that it determines. The "bar" of "Bestimm*bar*keit" therefore stands for the continuous condition of the emergence of new determinations that are produced retroactively. This is how I read central aspects of what Badiou calls "subtraction". See: Alain Badiou, *Conditions*, pp. 113–29.

33 A further development of this logic I have undertaken in *Von der Treue als subtraktiver Institution*, in *Ereignis und Institution*, ed. by Gernot Kamecke/Henning Teschke, Tübingen: Narr 2008. The objection that Marx would be haunted by the Hegelian rabble-problem in his distinction of proletariat and lumpenproletariat, i.e. by the excluded of the excluded, reads Marx's description of universal production in the sense of a stable concept of production and misses the Bestimm*bar*keit of the process. Rather in the double of proletariat-lumpenproletariat the double of absolute and resentment-rabble is repeated because the lumpenproletariat is first and foremost marked by its self-seeking particular interest which throws it into the revolutionary movement hoping for a re-establishment of the bourgeois property order and for the restitution of that which it had lost.

34 Such a concept of life that immanently related to itself opposes the national-economic dublication of man into bourgeois and citoyen. A commentary of the critique of this in early Marx can be found in Helmut Reichelt, *Zur logischen Struktur des Kapitalbegriffs bei Karl Marx*, Frankfurt a. M. 1973, pp. 19–72.

35 Michael Theunissen, *Sein und Schein*, p. 477.

36 Étienne Balibar, *Ambiguous Universality*, in *Politics and the Other Scene*, London/New York: Verso 2002, p. 174.

37 Georg Lukacs, *History and Class Consciousness. Studies in Marxist Dialectics*, London: Marlin Press, p. 149.

38 See for example Erich Fromm, *Marx's Concept of Man*, London/New York: Continuum 2003. Also Frank Ruda, *Humanism Reconsidered*, pp. 175–93.

39 *Briefe von und an Hegel*, ed. by F. Nicolin, Hamburg 1977, Bd. 4, S. 136. Translated this phrase means: "If there were a government of angels, they would govern themselves democratically."

40 Alain Badiou, *Pocket Pantheon. Figures of Postwar Philosophy*, London/New York: Verso 2009, p. VIII.

[41] Here one could add a detailed discussion concerning the difference of the political thought of Giorgio Agamben and Alain Badiou. But a short, speculative footnote has to suffice: If Agamben thinks the irruption of a complete indeterminacy into the existing structures organized in identities or units by the state as an event which makes a form of unconditioned belonging visible, he shares this point with Badiou. Both—all their differences set aside—agree that an event consists in an irruption—of a mere belonging, of the void of the situation (Badiou) or of a pure belonging of any singularity to language (Agamben)—into a consistent, closed structure which generates its consistency via the assigning of determinations, qualities, and properties. With both of them one can therefore think the Hegelian rabble-problem. But Agamben does not identify the rupture of the event only with that which will have been logically 'before' the genesis of structures—the event as irruption of this retroactive 'before'—but also he identifies such an event with the truth that therefore is always the truth of being. The event which introduces a pure belonging of anyone is always a event of truth and this truth is the truth of being repressed by the structure. Any event, any irruption of indeterminacy into the structures distributing determinations, thus expresses the same truth (of being)—a Heideggerian heritage. This is why Agamben can think politics against the background of political (or economical) theology and assign a messianic character to these evental irruptions. For there is *one* truth of being. In Badiou one finds in contrast a different conception of the relation of being, event and truth. Although it might be said that being is that which as indeterminacy (as void) breaks into the consistent structures, truth is separated from the event and also from being. The event is the 'structural place' of an emerging possibility (of a truth) inexisting previously which *after* the event has to be unfolded by a subject. Thus truth is always a subjective construction in each and always singularly historical situations. This is why Badiou insists on the necessity of the concept of the subject, as agent of the deployment of a truth in singular situations and on the primacy of (political, artistic, etc.) practice against philosophy. One can resume the difference between the two thinkers shortly: for Agamben is a *multiplicity* of singular event as ruptures of the given which always expose *one and the same* truth (of being); for Badiou there is a *multiplicity* of singular events in singular situations which also enable a *multiplicity* of truths unfolded by 'faithful' subjects. For Agamben there is *one* truth (of being) which shows itself in a multiplicity of events in singular situations; for Badiou there are (infinitely) *multiple* truths whose subjective unfolding will have been possible by a multiplicity of events in singular situations. Could one not say something quite similar about the relation between Rancière (as anti-philosophical Agamben) and Žižek? And: Could one not against the background of the previous investigation claim that the difference between the invariance of one truth of being and a thinking of the practical unfolding of truths by subjects, is the difference between the Hegelian rabble and the Marxian proletariat?

Bibliography

Adorno, W. Theodor, *Minima Moralia. Reflections on Damaged Life*, London/New York: Verso 2005.
—, *Negative Dialectics*, London: Routledge 1990.
—, *Three Studies*, Cambridge/London/Massachusetts: MIT Press 1993.
—, *Sexual Taboos and Law Today*, in *Critical Models: Interventions and Catchwords*, New York: Columbia University Press 2005, pp. 71–89.
—, *Kant's Critique of Pure Reason (1959)*, Stanford: Stanford University Press 2001.
—, *Problems of Moral Philosophy*, Stanford: Stanford University Press 2001.
Agamben, Giorgio, *The Man without Content*, Stanford: Stanford University Press 1999.
—, *Homo Sacer. Sovereign Power and Bare Life*, Stanford: Stanford University Press 1998.
—, *The Open: Man and Animal*, Stanford: Stanford University Press 2004.
Alain, Chartier Émile, *Idées. Introduction à la philosophie. Platon – Descartes – Hegel – Comte (1939)*, Paris: Flammarion 1983.
Althusser, Louis, *For Marx*, London/New York: Verso 2005.
Anderson, Joel, *Hegel's Implicit View on How to Solve the Problem of Poverty: The Responsible Consumer and the Return of the Ethical to Civil Society*, in *Beyond Liberalism and Communitarianism. Studies in Hegel's Philosophy of Right*, ed. by Robert R. Williams, New York: State University of New York Press 2001, pp. 185–205.
Avineri, Shlomo, *Hegel's Theory of the Modern State*, Cambridge/London: Cambridge University Press, 1972.
Badiou, Alain, *Théorie de la contradiction*, Paris: F. Maspero 1975.
—, *Peut-on penser la politique?*, Paris: Éditions du Seuil 1985.
—, *Entretien avec Christine Goémé*, France Culture 10.02.95.
—, *Ethics. An Essay in the Understanding of Evil*, London/New York: Verso 2001.
—, *La volonté. Cours d'agrégation (2002–2003)*, on http://www.entretemps.asso.fr/Badiou/02–03.2.htm.
—, *Saint Paul. The Foundation of Universalism*, Stanford: Stanford University Press 2003.
—, *Being and Event*, New York/London: Continuum 2005.
—, *Metapolitics*, London/New York: Verso 2005.
—, *Séminaire sur: S'orienter dans la pensée, s'orienter dans l'existence (2)*, on http://www.entretemps.asso.fr/Badiou/05–06.2.htm.
—, *Circonstances 3. Portées du Mot «Juif»*, Paris 2006.
—, *The Century*, Cambridge/Malden: Polity Press 2007.
—, *Intervention dans le cadre du Collège international de philosophie sur le livre de Giorgio Agamben: la Communauté qui vient, théorie de la singularité quelconque*, on http://www.entretemps.asso.fr/Badiou/Agamben.htm.

—, *Number and Numbers*, Cambridge/Mladen: Polity Press 2008.

—, *Theory of the Subject*, London/New York: Continuum 2009.

—, *Pocket Pantheon. Figures of Postwar Philosophy*, London/New York: Verso 2009.

—, *Conditions*, London/New York 2009.

—, *Logics of Worlds. Being and Event 2*, London/New York: Continuum 2009.

—, *The Communist Hypothesis*, London 7 New York: Verso 2010.

—, *Politics: A Non-Expressive Dialectics*, in *Beyond Potentialities? Politics between the Possible and the Impossible*, ed. by Mark Potocnik/Frank Ruda/Jan Völker, Zurich: diaphanes 2011.

Balibar, Étienne, *Marx, the Joker in the Pack*, in *Economy and Society*, 14: 1, February 1985, pp. 175–93.

—, *Für Althusser*, Mainz: Decaton 1994.

—, *The Philosophy of Marx*, London/New York: Routledge 2007.

Bavaresco, Agemir, *La théorie hégélienne des l'opinion publique*, Paris: L'Harmattan 2000.

Bean, Philip, *Law, Order and Welfare*, in *In Defence of Welfare*, ed. by Philip Bean/John Ferris/David K. Whynes, London/New York: Routledge 1985, pp. 206–26.

Benhabib, Selya, *Obligation, Contract and Exchange: On the Significance of Hegels's Abstract Right*, in *The State & Civil Society: Studies in Hegel's Political Philosophy*, ed. by Z. A. Pelczynski, Cambridge: Cambridge University Press 1984, pp. 159–77.

Berlin, Isaiah, *Two Concepts of Liberty*, Oxford: Clarendon Press 1958.

Cantor, Georg, *Beiträge zur transfiniten Mengenlehre*, in *Mathematische Annalen 46*, 1895, pp. 481–512.

Cesa, Claudio, "Liberté et libertépolitique de Fichte à Hegel," in *Autour de Hegel. Hommage à Bernard Bourgeois*, ed. by François Dagognet / Pierre Osmo, Paris: Vrin 2000

Chiesa, Lorenzo, *The Body of the Structural Dialectic, or, the Partisan and the 'Human Animal'*,Typescript.

Comay, Rebecca, *Dead Right: Hegel and the Terror*, in *South Atlantic Quarterly*, 103:2/3, Spring/Summer, Durham NC 2004, pp. 375–95.

Conze, Werner, *Proletariat – Pöbel, Pauperismus*, in *Geschichtliche Grundbegriffe. Historisches Lexikon zur politisch-sozialen Sprache in Deutschland*, Stuttgart: Klett-Cotta 1984, vol. 5.

—, *Vom Pöbel zum Proletariat. Sozialgeschichtliche Voraussetzungen für den Sozialismus in Deutschland [1941]*, in *Gesellschaft – Staat – Nation. Gesammelte Aufsätze*, Stuttgart: Klett-Cotta 1992, pp. 232–46.

Dallmayr, R. Fred, *G.W.F. Hegel. Modernity and Politics*, New York/Oxford: Sage Publications 2002.

Derbolav, Josef, *Hegels Theorie der Handlung*, in *Materialien zu Hegels Rechtsphilosophie*, Vol. 2, ed. by Manfred Riedel, Frankfurt a. M.: Suhrkamp 1975, pp. 201–16.

Derrida, Jacques, *The Pit and the Pyramid: Introduction into Hegel's Semiology*, in *Margins of Philosophy*, Sussex: University of Chicago Press 1982, pp. 69–108.

Dolar, Mladen, *Cogito as Subject of the Unconscious*, in *Cogito and the Unconscious*, ed. by Slavoj Žižek, Durham/London: Duke University Press 1998, pp. 11–40.

Düttmann, Garcia Alexander, *Between Cultures: Tensions in the Struggle for Recognition*, London/New York: Verso 2000.

Eves, Howard, *An Introduction to the History of Mathematics*, New York: Brooks Cole 1975.

Fleischmann, Eugène, *La philosophie politique de Hegel: sous la forme d'un commentaire des Fondements de la philosophie du droit*, Paris: Gallimard 1964.

Foucault, Michel, *History of Madness*, Oxon: Routledge 2006.

Fraenkel, Adolf, *Einleitung in die Mengenlehre. Eine gemeinverständliche Hinführung in das Reich der unendlichen Grössen*, Berlin/Heidelberg/New York: Kessinger Pub. 1972.

Frege, Gottlob, *The Foundations of Arithmetic: A Logico-Mathematical Enquiry into the Concept of Number*, Evanston: Northwestern University Press 1980.

Fromm, Erich, *Marx's Concept of Man*, London/New York: Continuum 2003.

Funke, Gerhard, *Gewohnheit*, Archiv für Begriffsgeschichte, vol. 3, Bonn 1961.

Gans, Eduard, *Naturrecht und Universalgeschichte. Vorlesungen nach G.W.F. Hegel*, Tübingen: Mohr Siebeck 2005.

Gans, Eduard, *Vorrede zu G.W.F. Hegels Werke*, Berlin 1833, Bd. 8.

Geremek, Bronislaw, *Poverty. A History*, Cambridge: Blackwell Publishers 1991.

Gulyga, Arseni, *Georg Wilhelm Friedrich Hegel*, Leipzig: Reclam 1980.

Habermas, Jürgen, *Hegel's Critique of the French Revolution*, in *Theory and Practice*, Beacon Press 1973, pp. 121–41.

—, *Knowledge and Human Interest*, Boston: Beacon Press 1972.

Hallett, Michael, *Cantorian Set Theory and the Limitation of Size*, Oxford: Oxford University Press 1996.

Hallward, Peter, *Badiou. A Subject to Truth*, Minneapolis: University of Minnesota Press 2003.

—, *Depending on Inconsistency: Alain Badiou's Answer to the "Guiding Question of All Contemporary Philosophy,"* in *Polygrpah. An International Journal of Culture and Politics*, 17 (2005), The Philosophy of Alain Badiou, pp. 7–21.

Hamacher, Werner, *The Right to Have Rights (Four-and-a-Half Remarks)*, in *South Atlantic Quarterly* 103:2/3, Spring/Summer, Durham NC 2004, pp. 343–56.

—, *The Right Not to Use Rights. Human Rights and the Structure of Judgments*, in *Political Theologies. Public Religions in a Post-Secular World*, ed. by Hent de Vries/Lawrence E. Sullivan, New York: Fordham University Press 2006, pp. 671–90.

Hegel, G. W. F., *Vorrede zu Hinrichs Religionsphilosophie*, in *Werke*, Frankfurt a.M.: Suhrkamp 1970, vol. 11, pp. 42–68.

Hegel, G. W. F., *The Positivity of Christian Religion*, in *Early Theological Writings*, Chicago: University of Chicago Press 1975

—, *Jenaer Realphilosophie I: Die Vorlesungen von 1803/04*, Leipzig: Meiner 1932.

—, *Jenaer Realphilosophie. Vorlesungsmanuskripte zur Philosophie der Natur und des Geistes von 1805–1806*, Berlin: Meiner 1969.

—, *Gesammelte Werke*, Frühe Schriften 1, vol. 1, Hamburg: Meiner 1989.

—, *On Natural Right and Political Science. The First Philosophy of Right. Heidelberg 1817–1818 with Additions from the Lectures of 1818–1819*, Berkeley/Los Angeles/London: University of California Press 1995.

—, *The German Constitution (1798–1802)*, in *Hegel. Political Writings*, Cambridge: Cambridge University Press 2004, pp. 6–101.

—, *On the Scientific Ways of Treating Natural Law, on its Place in Practical Philosophy, and its Relation to the Positive Sciences of Right (1802–1803)*, in *Hegel. Political Writings*, op. cit., pp. 102–80.

—, *Briefe von und an Hegel*, Hamburg: Meiner 1969–81, vol. 4.

—, *Politische Schriften*, Frankfurt a. M.: Suhrkamp 1966.

Heyde, Ludwig, *Sittlichkeit und Ironie. Hegels Kritik der modernen Subjektivität in den Grundlinien der Philosophie des Rechts*, in *Die Folgen des Hegelianismus. Philosophie, Religion und Politik im Abschied von der Moderne*, ed. by Peter Koslowski, Munich: Fink 1998, pp. 303–19.

Hocevar, Konrad Rolf, *Stand und Repräsentation beim jungen Hegel. Ein Beitrag zu seiner Staats- uns Gesellschaftslehre sowie zur Theorie der Repräsentation*, Munich: Beck 1968.

Hoffmeister, Johannes, *Wörterbuch der philosophischen Grundbegriffe*, Hamburg: Meiner 1955.

Hösle, Vittorio, *Der Staat*, in *Anspruch und Leistung von Hegels Rechtsphilosophie*, ed. by Christoph Jermann, Stuttgart/Bad-Cannstatt: frommann holzboog 1987, pp. 183–226.

Hyppolite, Jean, *Genesis and Structure of Hegel's Phenomenology of Spirit*, Evanstan: Northwestern University Press 1974.

Ilting, Heinz Karl, *Aufsätzeüber Hegel*, ed. by Paolo Becchi/Hansgeorg Hoppe, Frankfurt a. M.: Humanities Online 2006.

James, David, *Hegel's Philosophy of Right. Subjectivity and Ethical Life*, London/ NewYork: Continuum 2007.

Kant, Immanuel, *Anthropology from a pragmatic point of view (1788)*, in Kant, *Anthropology, History, and Education*, Cambridge: Cambridge University Press 2007.

Kimmerle, Heinz, *On Derrida's Hegel Interpretation*, in *Hegel after Derrida*, ed. by Stuart Barnett, London/New York: Routledge 1998, pp. 227–38.

Kiss, Endre, *Die Begriffsvariationen der Gesinnung in Hegels Denken*, in *Phänomenologie des Geistes. Hegel-Jahrbuch 2002. Zweiter Teil*, ed. by Andreas Arndt/Karol Bar/ Henning Ottmann, Berlin: Akademie 2002, pp. 100–8.

Kluge, Friedrich, *Etymologisches Lexikon der deutschen Sprache*, Berlin: Gruyter 1989.

Knowles, Dudley, *Hegel and the Philosophy of Right*, London: Routledge 2002.

Kouvelakis, Stathis, *Philosophy and Revolution. From Kant to Marx*, London/New York: Verso 2003.

Krug, Traugott Wilhelm, *Allgemeines Handwörterbuch der philosophischen Wissenschaften nebst ihrer Literatur und Geschichte*, Leipizg: Brockhaus 1833, vol. 2.

Laclau, Ernesto, *Why Constructing a People Is the Main Task of Radical Politics*, in *Critical Inquiry*, 32 (Summer 2006), pp. 646–80.

Landau, Peter, *Hegels Begründung des Vertragsrechts*, in *Materialien zu Hegels Rechtsphilosophie*, Bd. 2, ed. by Manfred Riedel, Frankfurt a. M.: Suhrkamp 1975, pp. 176–200.

Lavine, Shaughan, *Understanding the Infinite*, Cambridge: Harvard University Press 1998.

Lazarus, Sylvain, *Anthropologie du nom*, Paris: Éditions du Seuil 1996.

Lenin, I. Wladimir, *Staat und Revolution. Die Lehre des Marxismus vom Staat und die Aufgaben des Proletariats in der Revolution (1917)*, in *Werke in 40 Bänden*, Berlin: Dietz 1955–1989, vol. 25, pp. 393–507.

Losurdo, Domenico, *Zwischen Hegel und Bismarck. Die achtundvierziger Revolution und die Krise der deutschen Kultur*, Berlin: Akademie Verlag 1993, pp. 157–234.

Löwith, Karl, *Hegel und die Sprache*, in *Sämtliche Schriften I. Mensch und Menschenwelt*, Stuttgart: Metzler 1981, pp. 373–98.

Löwy, Michael, *The Theory of Revolution in the Young Marx*, Chicago: Haymarket 2005.

Luhmann, Niklas, *Inklusion und Exklusion*, in *Soziologische Aufklärung 6. Die Soziologie und der Mensch*, Opladen: Westdeutscher Verlag 1995, pp. 237–64.

—, *Die Gesellschaft der Gesellschaft*, Frankfurt a. M.: Suhrkamp 1998.

—, *Jenseits der Barbarei*, in *Gesellschaftsstruktur und Semantik. Studien zur Wissenssoziologie der modernen Gesellschaft*, Frankfurt a. M.: Suhrkamp 1999, vol. 4, pp. 138–50.

Lukacs, Georg, *History and Class Consciousness. Studies in Marxist Dialectics*, London: Marlin Press 1999.

Machiavelli, Niccolo, *The Prince*, London: Penguin 2003.

Macpherson, C. B., *The Political Theory of Possessive Individualism. Hobbes to Locke*, Oxford: Oxford University Press 2011.

Malabou, Catherine, *The Future of Hegel. Plasticity, temporality and Dialectic*, Oxfordshire/New York: Routledge 2004.

Marcuse, Herbert, *Reason and Revolution. Hegel and the Rise of Social Theory*, London: Routledge 1955.

Marx, Karl, *Debates on the Law on Thefts of Wood*, on http://www.marxists.org/ archive/marx/works/1842/10/25.htm.

Marx, Karl/Engels, Friedrich, *The German Ideology*, New York: Prometheus Books 1998.

Marx, Karl/Friedrich Engels, *The Holy Family*, Moscow: Progress Publishers 1975.

McCumber, John, *The Company of Words: Hegel, Language, and Systematic Philosophy*, Evanston: Northwestern University Press 1993.

Menke, Christoph, *Tragödie im Sittlichen. Gerechtigkeit und Freiheit nach Hegel*, Frankfurt a. M.: Suhrkamp 1996.

Mercier-Josa, Solange, *Übergänge von Hegel zu Marx. Philosophie, Ideologie und Kritik*, Köln: Pahl-Rugenstein 1989.

Nancy, Jean-Luc *Hegel. The Restlessness of the Negative*, Minneapolis: University of Minneapolis Press 2002.

Neocleous, Mark, *Administering Civil Society. Towards a Theory of State Power*, London/ New York: Palgrave Macmillan 1996.

Nietzsche, Friedrich, *Thus spoke Zarathustra. A Book for All and None*, Cambridge: Cambridge University Press 2006.

—, *Beyond Good and Evil. Prelude to Philosophy of the Future*, Cambridge: Cambridge University Press 2002

—, *Ecce Homo. How one becomes what one is*, Oxford: Oxford University Press 2009.

Nuzzo, Angelica, *Freedom in the body*, in *Beyond Liberalism and Communitarianism. Studies in Hegel's Philosophy of Right*, ed. by Robert R. Williams, New York: State University of New York Press 2001, pp. 111–24.

214   Bibliography

Pippin, B. Robert, *Hegel's Political Argument and the Problem of Verwirklichung*, in *Political Theory*, vol. 9, no. 4 (Nov. 1981), pp. 509–32.

—, *Hegel, Freedom, The Will*, in *Grundlinien der Philosophie des Rechts*, ed. by Ludwig Siep, Berlin: Akademie 1997, pp. 31–54.

—, *Hegels Praktischer Realismus. Rationales Handeln als Sittlichkeit*, in *Hegels Erbe*, ed. by Christoph Halbig/Michael Quante/Ludwig Siep, Frankfurt a. M.: Suhrkamp 2004, pp. 295–323.

Rancière, Jacques, *Le concept critique et la critique de l'économie politique des "Manuscrits de 1844" au "Capital"*, in *Lire le Capital*, ed. by Louis Althusser/Étienne Balibar/Roger Establet/Pierre Macherey/Jacques Rancière, Paris: PUF 1996, pp. 81–199.

—, *Disagreement. Politics and Philosophy*, Minneapolis: University of Minnesota Press 2004.

Rauch, Leo "Hegel, Spirit and Politics," in *Routledge History of Philosophy, Volume IV, The Age of German Idealism*, London/New York: Routledge 2003

Reichelt, Helmut, *Zur logischen Struktur des Kapitalbegriffs bei Karl Marx*, Frankfurt a. M.: Ca Ira 1973.

—, *Die Marxsche Kritik der Hegelschen Rechtsphilosophie*, on www.marxforschung.de/docs/0703_reichelt.pdf (10.08.2008).

Reid, Constance, *Hilbert*, London: Springer 1970.

Riedel, Manfred, *Studien zu Hegels Rechtsphilosophie*, Frankfurt a. M.: Suhrkamp 1969.

—, *Einleitung*, in *Materialen zur Hegelschen Rechtsphilosophie*, Frankfurt a. M.: Suhrkamp 1975, pp. 11–47.

—, *Zwischen Tradition und Revolution. Studien zu Hegels Rechtsphilosophie*, Stuttgart: Klett Cotta 1982.

Ritter, Joachim, *Metaphysik und Politik. Studien zu Aristoteles und Hegel*, Frankfurt a. M.: Suhrkamp 2003.

Rockmore, Tom, *Marx after Marxism. The philosophy of Karl Marx*, Oxford: Wiley-Blackwell 2002.

Rosenzweig, Franz, *Hegel und der Staat. Zweiter Band. Weltepochen (1800–1831)*, Frankfurt a. M.: Suhrkamp 1962.

Ruda, Frank, Namenlosigkeit. Von nichts zu Nichts oder vom Pöbel zum Proletariat, in *Latenz. 40 Annäherungen an einen Begriff*, ed. by Stefanie Dieckmann/Thomas Khurana, Berlin: Kadmos 2007, pp. 158–63.

—, *Von der Treue als subtraktiver Institution*, in *Ereignis und Institution*, ed. by Gernot Kamecke/Henning Teschke, Tübingen: Narr 2008, pp. 69–93.

—, *Alles verpöbelt sich zusehends! Namenlosigkeit und generische Inklusion*, in *Soziale Systeme. Zeitschrift für soziologische Theorie*, Jg. 14, (2008), ed. by Sina Farzin/Sven Opitz/Urs Stäheli, pp. 210–28.

—, *Was ist ein Marxist? Lenins Wiederherstellung der Wahrheit des Namens*, in *Namen. Benennung, Verehrung, Wirkung (1850–1930)*, ed. by Syvlia Sasse/Tatjana Petzer/Sandro Zanetti, Berlin: Kadmos 2009, pp. 225–42.

—, *Humanism Reconsidered, or: Live living Life*, in *Filozofski vestnik, What is it to live?*, XX: 2, 2009, pp. 175–96.

—, *Back to the Factory. A Plea for a Renewal of Concrete Analysis of Concrete Situations,* in *Beyond Potentialities? Politics between the Possible and the Impossible,* ed. by Mark Potocnik/Frank Ruda/Jan Völker, Berlin: Diaphanes 2011.

—, *The Name of the Monarch: Hegel's Communist Conception of the State* (in preparation).

Russell, Bertrand, *Introduction to Mathematical Philosophy,* London: Simon & Schuster/Touchstone 1920.

Santner, Eric, *On the Psychotheology of Everyday Life. Reflections on Freud and Rosenzweig,* Chicago: University of Chicago Press 2001.

Schalow, Frank, *The Question of Being and the Recovery of Language within Hegels Thought,* in: *The Owl of Minerva,* 24, 2 (Spring 1993), pp. 163–80.

Schmidt, Steffen, *Hegels System der Sittlichkeit,* Berlin: Akademie Verlag 2006.

Schnädelbach, Herbert, *Hegels praktische Philosophie. Ein Kommentar der Texte in der Reihenfolge ihrer Entstehung,* Frankfurt a.M.: Suhrkamp 2000.

Schroeder, L. Jeanne, *The Vestal and the Fasces. Hegel, Lacan, Property and the Feminine,* Berkeley/Los Angeles: University of California Press 1998.

Stewart, Jon, *The Hegel Myths and Legends,* Evanston: Northwestern University Press 1996.

Stillman, G. Peter, *Property, Contract and Ethical Life Property, Contract, and Ethical Life in Hegel's Philosophy of Right,* in *Hegel and Legal Theory,* ed. by Drucilla Cornell/ Michel Rosenfeld/David Gray Carlson, London New York: Routledge 1991, pp. 205–27.

Theunissen, Michael, *Sein und Schein. Zur kritischen Funktion der Hegelschen Logik,* Frankfurt a. M.: Suhrkamp 1980.

—, *Die verdrängte Intersubjektivität in Hegels Philosophie des Rechts,* in *Hegels Philosophie des Rechts,* ed. by Dieter Henrich/Rolf-Peter Horstmann, Stuttgart: KlettCotta 1982, pp. 317–81.

Tillich, Paul, *Vorlesung über Hegel (Frankfurt 1931/32),* Berlin/New York: Gruyter 1995, vol. 8.

Tugendhat, Ernst, *Self-Conscious and Self-Determination,* Cambridge/London: MIT Press 1989.

Völker, Jan, *Ästhetik der Lebendigkeit. Kants dritte Kritik,* München: Fink 2011.

Wandschneider, Dieter, *Raum, Zeit, Relativität: Grundbestimmungen der Physik in der Perspektive der Hegelschen Naturphilosophie,* Frankfurt a. M.: Klostermann 1982.

Weil, Eric, *Hegel et l'Etat. Cinq conférences suivies de Marx et la philosophie du droit,* Paris: Vrin 2000.

Williams, Robert, *Beyond Liberalism and Communitarianism. Studies in Hegel's Philosophy of Right,* New York: State University of New York Press 2001.

Won, Jun-Ho, *Hegels Begriff der politischen Gesinnung. Zutrauen, Patriotismus und Vertrauen,* Würzburg: Königshausen & Neumann 2002.

Zermelo, Ernst, *Untersuchungen über die Grundlagen der Mengenlehre,* in *Mathematische Annalen* 65, 1908, pp. 261–81.

Žižek, Slavoj, *The Sublime Object of Ideology,* London / New York: Verso 1989.

—, *Looking Awry. An Introduction to Jacques Lacan through Popular Culture,* Massachusetts: MIT Press 1992.

—, *Tarrying with the Negative. Kant, Hegel, and the Critique of Ideology*, Durham/London: Duke University Press 2003.

—, *Le plus sublime des Hystériques. Hegel passe*, Paris: Erès 1999.

—, *The Ticklish Subject. The Absent Centre of Political Ontology*, London/New York: Verso 2000.

—, *For they know not what they do. Enjoyment as a Political Factor*, London/New York: Verso 2002.

—, *Did Somebody say Totalitarianism? Five Interventions into the (Mis)Use of a Notion*, London/New York: Verso 2002.

—, *Organs without Bodies. Deleuze and Consequences*, New York/London: Routledge 2004.

—, *Die politische Suspension des Ethischen*, Frankfurt a. M.: Suhrkamp 2005.

—, *The Metastases of Enjoyment. On Women and Causality*, London/New York: Verso 2005.

—, *Against the Populist Temptation*, in *Critical Inquiry*, 32 (Summer 2006), pp. 551–74.

—, *The Parallax View*, Cambridge: MIT Press 2006.

—, *Disciplines between two Freedoms – Madness and Habit in German Idealism*, in *Mythology, Madness, and Laugther. Subjectivity in German Idealism*, ed. by Markus Gabriel/Slavoj Žižek, London/New York: Continuum 2009, pp. 95–121.

—, *In Defense of Lost Causes*, London/New York: Continuum 2010.

Zupančič, Alenka, *The 'Concrete Universal' and what Comedy can tell us about it*, in *Lacan: The Silent Partners*, ed. by Slavoj Žižek, London/New York: Verso 2006, pp. 171–97.

Index

Made in the USA
Lexington, KY
17 July 2017